ALASKA
PUBLIC POLICY

CURRENT PROBLEMS AND ISSUES

Edited by Gordon Scott Harrison

Institute of Social, Economic and Government Research
University of Alaska

Published by
Institute of Social, Economic and Government Research
College, Alaska
1971

Throughout its ten years of existence, the University of Alaska's Institute of Social, Economic and Government Research has made a continuing effort to inform Alaskans—and others concerned with Alaska—of the public policy issues facing the state. In furtherance of this effort, a large variety of studies and publications have been produced to provide information about the state and its people. At the present time, ISEGR sponsors four publication series: the *Alaska Review of Business and Economic conditions*, *Occasional Papers*, *Research Notes*, and *Research Reports*. These are distributed to public and private officials and agencies, to other research scientists, and to the general public.

The staff of ISEGR represents a unique interdisciplinary group of social scientists, duplicated in scope in few, if any, other university research institutions. Though small, the staff has done a broad range of policy research in Alaska. Individually or as teams, institute members have pursued areas of special social need and of general personal interest. In all cases, following established academic tradition, members have been encouraged to report their research and express their conclusions freely, regardless of the controversiality of the issues or of their individual statements and opinions about them. This publication thus reflects no special attempt to include "pro and con" viewpoints on any given issue, other than what may be included in the individual articles themselves. The approach generally taken by the authors is analytical rather than adversary; the purpose, to stimulate thought and discussion rather than provide ultimate answers.

The present volume follows in the tradition of the Institute's public policy research and discussion, but falls outside its regular publication program. As happens with much university professional work, papers are often presented at meetings and published in journals outside the state. Also, occasional talks given by staff members to groups in Alaska do not reach a broader audience interested in them. It was therefore thought that a useful purpose would be served by collecting in a single volume several of these articles, papers, and speeches by members and associates of ISEGR. By publishing them in one place, scholars, students, administrators, legislators, and the interested public are provided with a reference source for ideas, information, and bibliography on the major public policy questions facing contemporary Alaska.

All of the articles were prepared before 1971; most in 1969 and 1970. One article by George W. Rogers, "Economic Development in Southeast Alaska and its Impact on Native Populations," was first published in 1963. No effort has been made to update the material in this article or in any of the others, so special note should be made of the date when they first appeared. However, the information and ideas in each of the articles selected for inclusion were deemed to have relevance to contemporary problems.

A number of critical policy decisions are expected in the near future, and these are bound to change the context and character of some of the policies and their implications as discussed in the following articles. Yet the basic development-related issues and conflicts in Alaska will remain, and even the articles affected by immediate future changes should retain continuing relevance to better understanding, analysis, and discussion of Alaska public policy.

Victor Fischer
Director, ISEGR
May 1971

TABLE OF CONTENTS

INTRODUCTION

Gordon S. Harrison

I

SECTION I: Overview

• State Government and Economic Development in Alaska   17
    Thomas A. Morehouse and Gordon S. Harrison

A Framework for Evaluating Use of Alaska's Land
    and Natural Resources   49
        Scott R. Pearson

Alaska's Economy in the 1960s   73
    George W. Rogers

Additional Reading   99

Contents

SECTION II: Land

Issues of Land Use Determination in Alaska:
  For an Alaska Omnibus Land Act   103
    Arlon R. Tussing

Alaska—The Federally Owned State   115
  George W. Rogers

An Alaskan Conservationist's View of the
  Public Land Law Review Commission's Report   137
    Robert B. Weeden

When the Land Freeze Ends   151
  Arlon R. Tussing

Additional Reading   163

SECTION III: Petroleum Development

Oil and Alaska's Economy   167
  Arlon R. Tussing

International Petroleum and the Economic
  Future of Alaska   175
    George W. Rogers

Alaska's Petroleum Leasing Policy   191
  Gregg K. Erickson

Additional Reading   219

SECTION IV: Environmental Quality

Wilderness and Development in Alaska   223
  George W. Rogers

Wilderness and Oil: A Survey of Critical
    Issues in Alaska   235
        Robert B. Weeden and David R. Klein

Man in Nature   259
        Robert B. Weeden

Additional Reading   271

SECTION V: Rural Development

• Rural Alaska's Development Problem   275
        Gordon S. Harrison and Thomas A. Morehouse

Economic Development in Southeast Alaska and
    Its Impact on the Native Population   289
        George W. Rogers

• Patterns of Migration, Urbanization and Acculturation   307
        Arthur E. Hippler

The Impact of a Native Land Claims Settlement on
    Economic Development in Alaska   315
        Arlon R. Tussing and Douglas N. Jones

Additional Reading   327

ABOUT THE CONTRIBUTORS   329

INTRODUCTION

Gordon S. Harrison

The major issues of public policy in Alaska today concern land use and natural resource development—or, generally speaking, economic development. Indeed, conflicts over land use and natural resource development have dominated Alaska's political life since the turn of the century. The underlying continuity of public policy debate in Alaska over the last seventy years is nicely illustrated by a comparison of the early twentieth century dispute over Alaska coal development and the contemporary dispute over arctic oil development; both involved similar conflicts over conservation, transportation, land, and federal regulation in Alaska's development, as well as conflicts over the distribution of benefits from development between and among public and private interests. The current dispute in Alaska over Native land claims is, like that of arctic oil development, largely a controversy over alternate patterns of land use, resource development, and distribution of benefits.

Thus, Alaska's resource development is the theme that links each of the seventeen articles in this volume. Although every aspect of the problem of economic development is not treated (consideration of the development of Alaska's marine resources is omitted, for example), the major issues of public policy are raised in one form or another. The book's division into five sections—one overview section and four sections on land, petroleum development, environmental quality, and rural development—imposes a measure of artificiality on the division of the subject matter. Environmental issues, for example, pervade the question of oil development. However, the demands for some kind of structural organization made these general divisions unavoidable.

The three articles of Section I provide, each in its own way, broad perspective on the problem of economic development in Alaska. These articles set the stage for the discussions in the succeeding sections. "Economic Development and State Government in Alaska" by Thomas A. Morehouse and Gordon S. Harrison points to the general issue of economic development as the lifeblood the Alaska's politics. The article traces the evolution of development-related conflicts in Alaska from territorial times to the present day. As a survey of the main public policy issues in Alaska, especially the current issues of Native land claims and petroleum development, it provides a point of departure for the more detailed treatment of these issues in following articles.

"A Framework for Evaluating Use of Alaska's Land and Natural Resources" by Scott R. Pearson provides conceptual tools for answering the critical questions to be asked of any proposed economic development activity, namely, what are its benefits and what are its costs? To whom do the benefits accrue and upon whom do the costs fall? It stresses that without a full understanding of the economic ramifications of various courses of action, an interest group might advocate policies that are counterproductive to its objectives and oppose others that are not ultimately harmful to them. In situations where policies and objectives are in irreconcilable conflict, political compromise is the only recourse. Pearson also discusses in theoretical terms the very important distinction between direct and indirect impacts, positive and negative, that typify developmental activity. This distinction is utilized by Arlon R. Tussing and George W. Rogers in their discussions of the impact of oil on Alaska's economy.

Introduction

"Alaska's Economy in the 1960s" by George W. Rogers points to the main economic trends in Alaska during the past decade. By providing a quantitative overview of Alaska's recent economic growth, this article offers pertinent factual background for subsequent discussions of economic activity in the state.

Section II deals with the question of Alaska's land, which is involved in one form or another in virtually every resource development issue in the state. Disputes over land ownership, control, classification, management, and disposal are very important in state politics, mainly because it is widely believed in Alaska that all successful development begins with full land ownership, as opposed to the mere possession of the right to harvest timber or extract minerals from it, and because exploration for and exploitation of Alaska's land-based natural resources threatens other land-related resources, such as wildlife, scenic beauty, and wilderness. With major oil and gas fields discovered, exploration for metallic minerals intensified, population increasing, urban areas expanding, and pressures mounting inside the state and outside for protection and preservation of Alaska's natural environment, the issue of land promises to remain at the center of development-related conflicts for the foreseeable future.

At the time statehood was granted, the federal government owned 99.8 per cent of Alaska's 365 million acres. Of this, almost a quarter had been withdrawn by administrative and executive order for national forests, wildlife ranges, Petroleum Resource No. 4, national parks and monuments, power resources, Indian reservations and reserves, and military reservations. Over 270 million acres remained under the control of the Bureau of Land Management as vacant, unappropriated public domain lands. These land holdings in Alaska amounted to approximately half of the entire land holdings of the federal government.

As part of the Statehood Act, Alaska was given 25 years to select almost 104 million acres of federal land in the state—102,550,000 acres from the vacant, unappropriated public domain for general purposes, 400,000 acres from national forests for community expansion and recreation, and 200,000 acres from the public domain for support of schools and a mental health program. Although generous in absolute terms, this grant will still leave two-thirds of Alaska's land under federal ownership and control when, and if, the state acquires its full allotment.

The state government began immediately to make land selections in accordance with the Statehood Act and these selections set the stage for a variety of conflicts. Native protests to state selections became the most critical of these. In late 1961 the Bureau of Indian Affairs filed protests on behalf of the Natives of Minto, Northway, Tanacross, and Lake Alegnagik against state selection of 1,750,000 acres. By mid-1968 there were over 40 official Native protests and claims to almost 300 million acres of land—virtually all of Alaska. As a result of these land claims the Bureau of Land Management has refused since early 1966 to process mineral lease offers on and state selections of land clouded by a Native claim; the Interior Department since early 1969 has temporarily withdrawn unreserved and unappropriated federal land in Alaska from any appropriation (Public Land Order 4582); and recently the federal courts in the Nenana case (State of Alaska v. Stewart L. Udall *et. al.*) have suggested that Native use and occupancy of federal land may remove it from vacant, unappropriated public domain status and hence from availability to state selection. The Native land claims await a congressional settlement.

Inasmuch as the Native land claims have effectively stopped the disposition of federal land, these claims constitute the overriding land conflict in Alaska today. However, other conflicts have developed over state land selections. For example, in the matter of setting priorities for state selections, conservationists and developmentalists have urged quite different sets of criteria. "Issues of Land Use Determination in Alaska: For an Alaska Omnibus Land Act" by Arlon R. Tussing discusses land administration in Alaska and surveys the current serious land-use conflicts. The major parties to these conflicts are the Alaska Native groups, developmentalists, conservationists, the state government, and the federal government. In this article Tussing proposes a package congressional solution to Alaska's current land problems that embodies a five-sided political compromise.

The administration of Alaska's land by the federal government has been criticized since shortly after the United States acquired possession of Alaska. Most of this criticism has charged that federal land laws have been much too restrictive and that economic development has been hindered as a consequence. In Alaska "there has never occurred the wholesale transfer of 'free land' which, despite possible inequities, would thereafter insure a chain of private reconveyancing and fuller use of the land resource," stated a publication of the territorial Alaska Development Board in 1948.

Others have argued that land use in Alaska has been and continues to be much too haphazard and erratic, and that more, not less, restrictive land laws and policies should prevail. These people have favored more land-use planning, classification, and other measures to insure wise and orderly utilization of Alaska's land.

These and other disputes over federal land policy prompted the formation of the Public Land Law Review Commission in 1964 to examine all federal land laws, policies, and regulations, and to recommend necessary changes to the President and Congress. The Commission's report, *One Third of the Nation's Land*, makes recommendations which if enacted into law would have far-reaching consequences for Alaska.

"Alaska—the Federally Owned State" by George W. Rogers and "An Alaskan Conservationist's View of the Public Land Law Review Commission" by Robert B. Weeden are two critical responses to the Commission's report. Both authors generally favor more land-use planning and classification by the federal government and both tend to favor federal retention of the federal public domain—except in Alaska, where the state selections are needed to support state programs and where the state government has formulated land laws and regulations that are considered more progressive than those of the federal government. Rogers develops his critique of the Commission's report into a critique of the notion that the development of Alaska should be patterned after the development of the older states. He argues for a new definition of "progress" in Alaska.

"When the Land Freeze Ends" by Arlon R. Tussing is a short article that argues for retention of some form of the current federally imposed land freeze after settlement of the Native land claims—that is, after disappearance of the conflict that precipitated the original freeze. The prospect of a land freeze extension is not greeted cheerfully by developmentalists, who regard the present freeze a major drag on economic development in the state. This article makes the case for some kind of extension. Tussing foresees a crisis of land policy and administration at the time the freeze is lifted; he predicts a rush of speculators and developers to acquire federal land under the public land laws, defensive selections by the state to prevent such disposition, and demands from within government, from conservationists, and from developers for unilateral executive or administrative withdrawals of public land in Alaska. Tussing argues for government action to forestall these and other problems from developing and to allow unhurried land-use planning to take place.

Section III treats the public policy issues of petroleum development, which in Alaska at the present time concern largely but not excludively arctic oil of Prudhoe Bay.

For a century it has been known that oil is to be found along the arctic coast of Alaska. Twenty-three million acres of land there were withdrawn for a Naval petroleum reserve over 40 years ago. But until recently, known deposits have not been commercially attractive. Atlantic Richfield's discovery in 1968 is significant because the size and other characteristics of the newly discovered field now make arctic oil economical to develop and produce. Despite the high costs of industry operations in the remote arctic, and despite the costs of transporting arctic oil great distances to markets in the United States and Japan, Alaska's North Slope suddenly appears to be, from the industry's standpoint, a source of very inexpensive crude oil.

Although recent uncertainty over construction of the trans-Alaska pipeline has slowed further exploration activity on the North Slope, the Prudhoe Bay discovery has spurred interest in searching for oil elsewhere in the state. Geophysical and/or wildcat drilling is underway in the Bering Sea, the Beaufort Sea, Bristol Bay, the Yukon Delta and upper Yukon regions, and the Alaska Peninsula.

But even if no additional commercially attractive fields are
discovered in Alaska, which seems unlikely, the state government can
look forward to considerable revenue from Prudhoe Bay oil after the
transportation problem is solved.

"Oil and Alaska's Economy" by Arlon R. Tussing and
"International Petroleum and the Economic Future of Alaska" by
George W. Rogers present complementary views of the impact of
North Slope oil on Alaska's economy. Both authors stress that the
main benefits of oil to the state will be in the form of public rather
than private payments. That is, bonuses, royalities, and taxes paid to
the state treasury will greatly outweigh industry purchases of labor,
goods, and services. Rogers traces in some detail the evolution of oil
activity in Alaska to the end of 1970, and points out that oil
industry activity has its own built-in boom-bust cyclical features.

While the impact of North Slope oil on the Alaska economy is of
foremost importance to Alaskans, it should be kept in mind that
Alaska crude oil is going to have major economic and political effects
outside the state as well. These are more difficult to speculate about,
however, because of the wide range of factors involved. It seems clear
that relatively cheap, plentiful, high-quality crude oil from Alaska
will put considerable pressure on the west coast energy market and
perhaps also the midwest and east coast markets. These markets are
now protected by market-demand prorationing policies of individual
oil-producing states (that limit the amount of domestically produced
oil) and oil import quotas maintained by the federal government
(that limit the amount of foreign oil coming into the United States).
These protectionist measures act together to support the domestic
price of oil at levels substantially above world prices. Oil industry
dislocations are certain to occur in the older petroleum-producing
states, and some alteration is likely in the current regulatory regime.
But the full dimension of these and other national and international
effects will become visible only after crude oil from Alaska begins to
reach the market.

Within the state, it remains to be seen whether pressure will arise
for prorationing or other production-restricting policies. This too will
depend largely on what happens after Alaska crude oil enters the
market. However, the many private land owners and speculators with

a direct stake in oil revenues, who comprise the political base for prorationing policies elsewhere in the United States, are not present in Alaska. The state collects 90 per cent of oil revenues from federal lands and 100 per cent of oil revenue from its own lands, and is the only significant landlord in the state.

Indeed, the fact that the state is the only effective landlord sets Alaska off from all of the other major oil-producing states, and it provides a political climate conducive to the formulation of wise long-range public oil policies. Alaska legislators and administrators are favorably disposed to development of the state but equally sensitive to economic exploitation by outside corporate interests. In setting public petroleum policies, both the legislature and administration have leaned heavily on advice from professional petroleum and business consultants. On balance, Alaska has gone a long way toward setting policies on the conservation, production, distribution, and marketing of its crude oil that are in the widest public interest.

One such policy is discussed by Gregg K. Erickson in "Alaska's Petroleum Leasing Policy," the last article of Section III. Erickson points out that Alaska's oil leasing policy is built around the mechanism of the economic marketplace. Among other things, Erickson discusses the controversy of competitive *vs.* non-competitive leasing, and he follows his main discussion with six "notes" that provide additional detail on present state policy and policy alternatives.

Section IV deals with the question of environmental quality in Alaska. As the foregoing discussions of land and petroleum development have indicated, this question is not easily separated from the other major public policy issues. Environmental and conservation issues are an inherent feature of every development-related conflict in Alaska.

With the environment an issue of sudden national importance and with the large amount of publicity surrounding several suits against developmental activity in Alaska by conservationist groups, it might appear to some that the issue of environmental protection is a new one in Alaska. In fact, a tug-of-war has been going on in the state between conservationists and developmentalists since the turn of the century. At that time conservation-oriented federal land policies in Alaska led to large withdrawals and reservations of land for general protective purposes, and many Alaskans charged that these land policies were obstacles to the economic advancement of the territory.

Now as then, the federal government is a leading participant in controversy over environmental and conservation issues in Alaska. In general, agencies of the federal government have been and are still more sensitive to these issues than agencies of the state government. (It should be pointed out, however, that the U.S. military has left more unsightly and potentially pollutant litter throughout Alaska than any other private or public organization—mostly rusting equipment, empty and unopened fuel drums, and Quonset huts in the arctic and Aleutian Islands.) It can be argued that federal agencies are more conservation minded than state agencies because they have not had the direct economic interest of the latter in developmental activities. Nonetheless, agencies at both governmental levels are sensitive to the costs of conservation, primarily through delayed or foregone development activities, as well as to the pressures of private interests with a direct financial stake in such activities. The main difference, however, is that federal agencies must respond to a much broader set of national interests and values than state agencies in Alaska, where the quest for development has reflected both governmental and private objectives. The National Environmental Policy Act of 1969 promises to reinforce federal involvement in development-environment conflicts, as the current matter of the trans-Alaska pipeline indicates.

Two of the articles in this section treat aspects of the environmental question apart from specific development conflicts. "Wilderness and Development in Alaska" by George W. Rogers traces the concept of wilderness and development from aboriginal to modern times in Alaska. He observes that the twin concepts would have been meaningless to the earliest residents in Alaska; that wilderness was regarded as an impediment to development for most of Alaska's history in modern times; and finally that there is an increasing awareness that the meaning of development must be expanded to include wilderness values.

"Man in Nature: A Strategy for Alaskan Living" by Robert B. Weeden describes an image of the "good society" in Alaska. Many Alaskans would surely identify with Weeden's ideal—a society that gives "exceptional recognition of Nature as an integral part of the human environment"—but what they would be willing to pay for its realization in terms of lost or deferred development activity is another question. For as the author stresses, if this image is to be achieved—or preserved, as some might say who feel that the contemporary style of Alaskan living substantially embodies Weeden's ideal—the state government must adopt policies that will limit Alaska's population, permit industrialization on a very selective basis, and cultivate a general "environmental consciousness."

The third article, in exploring the impact of oil development on the state's wildlife, raises broad questions of environmental protection in Alaska. "Wilderness and Oil: A Survey of Critical Issues in Alaska" by Robert B. Weeden and David Klein presents a comprehensive review of present and potential conflicts between petroleum development and wildlife populations in the state. The authors discuss the issues of renewable resource management that are raised by these conflicts and assess efforts being made to resolve or minimize them.

Section V raises the question of economic development in the rural areas of the state, where approximately 70 per cent of Alaska's Native population lives in over 175 small villages. Rural Alaska has shared little in the benefits of Alaska's economy growth. Actually, there are so few economic linkages between urban and rural Alaska that the areas may be thought to have separate economic systems. Native communities in rural Alaska are largely outside the investment and spending streams of the dominant, urban-centered economy of the state.

There has been, in general, a failure on the part of government agencies to realize or to admit the fundamental economic division of the state. This is reflected in the widespread assumption that the benefits of growth and development in the urban economy will reach the predominantly Native rural areas of the state. It is also reflected in the widespread notion that economic growth can take place in rural Alaska according to the same economic dynamic that propels it in urban Alaska. That is, most rural development programs of both state and federal agencies hold out the prospect of economic *viability* in the rural areas. Power systems are built, sewer systems are installed, and marketing cooperatives formed, all with a view to providing an economic sub-structure from which economic growth can emerge with its own self-sustaining dynamic. Some rural development programs place special emphasis on "human development" or "social modernization," but this means little more than encouraging habits of thought and action that support Western economic forms, such as management, entrepreneurship, deferred consumption, saving, formal education, and the like.

Rural development programs in Alaska have the potential for raising significantly the income levels and living standards of rural Natives. However, it seems quite unrealistic to assume that rural areas of the state will ever have a viable indigenous economy. Mines may open up, more profitable fish processing techniques may be devised, petroleum deposits may be discovered, logging may be initiated or accelerated and new pulp mills constructed, bringing, perhaps localized economic benefits to rural Natives. But sizable development of this kind will only result from economic forces external to the region and probably external to the state as well. Locally generated economic activity will be marginal at best and will require outside subsidization in the form of grants and/or low interest loans.

"Rural Alaska's Development Problem" by Gordon S. Harrison and Thomas A. Morehouse discusses government development efforts in rural areas of the state. The authors are generally critical of the administration of state and federal programs, and they project a rather pessimistic future. Mindful of the upper economic limits of any rural development effort, they assert that rural economic development programs have been isolated, short-term affairs rather than interlocking components of a viable, comprehensive strategy. Indeed, neither an over-riding development strategy nor development planning process now exists and no agency of the state or federal government is capable of bringing either about.

"Economic Development in Southeast Alaska and its Impact on the Native Population" by George W. Rogers is a seminal article on the economic situation confronting Alaska Natives. The sting of this article, which first appeared in 1963, is that contrary to official expectations, the development of major timber industries in Southeast Alaska in the 1950s did not have an appreciable effect on local Native employment. The case of Southeast Alaska illustrates the fallacy of thinking that modern industrial development and economic activity *per se* will contribute to the economic advancement and well-being of rural Natives.

Although Arthur E. Hippler's paper, "Patterns of Migration, Urbanization and Acculturation" does not deal directly with issues of rural development policy, it does bear on a discussion of appropriate rural economic development tactics and strategies. Hippler's data are incomplete and his conclusions tentative, but he has found much convincing evidence that Native villages will continue to exist at their present general population levels for an indefinite future even as the rate of out-migration increases. In addition, he suggests that few rural immigrants to the cities successfully urbanize. This is due in part to racial discrimination and in part to lack of educational and vocational training, both of which block access to full economic and social participation in urban life. The full implications of these observations for development policies are not clear. However, the findings tend to discredit the widely held notion that villages are disappearing and consequently that further investment in them is both unnecessary and unwise. Also, they point out that meaningful employment opportunities are a minimum prerequisite for successful urbanization and acculturation of rural Alaska Natives.

Nothing is known at the present time about the impact of rural development projects on contemporary migration and settlement patterns. To what extent does the provision of water and sewer systems, low cost housing, and social services in regional centers attract people away from the villages? To what extent does the extension of these amenities to the villages encourage people to remain in the villages? Development agencies often assume that their programs significantly affect rural Native migrations. But only scattered anecdotal evidence supports this assumption. Convincing research has yet to be done on the question of development efforts and Native residential preference. However, a survey conducted in 1970 by the Alaska State Department of Labor is very suggestive. It found that slightly more than 30 per cent of the rural residents would be willing to move for temporary employment or vocational training, and that only about 20 per cent would be willing to move for permanent jobs.

"The Impact of a Native Land Claims Settlement on Economic Development in Alaska" by Arlon R. Tussing and Douglas N. Jones is derived from Chapter VI of the massive report, *Alaska Natives and the Land.* This report was prepared by the Federal Field Committee for Development Planning in Alaska at the request of Senator Henry M. Jackson (D, Washington) who, as chairman of the Senate Committee on Interior and Insular Affairs, was charged with holding hearings and collecting information on various proposals for settlement of the Native land claims. Common to these legislative proposals was compensation paid to Alaska Natives in the form of land grants from the federal treasury and various oil revenue sharing schemes. Compensation was to be made for different purposes to individuals, villages, and a Native development-investment corporation. Tussing and Jones assess the likely impact of various possible legislative provisions on the economic development of rural areas and the state as a whole.

It should be noted that whatever its ultimate economic impact, a land claims settlement is bound to precipitate future conflicts over land use and resource development. There are likely to be conflicts, for example, between Native groups and the state government over land selections, and between Native groups and conservationists over the environmental impact of certain Native development programs as well as over land selections and generally.

These articles, individually and collectively, highlight the major issues and public policy in Alaska today. Although they do not reflect every point of view on each issue, hopefully they provide a point of departure for further, more informed discussion and debate on Alaska public policy questions.

SECTION I: OVERVIEW

A somewhat different version of this article appeared in State Government, published by the Council on State Government, Vol. XLIII no. 4 (1970) and Vol. XLIV no. 1 (1971).

A somewhat different version of this article appeared in *State Government* (published by the Council of State Governments), Vol. XLIII no. 4 (1970) and Vol. XLIV no. 1 (1971).

STATE GOVERNMENT AND ECONOMIC
DEVELOPMENT IN ALASKA

Thomas A. Morehouse and Gordon Scott Harrison

Alaska's 586,400 square miles make it one-fifth the size of the continental United States—as large as Texas, California, and Montana combined. Barrow, at the northern tip of the state, is 1,300 miles from Ketchikan in the southeast; Attu, at the far end of the Aleutian chain, is over 2,000 miles from the state capital at Juneau. But with only 300,000 people, Alaska is the smallest state in population, smaller than 80 U.S. metropolitan areas. Except for Eskimos, Indians and Aleuts—who live mainly in rural villages scattered throughout the state and comprise about a fifth of the population—Alaska's people are concentrated in a small number of urban communities. Anchorage, the largest urban area, itself accounts for over two-fifths of the state's population.

Reflective of Alaska's physical and socio-economic peculiarities are unique structural features of state government such as a state Department of Education that directly administers a rural schools system covering an area almost as large as the state itself; a Division of Marine Transportation that operates a fleet of ferries on a "marine highway" system serving the southcentral coast and linking southeast Alaska with Seattle and Canadian ports; and a Division of State Troopers responsible for law enforcement and police protection not only at the state level, but also locally in all but the largest communities.

Also uniquely "Alaskan" is a massive federal presence: the U.S. military establishment operates the largest single Alaskan enterprise, public or private; the Bureau of Land Management and several other agencies control the 95 per cent of Alaska's land area owned by the federal government; the Bureau of Indian Affairs and the Public Health Service directly administer education, health, and welfare programs for the Eskimos, Indians, and Aleuts of village Alaska; and the Interior Department runs the Alaska Railroad.

Yet, when these and other peculiarities are added together, they reveal little about the basic patterns and dynamics of the state's government. Most of what is significant about state government in Alaska can be discovered and understood not by describing its institutions, but by focusing on its distinctive problems of public policy and how they have been defined, confronted, and coped with by Alaska's people and their governing officials. In Alaska, these have been problems of economic development.

Political Culture

Government in Alaska is shaped to a large extent by the state's "political culture"—a distinct and assertive set of attitudes, beliefs, and social-political orientations on the part of the dominant population.

Prevalent among the state's resident white population is a highly developed social and political identity. Alaskans tend to view their state as one quite different from, and in many ways superior to, the other states of the union. Popular references to the other states—such as the "lower 48," the "smaller states," or simply the "outside"—have a thinly veiled ethnocentric and patronizing tone. Self-imagery of rugged individualism is widespread. Strains of popular thought celebrating rural virtues are associated with a sense of innocence vis-a-vis the rest of the nation. In addition to early

American pioneer and Calvinist elements, the political culture of Alaska includes traces of turn-of-the-century populism. The many small, independent, and vulnerable fishermen, miners, and merchants tend to be hostile to "big city" corporate power and massive bureaucracies that are regarded as threats to a healthy, hard-working, and honest folk.

A firm sense of identity with and loyalty to Alaska is held by a population that consists largely of recent immigrants from other parts of the United States. Almost half of Alaska's entire population in 1960 resided outside the state five years earlier.[1] Alaska patriotism may well be reinforced by the "newcomer" nature of the resident population. In one sense or another, most immigrants to Alaska have sought a "new beginning" in Alaska, and, as the earlier experience of European immigration to America demonstrates, new loyalties can be rapidly acquired by a recently settled population.

If asked what they find most attractive about the state, Alaskans will almost unanimously refer to its natural beauty and sparse population.[2] At the same time, however, most Alaskans do not seem to want natural beauty preserved for its own sake and are interested in bringing as many settlers and tourists to the state as possible. This is because "development" of Alaska is regarded as the highest public and private good, and few contradictions are associated with it.

Alaska's development is the central issue that unifies the state at every political tier, in much the way that the civil rights issue unifies southern states at each of their political levels. From the state's viewpoint, Alaska's congressional delegation has a single major purpose, and that is to promote Alaska development through federal channels. Otherwise, the state's two senators and one representative are relatively free agents in Washington who can assume, with more or less equanimity, conservative or liberal positions on most national issues. In general, national political questions have low saliency among most Alaska residents.[3] Alaska is isolated from the rest of the country not only physically but politically as well.

Contrasted with other states of the union, Alaska state politics command inordinate attention. This, too, is probably a function of the state's isolation, but also of its small population. State political actors tend to be well-known and they bring individual, personal styles to the drama of state politics. Face-to-face political communication is certainly more pervasive in Alaska than in other states, where population size and density make effective communication possible only through mass media.

Although still clearly discernible, the outlines of Alaska's political culture are undergoing change. The Native people of Alaska are becoming a significant political force; population patterns, previously shaped by boom-bust economic conditions, have tended to stabilize in recent years; a new political-economy, based on the production of vast oil reserves, is beginning to emerge. How these and related forces will change existing patterns of political culture remains to be seen.

The Economy and Economic Development Policies

Recent oil discoveries on the state's North Slope, and significant exploration activity elsewhere, will undoubtedly have major impacts on the economic and political life of Alaska. But today, Alaska's economy is still "underdeveloped" in a sense analogous to that used to describe the economies of large areas of Africa, Asia and Latin America. Alaska does not have a broad, self-sustaining economic base. The economy is, in general, insular, non-diversified, service oriented, structurally fragmented, and capital intensive. Outside of the southeast panhandle, economic activity is also highly seasonal. Because of pervasive leakages to the lower states, Alaska's income multiplier is very small. A breakdown of the various categories of economic activity by percentage of the state's gross product reveals the unbalanced and underdeveloped character of Alaska's economy.[4]

Alaska's Economic Activity	Percentage of Gross Product
Government and government enterprise	36.2
Wholesale and retail trade	12.3
Contract construction	11.4
Manufacturing	8.0
Finance, insurance and real estate	7.5
Transportation	5.5
Communications	5.3
Mining	3.7
Electric, gas and sanitary services	2.0
Agriculture, forestry and fishing	0.8

The largest industry in Alaska is government. Direct government activity and government supported service and construction activities account for more than half of all economic activity in the state. Supportive industries (construction, communication, transportation, utilities, banking, insurance, etc.) account for one-half of the total volume of economic activity in the private sector. While there is a general expectation that Alaska's future economy will be resource-based, agriculture, forestry, fishery, and mineral products accounted for only five per cent of the total gross domestic product in the mid 1960's.

Prior to the Second World War, Alaska had a "colonial" economy based on the exploitation of furs, salmon, and gold by absentee interests. Capital financing was non-resident; most of the seasonal labor force was non-resident; products were all exported; and no efforts were made to develop local economies beyond that required to support extractive industries.

With World War II came military construction and other defense-related spending in Alaska that gave the state's economy a new dimension. Development of the state's strategic potential meant investment in communication and surface transportation networks as well as a quantum jump in population. The postwar economy was, however, still unstable in that the infra-structural and other development did not rest upon an indigenous economic base. Wartime and postwar military spending led to the creation of a sizeable resident construction industry, but it stimulated only limited secondary economic growth. The resulting economy was essentially consumption oriented.

Further growth of Alaska's economy is tied to development of the state's natural resources, particularly its oil and gas deposits. It is also expected that expansion of the fishery, forestry, and mineral industries will help broaden, balance, and stabilize the entire economy through the simulation of complementary manufacturing and service activity. The development strategy of successive state administrations since statehood has been to encourage Alaska's export, natural resource sector through such policies as increased Japanese trade and investment, first-stage processing of natural resource products in Alaska, industrial tax concessions, and extension of the rail and road networks.

Encouragement of Japanese Trade and Investment

Japan, with a prosperous national economy dependent upon raw material imports, has become Alaska's first significant international trade partner. In 1970 over 80 per cent of Alaska's approximately $70 million in annual exports were to Japan. Timber, fish and liquified natural gas accounted for the bulk of these exports. Japanese companies own outright or have major investments in several of Alaska's largest pulp mills and shore-based fish processing facilities. A $200 million venture including Phillips Petroleum, Marathon Oil, and the Tokyo Gas Company has recently brought Cook Inlet-Kenai gas fields into commercial export production (through the liquification process), and Japanese utilities are exploring other potential energy sources in Alaska.[5]

Requirement of Primary Processing of Natural Resource Products in Alaska

Each of Alaska's post-statehood administrations has pursued a policy requiring the "primary processing" of natural resource products in Alaska prior to their export from the state. This primary processing policy actually originated in territorial times with the United States Forest Service, which applied a similar requirement to log exports. The policy is justified as a defense against "colonial" exploitation of the state's natural wealth, and as a device for providing employment to state residents. It underlies current development objectives such as the construction of oil refineries.[6]

Industrial Tax Concessions
The single largest tax concession now in effect is an industrial incentive law which allows a corporate tax credit equal to 50 per cent of the original investment. Other forms of preferential tax treatment are a generous depletion allowance for oil and mineral production, and absence of royalty payments for metallic minerals extracted from state lands as well as absence of lease or rental payments for lands so used.

Extension of Rail and Road Network
    It is currently thought that development of mineral deposits in Alaska— particularly the known deposits in the remote Brooks Range of northern and interior Alaska—is thwarted by the lack of adequate road and rail facilities. Extension of the Alaska Railroad beyond Fairbanks and construction of an all-weather road to the North Slope oil fields have become high priority objectives. Although still in the proposal stages, such surface transportation facilities are considered valuable social overhead capital and are thought to serve as a "lead" for development. Public investment in them is justified on those grounds.[7]

    In pursuing these and other development policy objectives, Alaska officials are, in part, reacting against the "colonial heritage" of federal government rule and resource exploitation by non-resident interests that characterized Alaska's development (or lack of it) for nearly a century before statehood.

Alaska as a Territory

    During the first half of Alaska's history as an American possession the region was handicapped by too little or no government; during the latter half, down to the time of statehood in

1959, it suffered from the accretion of too many "governments," both territorial and federal, but without any effective center of governance. Federal and territorial agencies divided administrative power while congressional committees and a territorial legislature shared legislative power. In both cases, the pattern of "sharing" was highly diffuse and unequal, with the federal government taking by far the largest part.

This long period of federal control produced a peculiar Alaska ideology in terms of which most, if not all, of the major problems of the territory were attributed to federal mismanagement, misrule, or neglect. The lack of development was attributed to the absence of Alaska self-government (i.e., control over its own development), and distortions of development (resource "skimming," exportation of wealth, etc.) were attributed to absentee control by fishing and mining industries whose interests were served by the governmental status quo. Thus, the federal government was faulted both for neglecting Alaska, insofar as resident interests were concerned, as well as for actively oppressing Alaska by monopolizing public authority over resource development and pursuing policies that favored the absentee corporate interests.

For seventeen years after the 1867 Treaty of Cession under which the United States purchased Alaska from Russia, there was no legal government in the region. A collector of customs was stationed in Alaska by the U.S. Treasury Department, and excesses of disorder were unevenly and periodically put down by itinerant U.S. Army and Navy units. Alaska's first "government" took the form of a "civil and judicial district" established by the Organic Act of 1884, but this consisted merely of a skeletal judicial system under federal control, and a presidentially appointed governor with extremely limited powers. The act was "specific in its limitations and prohibitions, indefinite and equivocal in its grants."[8] Federal legislation for Alaska would be shaped within this extremely restrictive mold until statehood 75 years later.

The last and most significant of the federal laws creating Alaska's basic governmental structure before statehood was the Organic Act of 1912. Under it, Alaska became a United States territory with its own legislature, but in keeping with the established pattern, the law severely limited territorial authority and prescribed the specific form, powers, and responsibilities of the legislature. The territory was denied authority over its fisheries and wildlife, it could not assume any debts without permission of congress, no provision was made for territorial land legislation, taxing powers were severely circumscribed, and the judiciary remained under direct federal control.

Designed to limit territorial power and to reinforce federal control, the system served for the next half century as a protective cover for the non-resident mining, fishing, and timber industries that were to reach favorable accommodations with the federal agencies and congressional committees retaining power in Washington. Alaska resource development policy was, in effect, made in piecemeal fashion through a series of such accommodations by remote federal officials and absentee private interests.

Over the years, both federal and territorial administrative agencies proliferated. On the federal side, there was little decentralization of authority from Washington to federal officials in the territory, and independent lines between central and field offices were jealously guarded and successfully maintained. Pro forma attempts were made by the Department of Interior to coordinate policy in Washington and operations in the field, but Interior could scarcely bring its own subordinate agencies together, let alone affect other federal departments such as Commerce and Agriculture.

On the territorial side of this administrative "system," the legislature created departments of health, agriculture, fisheries, mines, education, and aviation to perform limited functions not pre-empted by their dominant federal counterparts. The legislature also established many minor agencies and boards, as well as independently elective offices of attorney general, auditor, highway engineer, and treasurer. The result was a highly fragmented territorial executive structure, deliberately insulated by the legislature from the federally appointed governor who was regarded as an outsider.

By the end of the 1940's there were over 100 different federal and territorial agencies, about 50 of each. The most important of them were various agencies of the U.S. Department of Interior asserting independent control over their subdomains of land, fisheries, mining, and other resources. To the extent that there was any recognizable and continuing center of government in the region itself, it was found in the territorial legislature using its powers of the purse and of administrative review, investigation, and reorganization. But federal restrictions and interest group pressures prevented the legislature from significantly changing the terms under which private absentee interests variously exploited or "locked up" resources according to their own calculations of profit and loss and of competitive advantage. Indeed, it was not until 1949 that the legislature overcame the opposition of the "Alaska Lobby" and enacted a tax program which, for the first time, enabled the territory to impose taxes on incomes and on the value of extracted resources.

The Statehood Movement

The Alaska statehood movement can be understood as a direct reaction to these economic and political pathologies which were perceived to be rooted in the established system of federal agency-absentee interest control over Alaska's resources. The basic features of this system were (1) the diffusion of public authority and the relative concentration of private economic power, and (2) the non-resident orientation of both the public and private elements. Alaskans viewed this pattern as exploitive economically and oppressive politically—with political oppression providing the necessary condition for economic exploitation. Therefore, if Alaskans were to change the system, they would have to capture political control over economic development.

The ultimate means to this would be for Alaska to become a state. Statehood thus became synonymous with development, and development was considered identical with "progress" in all dimensions—economic, social, and political.[9] Since development under state control could be redirected in the interests of resident

Alaskans, an idealistic demand for democratic self-government was easily coupled with economic self-interest.

As indicated, the Second World War and military construction triggered major transformations in Alaska's population and economy. These developments also gave a strong push to the statehood movement. Between 1940 and 1950, territorial population grew from 75 thousand to 129 thousand, an increase of 77 per cent. (From 1930 to 1940, the rate of increase was only 22 per cent.) This growth was concentrated largely in Alaska's "railbelt" between Seward in the southcentral part of the territory and Fairbanks in the interior, and its focus was on Anchorage. These trends in population growth and distribution continued strongly into the 1950's.

The result was that the southcentral region, and particularly Anchorage, became Alaska's economic center, attracting large numbers of young professionals, white collar, and service workers from the "lower 48." By contrast, the southeastern panhandle, traditionally identified with Seattle-based fishing, timber and shipping interests—and, consequently, with the territorial status quo—was lagging behind. Moreover, fishing and mining, in the past the most important industries controlled by the older absentee interests, were themselves declining rapidly, and a more resident oriented construction industry was displacing them as dominant private interest groups in the Alaska political system.

Anchorage in the process became the home base of the Alaska statehood movement. Here were tapped the energies and idealism of a growing number of educated and youthful newcomers who believed that self-government was a natural right of Americans, and, in effect, that Alaska's territorial status was unnatural and demeaning. As reflected in successive public opinion polls during the 1950's, the sentiments of Americans elsewhere in the country were increasingly with them.

The stage was thus set for the final push to statehood: the old industries were slumping, newcomers from the existing states were leading the cause, and federal control was being sharply challenged not only for holding back "development," but on the moral grounds of democracy as well. However, a minority of Alaskans (particularly residents of Juneau, Sitka, and Ketchikan in the southeast) remained opposed to statehood for several reasons. In addition to the identification with absentee interests and the governmental status quo, there was also a well-grounded fear of the likely financial burden of statehood as well as resentment of a growing Anchorage and its apparent drive towards governmental and economic hegemony.

In the 1956 election to ratify the state constitution prepared earlier that year by the Alaska Constitutional Convention—more a vote on the statehood question than on the constitution itself—the proponents prevailed by a two-to-one margin statewide, while the southeast showed the strength of the opposition in a split vote. Reflecting the pre-eminence of the resource development issue, Alaskans in the same election approved an ordinance abolishing commerical fish traps[10] by a margin of six to one. Resident fishermen had, in fact, been vigorous proponents of statehood. To them, statehood meant resident control of the fisheries, just as it meant to most Alaskans the capture of control over resource development generally.

Congress passed the Alaska Statehood Act two years later; Alaskans again ratified statehood, this time by a six-to-one margin; and the act was signed by President Eisenhower on January 3, 1959.[11]

Development After Statehood

The economic development aspirations of the statehood movement were expressed in an article of the state constitution dealing with fundamental policy objectives for resource development. According to the constitution's Article VIII on natural resources, "It is the policy of the State to encourage the settlement of its land and the development of its resources by making them available for maximum use consistent with the public interest." Other sections of the article indicate that in pursuing this objective state officials should seek to eliminate the abuses of past absentee control, re-orient development to resident interests, and keep critical decision making powers within the state wherever possible.

Alaska's "model" constitution also provided the institutional and legal framework for development. Executive power, previously diffused in several directions, was concentrated in the office of the governor. Except for a lieutenant governor who is elected as the governor's running mate in the general election, there are no other elective administrative officials. Administrative functions are grouped by major purpose in fourteen principal departments (the constitution limits the number to 20) headed by officials appointed by and directly responsible to the governor.[12] The legislature, consisting of a 40-member house and a 20-member senate, is empowered to meet annually in sessions of unlimited length. There are fewer standing commitees than in any other state legislature except Nebraska's unicameral body. These and other characteristics of the state's governmental structure convey, overall, a sense of modernity and efficiency.

But in the years immediately after Alaska became a state, it became clear that statehood, even with the most modern institutions, was not automatically going to lead to the kinds and scale of development that most Alaskans envisioned. Control over development was one thing; making it happen was another. The economy, as described earlier, was heavily dependent on government and various supportive and tertiary service industries. Mining and fishing were continuing on their declines, and the military construction boom had been spent. Resource deposits were known to exist, but either full assessments of their commercial value had not been made or inaccessibility made their production uneconomical. Thus, the state, through most of the decade of the 1960's, faced persistent financial crises as federal agency responsibilities were transferred to the state, and a formally "strong" governor and an efficiently organized legislature were preoccupied with maintaining state government solvency. It was not a time for bold schemes of development. One of the most significant state government actions in these first years was establishment of the state ferry and marine highway systems. Though sound institutional and legal mechanisms of state control of development activities now existed, the state could not itself bring any large scale development into being.

The federal government helped the new state through this early period with transitional grants totaling $28 million from 1960 to 1965. It pumped large sums of money and technical expertise into the state after the disastrous earthquake of 1964 which hit the southcentral region, including Anchorage. Moreover, based on the earthquake reconstruction experience, it established the Federal Field Committee for Development Planning in Alaska, a body which has played an important role in development policy research and federal program coordination during a period when the state's own capabilities have not been adequate to the task. Most important, the federal government had, under provisions of the statehood act, authorized the state to select 104 million acres of land from the federally owned public domain which included, outside of the cities, virtually all of Alaska's 365 million acres. The state was also authorized to receive 90 per cent of the revenues from federal oil and mineral lease sales, rentals, and royalties.[13]

Federal land grants and financial support were not sufficient in themselves, however, to push the state into any self-sustaining process of economic growth, resident oriented or otherwise. But all this apparently changed with the discovery of oil in unprecedented commercial quantities on Alaska's North Slope in 1968. Then the state's authority to select from the federal lands obviously became the most critical state development power it possessed. Development of the oil fields would depend upon this power and control over new discoveries would require it.

The catch was that the federal government had, in 1966, imposed a "freeze" on further state selections in order to protect Alaska Native rights in and claims on the land. Moreover, environment had become a national issue, and the federal government was emerging as a regulator of Alaska's development in the interests of environmental protection. Given the federal government's direct interest and responsibility, development of the oil fields and related transport facilities in Alaska had become something of a national test case. Consequently, the old issue of who shall control resource development in Alaska had arisen in new form. In the territorial period, the fight was a relatively simple one between resident and nonresident development interests. Today the struggle revolves around economic development goals, ecological and social values, and Native rights — each involving alliances of Alaskans and "Outsiders."

Oil Exploration and Development in Alaska

In mid-1968, the Atlantic Richfield Company announced that it had discovered "one of the largest petroleum accumulations known to the world today" in Alaska near Prudhoe Bay on the North Slope of the Brooks Mountain Range. A single competitive sale of drilling rights on the North Slope in September 1969 brought the state of Alaska over $900 million. Upwards of $300 million per year is anticipated to flow into the state's treasury from royalties and severance taxes within a few years after arctic oil comes into commercial production in the mid-1970's. These sums contrast with Alaska's total state budget for fiscal year 1969-70 of $200 million. Interest alone on the state's $900 million is approximately $60 million per year.

In Alaska, neither oil nor oil on the North Slope were unknown prior to Atlantic Richfield's major discovery. Petroleum exploration on the arctic plains of north Alaska and in other parts of the state has been conducted since the turn of the century. Oil seeps on the arctic coast east of Barrow (first observed in the mid-1800s) led to the designation of 37,000 square miles of North Slope land as Naval Petroleum Reserve No. 4 in 1923. However, commercial production of oil did not begin until the late 1950s when new discoveries of significant petroleum deposits were made on the Kenai Peninsula south of Anchorage. In 1969 Alaska ranked eighth among the oil producing states, with a flow of almost 200 thousand barrels of crude oil per day from land and offshore fields in the Kenai Peninsula and Cook Inlet regions.

But discovery of the Prudhoe Bay field dwarfed all previous oil discoveries in the state. The state government, knowledgeable of geologic formations on the North Slope favorable to oil accumulation and mindful of industry interest in exploring the area, acquired from the federal domain large tracts of land around Prudhoe Bay prior to Atlantic Richfield's major strike in 1968. This strike set off a rush to explore and acquire drilling rights by other oil companies, such as British Petroleum, Standard of California, Texaco, Home, Hamilton Brothers, Pan American, McCulloch, and Gulf. The state's acquisition of North Slope acreage and its insistence on competitive bidding for drilling rights in the face of strong protests from private lease speculators and brokers, allowed the state government to earn in excess of $900 million in a single day of auctioning.

It is an industry assumption that between 500 and 600 thousand barrels of crude oil per day can be extracted from the Prudhoe Bay field as soon as a means can be devised for transporting it to market. Indeed, transportation is the rub, technically, economically, and political-legally.

A variety of schemes for transporting arctic crude oil to market were proposed and studied, including ice-breaking tankers that could penetrate the Northwest Passage, railroad cars travelling to Prudhoe Bay via an extension of the Alaska Railroad, and even submarine tankers with submersible trailers that could duck beneath the polar ice cap. But from the beginning, a pipeline carrying heated oil seemed to be the most feasible mode from an economic and engineering standpoint. Several oil companies with North Slope holdings, prominent among them British Petroleum, Atlantic Richfield, and Humble Oil, proposed to build a 48-inch diameter pipeline 800 miles across Alaska at an estimated cost of $1.5 billion. This consortium, referred to along with the pipeline project itself as the Trans-Alaska Pipeline System (TAPS), filed on June 10, 1969, an application with the Anchorage office of the Department of Interior's Bureau of Land Management for a right-of-way permit, requesting a favorable reply "by July."

Industry plans called for completion of the pipeline by 1972. Pipe was ordered from Japanese manufacturers and construction contracts were let. An Alaska oil boom appeared to be fully underway, and the oil companies, the state, the Alaska construction industry, labor unions, and other interests were anxious to cash in. For its part, the state sought to facilitate North Slope drilling activity by building a winter haul-road to connect Prudhoe Bay with the interior city of Fairbanks, which serves as the industry's staging area for northern oil development.

But the state, the oil industry and others were soon disappointed. The pipeline had to cross federal land, and in exercising its jurisdiction over this land, the federal government was forced to consider the questions of environmental protection and Native land claims in a different light from that of the state government. Consequently, several obstacles were raised to construction of the pipeline—obstacles that were, even a year and half later (at the end of 1970), only partially surmounted.

The Pipeline and Environmental Protection

The oil companies were unable to convince the Department of the Interior that they could safely build an 800-mile, hot-oil pipeline through some of the world's most severe terrain—from the Arctic Ocean to the port of Valdez on the Gulf of Alaska. Environmental protection was now a major political issue. National attention had been drawn to the emerging confrontation in Alaska between oil development and conservation interests, Congress passed the Environmental Policy Act of 1969, and the trans-Alaska pipeline scheme was challenged in the federal courts by national conservationist organizations. Finally, if the engineering-environmental problems were not themselves ultimately insurmountable, another barrier to pipeline construction was the federal government's freeze on any major land transactions or developments involving Alaska's public domain, pending resolution of the Alaska Native land claims by Congress. Thus, before a permit could be granted and construction of the pipeline could begin, conflicts between five major interests would need to be resolved: the oil industry, the state of Alaska, federal government, Alaska Natives, and national as well as Alaska-based conservation groups.

The oil companies had to put their own house in order even as they proceeded to negotiate with the Department of the Interior for a right of way permit. TAPS was nothing more than a very loosely organized consortium of nine oil companies owning exploration and development leases on Alaska's North Slope. As such, TAPS was not authorized to set policy or take any action without the separate concurrence of at least its major participants. Nor did TAPS itself possess the capability to deal effectively with the Department of Interior or the State of Alaska, and to meet the political and legal challenges of the conservationists. It was only after more than a year of disorganization and frustration that the companies dissolved TAPS and established the Alyeska Pipeline Service Company (ALPS) as a single legal entity to build and operate the pipeline.

When TAPS applied for a right-of-way permit in June 1969, its application not only lacked engineering details but failed to mention basic environmental problems. The Department of Interior responded not with a right-of-way permit, but with a long list of questions about the design of the pipeline and its environmental impacts.[14] The key design problem was how a 48-inch, hot oil pipeline could be securely buried in ground laced with ice wedges, containing extensive areas of permafrost, and subject to sharp earthquakes. Interior Department engineers doubted the feasibility of burying a hot oil pipeline in permafrost. Thawing would jeopardize the structural security of the pipeline, and threaten virtually irreversible environmental damage. (The pipeline is designed to carry up to two million barrels of oil a day. A break could result in a gravity drain of about one-half million gallons of oil per mile of line. The Santa Barbara Channel oil leak in January 1969 was only 20,000 gallons a day.)

Increasingly sensitive to the environmental issue and conservationist pressures, the Department of Interior initiated a lengthy period of technical studies, discussions, and negotiations with the oil companies. With the assistance of a federal inter-departmental task force on Alaska Oil Development, and technical support of the U.S. Geological Survey, the Department prepared a comprehensive set of environmental and engineering stipulations that TAPS would be required to meet in the construction and operation of the pipeline. In public hearings on the issue, state government officials claimed that they could "take care of environmental problems," and tended to downplay the significance of such problems. Their testimony was ignored.

Negotiations between the oil companies and the Department continued into 1970, with the most acute problems apparently revolving around the permafrost question and the related issue of what length of the pipeline should be above ground and what length below. The TAPS position was that most of the line could and should be buried, but Department engineers and scientists remained unconvinced that this could be done to the extent TAPS wanted without extreme risk.[15]

While the permafrost issue was emphasized by government technicians, it was not the only environmental consideration to be faced. Conservationists in particular kept several other issues in public view: The line would pass through or over several earthquake fault zones; above ground portions of the line might hamper caribou migrations; timber clearing, gravel excavation, and access road construction would disrupt natural habitat and silt streams and fish spawning grounds. Even with a trouble free and carefully constructed pipeline, there would almost certainly be accidental oil spills from the huge tankers that would operate out of the port of Valdez. And, finally, the oil and construction boom, new access roads and airstrips, and temporary and permanent settlements would, in the absence of adequate planning and controls, generate haphazard land development, speculation, and intensified resource exploitation.

Engineering and environmental problems became the subject of numerous technical studies and research and development projects by federal agencies and oil companies. Both government and industry, in turn, have also funded the work of a large number of scientists, engineers, and other researchers in universities and private consulting firms. It appears, however, that most of this work has been for the purpose of perfecting the means by which the pipeline will be built and anticipating and minimizing the environmental damage that it may cause. The question, as far as most of the parties are concerned, has not been whether but how. Neither in government and industry research, nor in government-industry public discussion, has the Prudhoe Bay-Valdez pipeline project itself been seriously questioned. While some conservationists have been adamantly opposed to any pipeline project, others have attempted to promote alternative routes (one through Canada) and modes (railroad), and still others have accepted the pipeline scheme provided it is not built prematurely and all possible precautions are taken. One unsuccessful candidate for statewide office during the 1970 primary election campaign suggested that the pipeline route should be altered (within Alaska) in the interests of both efficiency and environmental protection. This was considered an act of political courage by some, since such critical thinking about the pipeline, and the further delay it implied, was likely to lose votes.

The grounds for at least a temporary delay—possibly beyond the time that would have been required to adequately dispose of the engineering and design problems—was provided to the conservation interests by the National Environment Policy Act of 1969. Early in 1970, the Interior Department indicated a readiness to grant the right-of-way permit to the oil companies, presumably because the major design problems were solved, or nearly so. Three national conservation organizations promptly went to the federal district court in Washington, D.C. In April 1970, they won a temporary injunction on the grounds that the department had not complied with provisions of the 1969 act requiring a detailed statement on the environmental impact of the proposed project and alternatives to it, broad circulation of the statement, and review and possible public hearings by the federal Council on Environmental Quality. Several months of additional work by the Interior Department and the oil companies followed. At the end of 1970, the Secretary of Interior indicated that the questions raised by the conservationists would soon be answered in the department's report; however, it would still remain for the courts to decide whether this met the terms of the law.

Throughout this whole period, from June 1969 to the end of 1970, almost all of the significant action on the pipeline problem took place outside of Alaska. After the euphoric $900 million lease sale of September 1969, many Alaskans, including some of their state political leaders, became increasingly confused, frustrated, and resentful. Signals filtering through from Washington, Houston, and other centers of federal agency and oil company activity stimulated alternating moods of hope and despair. And the moods often bore little relation to the actual short run prospects of pipeline construction, which did not change. The state's attempt to circumvent federal restrictions and authorize construction of a pipeline access road in the summer of 1970 appeared to be an act more of desperation than ingenuity; such a road was subject to challenge in the courts as was the pipeline itself, and the oil companies did not want it under the circumstances. Similarly, the appointment of a Pipeline Commission to consider state ownership of the pipeline, and the dispatch of a 100-man "Alaska task force" to Washington in early 1970, were futile gestures. The pipeline problem was out of state hands.

Native Land Claims

If any doubts remained that the ultimate fate of the pipeline was beyond the control of Alaska's state government and the oil companies themselves, such doubts should have been totally dispelled when the Ninety-first Congress adjourned at the end of 1970 without enacting Alaska Native land claims settlement legislation. Indeed, congressional hearings, deliberations, and reports on proposed legislation in 1969 and 1970 showed clearly that little else would move in Alaska until a settlement was reached. As stated by the Senate Committee on Interior and Insular Affairs:

> Until Congress resolves the Native land claims each Senate land selection, mineral lease offer, homestead entry, mining claim, application for a right-of-way, for a use permit, and for purchase or lease of land and other property may be challenged.[16]

Alaska officials knew they were barred from proceeding with further selections of land from the federal domain, as authorized in the Alaska Statehood Act, after a "freeze" was first imposed because of the accruing protests by Alaska Native groups—Eskimos, Indians, and Aleuts, who compose about one-fifth of the population, and most of whom live in some 200 rural villages scattered throughout the state. But state government leaders did not seem fully aware that the pipeline, as well as any other major land development or transaction, was similarly blocked by the Alaska land freeze. At the end of 1970, however, state government and oil industry attention began to shift to the land claims issue and the freeze.

The source of the land claims problem lay in the fact that Native rights in the land, based on aboriginal use and occupancy, were recognized but never clearly defined and resolved after the American purchase of Alaska in 1867. Unlike the Indians of the lower states, Alaska's Natives had not been defeated in war, treaties were not made, and reservations generally were not established. The Alaska Organic Act of 1884 provided the legal foundation for the land issue. According to the act, Alaska Natives were not to be "disturbed in the possession of any lands actually in their use or occupation or now claimed by them but the terms under which such persons may acquire title to such lands is reserved for future legislation by Congress."

Congress had not yet acted on the issue when Alaska became a state 75 years later. However, in the 1958 Statehood Act, Native rights were reaffirmed even as the state was authorized to select 104 million acres of land from a public domain of some 365 million acres. The act thus provided that "the State and its people . . . forever disclaim all rights and title . . . to any lands or other property . . . the right and title to which may be held by Indians, Eskimos, or Aleuts." Congress again reserved to itself the power to define and resolve the problem of Native claims, but did not exercise this power. Instead, it took the apparently contradictory position of authorizing state land selections while attempting to maintain the status quo with respect to Native land rights. This set the stage for direct clashes between the state government and the Native people. The state began to select lands and Native protests followed.

At the time the land freeze was imposed in 1966, the state held title to only six million acres and had applied for title to some 20 million more. Meanwhile, Native regional associations, now organized into a statewide federation called the Alaska Federation of Natives, formed around the land issue, protesting state selection and asserting their own rights to 80 per cent of the total land area of Alaska. The federal courts have since reinforced both the congressionally declared status quo and the administrative land freeze,[17] but do not themselves have the jurisdiction necessary to impose a settlement, since that authority has been retained by Congress. If the land freeze is lifted before a legislative settlement is reached, it is almost certain that the Native organizations would be able to tie the entire matter up in the courts for an indefinite period.[18]

The timing and content of a claims settlement will depend in part on how well the state, the Natives, and conservation interests are able to reconcile their divergent interests. Another factor is how much political pressure the oil companies might bring to bear in Congress. Finally, of course, federal executive agencies and congressional committees will be at the center of the process. A bill (S. 1830) passed by the Senate in 1970, but not acted upon by the House, indicates the basic elements likely to compose a legislative settlement.

A land claims settlement will consist of both money and land. The Senate bill would have provided a total cash payment of $1 billion and about 10 million acres of land. Under the bill, cash payments would have consisted of $500 million from the federal treasury over a period of twelve years, plus two per cent of federal and state mineral lease revenues, up to a total of $500 million, to be paid out over a period of about 30 years. This, of course, would be unprecedented compensation in the history of the U.S. government relations with its Indian populations elsewhere. However, as is generally agreed, that history has not set a high standard.

Granted its impressive terms, the Senate proposal itself would still not fundamentally transform the economic and social condition of Alaska Natives. As acknowledged by the Senate Committee on Interior and Insular Affairs in its report on the land claims bill, "the

Natives of Alaska are in general a long distance from economic self-sufficiency and will be so for many years, notwithstanding this settlement."[19]

For a Native family of five, cash benefits might reach $1,000 annually within the first decade after a settlement. With a median family income of about $4,000, and where the cost of living is generally twice as high as that in the lower states, it is clear that life will not radically be altered. (Moreover, it is not clear to what extent such payments might substitute for current federal and state welfare benefits and social and economic development programs.)[20]

The Native groups, however, expressed strongest opposition to the land rather than the money provisions of the Senate bill. Emphasizing their heavy dependence on fish and wildlife for subsistence and the extensive area in the arctic environment required to support the natural habitat, the Natives sought title to 40, then 60, million acres of land. The state, on the other hand, objected most strenuously to that part of the proposed money settlement requiring a state contribution of two per cent of the funds from mineral leases, almost all of which would accrue to the state rather than to the federal government.

Despite their interest in obtaining an immediate settlement to clear the way for oil development, state government officials took a generally negative stance on settlement proposals, insisting most clearly that resolution of the claims issue was exclusively a federal responsibility. The state's position may have helped delay action on the bill.

For their part, the conservationists and oil companies were engaged on another front during the land claims debate, although, as has been seen, their interests in the claims issue were substantial. The land claims impasse provided the conservationists with insurance against a start on the pipeline project. Conversely, the oil companies and the state administration faced the double barrier of the environmental protection law and the land freeze. After the November 1970 elections, it appeared that a new state administration was preparing to be more "flexible" on the land claims issue, and the oil companies were indicating serious interests in an early settlement.

Policy Issues for the Future

Looking beyond the land claims and pipeline issues, the main task facing administrators and legislators in Alaska is one of maximizing public benefits of oil and oil-related development in the state. Since discrepant social and political values as well as technical expertise will be used in assessing the benefits of, and thus selecting among, various policy alternatives, it is impossible to predict the direction of development policy in Alaska. However, the general questions over which conflict is likely to arise are clear. Some of these questions emerged in the pipeline right-of-way and the Native land claims controversies. Others are linked, directly or indirectly, to economic changes brought about by oil development.

Before turning to an examination of the critical issues facing policy makers in the state, it should be pointed out that whatever position the state assumes on these issues, it will continue to conflict at times and places with the policies and activities of non-Alaskan or "outside" interests. First among these outside interests are the oil companies themselves, which are some of the largest national and international corporate organizations. The rate at which these companies choose to develop North Slope oil and to search for and develop other fields in Alaska, for example, will depend as much on policies of the state as those of the Canadian federal and provincial governments regarding petroleum exploration and development in the Canadian arctic, world supply and demand for petroleum, the commercial policies of the United States (oil import quotas) and other countries, and additional factors.

Second among important outside interests is the federal government, which will continue to own and manage up to two-thirds of the state even after Alaska has completed its selection of 104 million acres under provisions of the Statehood Act and the Native land claims are settled. Federal mineral leasing and homesteading laws will continue to apply to federal lands in Alaska, as will federal environmental quality laws such as the National Environmental Policy Act of 1969.

Third among outside interests likely to be in conflict with state development policies are national conservation organizations, which have taken a keen interest in Alaska's development activities inasmuch as these activities involve some of the finest wilderness and wildlife preserves left in the nation. So far, two significant legal actions have been brought by conservation groups against developmental activity in the state. One involves a federal injunction against issuance of a pipeline right-of-way permit (discussed above); the other involves a suit brought in U.S. District Court in Juneau by the Sierra Club against the U.S. Forest Service for the sale of over a million acres of timber in the Tongass National Forest to a private lumber and pulp company.[21]

We have seen that the state government has been largely unable to guide and control by itself oil development within its own boundaries. If outside interests or alliances of them continue to thwart major objectives of the state, the issue of "outside domination" of the economic life of Alaska is likely to acquire even greater significance in state politics than it has had in the past.

Within the state, policy conflicts are likely to emerge over methods available to the government for maximizing its direct financial profit from oil and gas development. An important issue is raised by state land selection policies, for example. To what extent should the state select land for the purpose of acquiring the right to lease competitively oil and gas drilling rights, and for the purpose of promoting other developmental activity? What importance should be attached to lands of scenic beauty but no mineral potential, such as sites for state parks, wildlife refuges, or portions of wilderness areas likely to be acquired by speculators or other private persons under federal mining and homesteading laws? Important issues are also raised by the state's petroleum leasing policy. To what extent should interests other than those of maximizing direct public revenue be considered in classifying lands for competitive leasing and in timing lease sales, for example? Other issues are raised by decisions affecting royalties and severance taxes. Should the State of Alaska defer compensation from private exploitation of its oil and gas resources by including royalty payments in leasing contracts, payments which may be uncertain and which would be receivable by the state only after commercial production begins, or should the state seek certain, immediate compensation through bonus lease bids that would be higher in the absence of royalty bidding provisions? When a legislature considers the severance tax rate too low and contemplates raising it, how much should it be willing to pay in the form of lost severance tax revenues for a stable investment climate?

More certain, however, is the likelihood of political conflict emerging over policies that emphasize either the direct or indirect benefits of petroleum development, one at the expense of the other. That is, there will be policy conflicts between courses of action that favor either generation of direct state revenue or creation of employment and secondary support activity. A current example of this conflict is the question of permitting offshore drilling in Bristol Bay, which has one of the most valuable salmon fisheries in the world. Fishermen oppose oil development there for fear that it might endanger the rich fishery. However, while the Bristol Bay fishing industry employs thousands of people, many of whom are locally resident Eskimos, it cannot compare with the oil industry in terms of generating state revenues. The same issue dominates the question of the extent to which Alaska should pursue petroleum development policies that foster employment and secondary economic activity. A requirement that petroleum be processed in Alaska, for example, would result in the initial employment of a number of construction workers and eventually of refinery workers, in addition to creating some secondary support activity. But because it would give rise to uneconomical refining, the requirement would have the effect of lowering the wellhead price of petroleum and ultimately reducing the state's income from royalty and severance tax payments and bonus bids. Local hire policies, which would necessitate public or private training programs and perhaps produce a work force of sub-optimal skill and efficiency, raise the same question: should individual employment be encouraged at the expense of general public revenues?

At issue in the question of direct vs. indirect benefits of oil development is how the state will redistribute to its citizens revenue it receives from oil and gas lease sales, royalties and taxes, and, in the event redistribution is not in the form of direct lump-sum payments, how the value of this redistribution is to be calculated. Indeed, the most critical set of policy issues facing Alaskans in future years concerns the allocation of oil revenues among competing demands for them. What portion of state oil and gas revenues is to be saved for future consumption? What portion is to be spent to meet immediate needs? Whose condition improves and whose worsens from saving? from spending? These and similar questions are going to be at the center of Alaska state politics and government in the future.

NOTES

[1]George W. Rogers and Richard A. Cooley, *Alaska's Population and Economy*, Vol. II (College, Alaska: Institute of Social, Economic and Government Research, 1963), table P-38, p. 47.

[2]See, for example, the report of a survey conducted by David R. Klein, "Alaskans and the Paths of Progress," *Alaska Sportsman*, August 1969.

[3]See Herman E. Slotnick, "The 1960 Election in Alaska," *Western Political Quarterly*, XIV, no. 1, part 2 (March 1961); Herman E. Slotnick, "The 1964 Election in Alaska," *Western Political Quarterly*, *XVIII, no. 2, part 2 (June 1965); Ronald E. Chinn, "The 1968 Election in Alaska, " Western Political Quarterly*, XXII, no. 3 (September 1969).

[4]Bradford H. Tuck, *An Aggregate Income Model of a Semi-Autonomous Alaskan Economy*, prepared for the Federal Field Committee for Development Planning in Alaska, Anchorage, 1967, p. 68.

[5]For further information on Japanese economic activity in Alaska, see Arlon R. Tussing, et. al., *Alaska-Japan Economic Relations* (College, Alaska: Institute of Social, Economic and Government Research, 1968).

[6]The assumptions underlying this policy have been questioned. See, eg., University of Wisconsin, School of Natural Resources, Center for Resource Policy Studies and Programs, *Federal Land Laws and Policies in Alaska*, Chapter III, "Timber" (Madison, Wisconsin: prepared for the Public Land Law Review Commission, 1969); and Gordon Scott Harrison, "Politics of Resource Development in Alaska: Primary Processing in the Salmon Industry," *ISEGR Occasional Papers*, No. 1, (July 1970).

[7]These assumptions are critically analyzed by Arlon R. Tussing and Gregg K. Erickson, *Mining and Public Policy in Alaska* (College, Alaska: Institute of Social, Economic and Government Research, 1969), pp. 65-72.

[8]Ernest Gruening, *The State of Alaska* (New York: Random House, 1968), p. 51.

[9]See George W. Rogers, *The Future of Alaska* (Baltimore: The Johns Hopkins Press, 1962), pp. 19, 146-48, 180ff.

[10]A fish trap consists of a frame net barrier, placed at strategic points in salmon migration routes, which directs the fish into a center hold. Owned mainly by non-resident cannery operators, the traps "were the tangible symbol of absentee control of Alaska's economy and demands for their abolition [was] one of the most powerful and frequently used of Alaska's political causes." (Rogers, *Future of Alaska*, pp. 178-79.)

[11]This was 43 years after the first statehood bill had been introduced in Congress by Alaska Delegate Wickersham in 1916.

[12]Two departments, Education and Fish and Game, are partial exceptions. They are headed by boards with limited non-administrative powers. The boards, themselves appointed by the governor, nominate an executive officer who must be acceptable to and approved by the governor. Although there are numerous other special boards and commissions with various advisory, examining, licensing, and limited regulatory and rule making functions, most are ex-officio or appointed by the governor, and are linked either directly to the governor's office or to the Department of Commerce.

[13]Federal agencies have also contributed substantial financial support to regularly budgeted state programs, accounting in recent years for about one-third of state revenues for such purposes. Most of these federal aids support state programs of highway construction, education, and health and welfare.

[14]See U.S. Senate, Committee on Interior and Insular Affairs, *Trans-Alaska Pipeline, Hearings*, 91 Congress, 1 Session Part 2, October 16, 1969, pp. 103 ff.

[15]Arthur H. Lachenbruch, *Some Estimates of the Thermal Effects of a Heated Pipeline in Permafrost*, Geological Survey Circular 632 (Washington: Government Printing Office, 1970). Also,

Ron Moxness, "The Long Pipe," *Environment*, Vol. 12, No. 7 (September 1970).

[16]U.S. Senate, Committee on Interior and Insular Affairs, *Alaska Native Settlement Act of 1970, Report*, 91 Congress, 2 Session, Report No. 91-925, June 11, 1970, p. 56.

[17]One of the suits was brought by a group of small Native villages to insure that no pipeline and access road right-of-way could cross lands through their village areas.

[18]For an authoritative discussion of the legal issues, see U.S. Senate, *Report*, pp. 56-61. At the end of 1970, when the freeze was scheduled to expire, it was extended by the Department of Interior for an additional six months. pending a claims settlement. If a claims bill is not passed within the period, it seems very likely that the freeze would be further extended.

[19]*Ibid.* p. 65; Federal Field Committee for Development Planning in Alaska, *Alaska Natives and the Land.* (Washington: Government Printing Office, 1968), pp. 11-26.

[20]See U.S. Senate, *Report*, pp. 99-111. It is estimated that the gross value per capita of the Senate bill to Alaska Natives (applying a discount rate of eight per cent for the period of years during which benefits would accrue), would be $6,526, a portion of which would be expended on community projects rather than cash payments to individuals.

[21]The suit claims that the Forest Service did not comply with the Multiple Use Act of 1965 in making the sale to U.S. Plywood-Champion Papers, Inc. It has been joined by other conservation groups and is still pending.

This article was prepared in the summer of 1970 while the author was a Research Associate at the Institute of Social, Economic and Government Research, participating in a project sponsored by the Ford Foundation entitled "A Survey of Environmental and Land Use Policy Issues in Alaska."

A FRAMEWORK FOR EVALUATING USE OF ALASKA'S LAND AND NATURAL RESOURCES

Scott R. Pearson

Over thirty years ago, the Alaska Resources Committee, chaired by Carl L. Alsberg, submitted a report to President Franklin D. Roosevelt which concluded that ". . . Alaska should be opened up as fast as and no faster than economic conditions warrant."[1] In an interesting footnote to this report, Henry A. Wallace, then Secretary of Agriculture, expressed the following opinion:[2] "I am impressed with the committee's emphasis of caution against the over-development of Alaska. It is clear that the committee has in mind that the mistakes made in the exploitation of natural resources in the early development of our states should be avoided in Alaska . . . In Alaska the rapid development policies dominant in the United States should be balanced by a policy of preservation." As contemporary Alaska prepares to embark on a petroleum boom whose significance is likely to outweigh the combined importance of all previous resource booms in Alaska's economic history, these earlier comments have a familiar and pertinent ring.[3]

The most crucial political and economic issue concerning contemporary Alaska involves determination of the pattern of future use of that state's land and natural resources.[4] Along with several agencies of the federal government and the State of Alaska, major interest groups concerned directly with resolution of this issue include proponents of rapid economic development, the petroleum and natural gas industry, defenders of wilderness and wildlife, and Alaska's Natives (Indians, Eskimos, and Aleuts). Because the Natives appear to have first claim to land in Alaska, the existing ambiguous situation regarding Native land claims must be cleared up before real progress can be made in furthering other interests.[5] But among those other interests, there is a hardening conflict between supporters of development and defenders of wilderness and wildlife.

There is no denying that a fundamental difference exists over determination of future use of Alaska's land and natural resources. At the same time, however, much of the debate seems to reflect an incomplete understanding of the likely magnitudes and distributions of benefits and costs that might be associated with alternative patterns of use. In particular, there is a widespread tendency for spokesmen from both sides to argue, at least implicitly, that their respective interests can only be served if use of specific areas is restricted to one activity rather than open to multiple uses.

The purpose of this paper is to provide an analytical framework to apply to multiple uses, i.e. one or more types of both developmental and conservationist activities, of Alaska's land and natural resources.[6] Discussion is principally carried on from the viewpoint of residents of Alaska, although the conflict between state and national interests is given explicit recognition.[7] In the first section alternative goals in determining patterns of use for natural resources are compared in an effort to indicate the importance of developing an evaluatory framework that could assist the evolution of political compromises. In the second section a general framework for evaluating benefits and costs associated with a particular pattern of resource use is developed with occasional references to specific examples from Alaska. The final section contains some speculations about the likely importance of land and natural resources in the economic development of Alaska.

Objectives in the Use of Natural Resources

Residents of the 49th state have an obvious and valid interest in the manner in which natural resources are employed in developing Alaska and in the extent to which these resources are preserved for other uses not directly related to economic growth. Although state, local, and private land holdings will amount at most to one-third of Alaska after the state completes its selection of land allowed under the Statehood Act, it is likely that the state will control areas containing the larger portion of Alaska's most valuable natural resources.[8] Other Americans are also concerned about the present and future use of Alaska's resources (and much less directly so are other North Americans as well as Asians, Europeans, etc.). This concern is given strong legal embodiment in the large federal land holding in Alaska, an area that will contain at least two-thirds of the state following the end of state selection.

Consider the use of Alaska's natural resources first from the viewpoint of Alaskans. These views can be characterized by a simplified but not unrealistic division into two broad groups of opinion—one whose principal goal is to increase economic development and/or current business activity within the state, and the other whose major objective is to conserve Alaska's rare and in some instances unparalleled resources of natural beauty, fish, and wildlife. People in the first group may not be opposed in principle to preserving a large part of Alaska in or near its current natural state. They simply do not gain as much pleasure from enjoying preserved natural resources as they would from increasing the level of economic activity in Alaska. Some in the group favoring development also point to the large numbers of poor and unemployed Alaskans and hope to better their current plight in the process of distributing a growing level of state income.

The second group, the conservationists, are not necessarily opposed in principle to economic development that would raise the real income of Alaskans. Instead they recognize the existence of important natural assets that have been wasted in other parts of the United States (and of the world) and hope to modify the pattern of economic growth in Alaska to allow for conservation of these assets.

There is nothing inherently unreasonable, irrational, or uneconomic in the stance of either group. Given their different objectives, each group rationally supports different patterns of use for Alaska's natural resources. Irrationality enters only if the true effects and implications of policies chosen to attain certain goals are very different from anticipated results.

Consider natural resource use in Alaska next from the point of view of Americans in general. Again it does not do a great injustice to reality to divide American opinion on this issue into two representative groups corresponding to the division of Alaskans. One group of Americans is interested mainly in the economic growth of the United States and hence of Alaska, even though the economy of Alaska is only a tiny portion of the total American economy. Important in this group are Americans from outside Alaska who might benefit from the economic development of that state, including the "taxpayer interest" now financing public works and welfare in Alaska, and those firms and individuals who have a desire to invest in or migrate to Alaska. Note that the goals of Americans who might invest in or migrate to Alaska may be in conflict with those of Alaskan proponents of development who desire to improve the welfare of people now residing in Alaska, not that of some future population swollen by migration. On the other hand, a significant body of American opinion is primarily concerned with preserving undeveloped portions of Alaska for use by all Americans (and foreigners) and with conserving the use of Alaska's natural assets in a way that might avoid environmental damage and prevent congestion to as large an extent as possible. As in the division of opinion among Alaskans, there is nothing inherently irrational in this conflicting view of the best way to use and manage Alaska's natural resources, if policies chosen to attain expressed goals are likely in fact to do so.

In this situation of conflict over goals and methods of achieving these goals, it is clear that political choices involving compromise must be a part of the decision-making process that plans the future use of Alaska's natural resources. But to speak convincingly about how such compromises might be attained, it is necessary to establish first whether all parties to each major issue correctly perceive the effects of policies that they support to achieve their objectives. Few people form their opinions on the basis of the general welfare of society as a whole. Self-interest plays a large role in the formation of opinion about public policy issues in Alaska as elsewhere. After the total benefits and costs that might be associated with a given pattern of resource use are identified, one must therefore consider the distribution of each in order to determine the extent to which desired objectives of major interest groups are achieved. Distribution of the gains from certain kinds of economic development, for example, may actually leave some supporters of development no better, or even worse, off. On the other hand, reservation of certain kinds of land areas for single purpose use, for example as a national park, may not be necessary for proper conservation and management, and may not, for that matter, assure that the natural assets are in fact conserved.

Even if all interest groups could correctly perceive the future distribution of gains and losses, some would have different objectives than others in deciding policies for the use of Alaska's natural resources. Within Alaska the proponents of development may be more influential than those of conservation. But among the Alaskan groups supporting development, wide divergences of opinion exist about what is an equitable distribution of the prospective gains, for instance, between some dominant white groups and Alaska's Natives. The balance of vocal public opinion elsewhere in the United States leans toward conservation rather than commercial development of Alaska's natural resources. To what extent do these differing objectives imply conflicts in evaluating policies for resource use?

In some instances direct and irreconcilable conflicts are inevitable. For example, by their very nature wilderness areas cannot support such developmental activities as hardrock mining, and vice versa.[9] In determining whether a given area of land should be preserved as wilderness or opened for large-scale development, the interests of conservation and development thus come into open and direct conflict. Political compromise in such incompatible instances involves swapping of interests in various land areas — that is, it entails yielding one's own self interest in one land area in return for attaining it in another.

In the large majority of instances, however, conflicts can be resolved by compromising within the area in question. At some additional cost, development can be carried out in ways that permit multiple purpose uses of land and do not entail significant environmental costs. From the opposite perspective, conservation for the most part requires thorough checks on the planning and procedures of developmental activities but not a complete absence of them. If additional costs imposed by moderate environmental quality controls cause the developmental activity to be uneconomic, then a reasonable conclusion is that such development should not be undertaken. An interesting example of successful coexistence of resource development and conservation within one land area has occurred in Alaska's Kenai National Moose Range, where petroleum exploration and production have taken place. As a result of careful procedures, it appears that petroleum development has had little or no adverse impact on on the wildlife in the refuge, although it has altered the scenery drastically in several places.

Because most multiple uses are reconcilable, apparent conflicts over use of Alaska's natural resources are in large part fueled by misinformation and unrealistic expectations. Improper or excessively strict or broad policies are advocated in attempts to achieve legitimate goals. Proponents of development often have false hopes about the magnitude and distribution of the gains from economic growth based on natural resources, and conservationists often have false fears of the extent of damage necessarily associated with developmental activities. Through understanding and political compromise, however, the objectives of most conservation groups and of most proponents of development can be achieved.

A Framework for Evaluating Natural Resource Use[10]

The governments of Alaska and the United States must make a series of coordinated or separate decisions about natural resource use in Alaska. The interests of both economic development and conservation will in varying degrees be served or compromised by these decisions. With these considerations in mind it is useful to construct an analytical framework to fulfill two objectives. The first is to discern whether each group's goals are likely to be attained through enactment of policies that it supports. The second is to aid in identifying and resolving resource conflicts when all interested parties rationally support policies that would attain their expressed goals. Although the scarcity of Alaskan data precludes strict empirical application of this framework, it can serve as a general analytical reference and assist identification of the types of data that would be essential for measuring benefits and costs associated with multiple use of Alaska's land and resources.

Statement of the Problem

Any pattern of multiple resource use will generate developmental and environmental benefits and costs.[11] A society considered in the aggregate presumably desires to maximize the present value (using an appropriate social discount rate) of a stream of net developmental and environmental benefits accruing to it over time.[12] However, within society, groups may weigh these effects differently.

In calculating these benefits, the concept of a social discount rate is important. A social discount rate is a rate of interest that embodies some weighted average of the time preferences of all groups in society. Some groups may have a strong preference for consumption of goods and services in the near future and others may choose to postpone their consumption. Some may consider only a specific number of future years, perhaps the period that it takes for an investment to depreciate completely, and others may have a much longer time horizon. In planning the future use of natural resources, each group's objectives and time preferences in association with future availability of desired goods and services will determine its own discount rate. These discount rates might differ considerably among various groups.

Measurement of future developmental and environmental benefits and costs attached to any specified pattern of use for natural resources is made difficult because the exact levels of these effects cannot be known with certainty. Because of uncertainty, future benefits and costs should be treated probablistically, not deterministically. In addition, the partial or total irreversibility implied by some modes of resource use has to be considered.[13] Construction of a dam, for example the proposed Rampart Dam, may be an almost irreversible act. Even if the dam were removed in the future, it is unlikely that the natural assets of the affected areas would return to their pre-construction status. Irreversible environmental costs might thus be incurred. Moreover, uncertainty surrounds the value of future developmental benefits. The value of anticipated future benefits associated with production of hydro-electric energy in Alaska was greatly reduced or eliminated, for example, when important sources of energy based on cheaper natural gas were discovered in Cook Inlet and subsequently on the North Slope. The effects of uncertainty are always present and may be reflected in the discount rates chosen by different groups in society.[14]

An additional difficulty in evaluating patterns of land use arises because no one has yet come up with a completely satisfactory set of methods to measure all types of conservationist uses of natural resources, including, among others, aesthetic values, outdoor recreation, scientific investigations, lack of congestion, and personal satisfaction gained from knowledge that a resource is preserved indefinitely. Techniques are available for computing an approximate value of the recreational use of a natural asset. Beyond this, all that has been done is to quantify net benefits associated with developmental land use and then to state that the opportunity cost of conservationist use must exceed the developmental benefits, if conservation is to increase the welfare of society as a whole.[15]

To give an example of how this line of reasoning might be applied to a potential resource conflict in Alaska, consider the possible use of a major portion of the Brooks Range for the proposed Gates of the Arctic National Park, and assume for sake of argument that the expoitation of minerals is deemed to be incompatible with the recreational purposes of the park. All prospective developmental uses of this area, including metallic mining and oil and gas production, would be evaluated using the framework presented below. This numerical guess, the expected present value of a future stream of developmental benefits, would serve as the opportunity cost of foregoing development. The incremental cost of foregone development must be less than the additional benefits from reserving this area for conservationist uses for the welfare of society to be increased. If the expected present value of the developmental benefits is small relative to competitive opportunities elsewhere in Alaska, or if the conservationist gains appear relatively large, then a clear *a priori* case can be made in favor of conservation even in the absence of detailed information about resource values.

In the discussion that follows, a framework is suggested specifically in terms of measuring developmental effects of land and resource use. Clearly, however, the approach applies as well to some kinds of "conservationist" uses—for example, outdoor recreation. In addition, it should be kept in mind throughout that the approach is meant to apply to instances of multiple land use, that is, joint use by one or more developmental and conservationist activities. For analytical reasons that will become apparent, however, comparisons sometimes must be made which assume a choice between or among individual developmental or conservationist uses. Finally, as noted in the introduction, emphasis is placed on the welfare of resident Alaskans rather than that of all Americans or some other group. Analytically, of course, the discussion could readily be altered to reflect a United States viewpoint.

Direct Effects

It is convenient to divide developmental effects into two categories—direct and indirect. Direct benefits arise from rents and other local factor incomes associated with exploitation of the natural resource (and hence use of the land). Rent in this context can be defined as the return to a natural resource employed in a productive use, that is, the resource owner's net revenue after meeting all costs of production, including profits. In Alaska the land and the land-(and sea-) based natural resources are mostly owned by the federal and state governments. By selling or leasing rights to private citizens or industries to exploit natural resources, the government, as landowner, attempts to capture portions of accruable rents. In instances where rents are expected to be large, the government, as sovereign, generally imposes special charges, for example, royalties on petroleum production or stumpage charges on timber production, to capture at least part of the rents generated in production.[16]

The public receives a direct benefit from private exploitation of natural resources when the government spends its share of the associated rents. The degree, kind, and distribution of benefits naturally depend on the budgetary decisions made by the state government. The state's expenditures could be "conservationist" in nature, such as provision for state parks. Alternatively, they could be developmental and provide for postponed and, it is hoped, increased consumption through investments in social overhead capital, human development, and directly productive activities, for example, roads, schools, and industries, respectively.

It is important to stress that the state's budgetary decisions, more properly the succession of budgetary decisions that it must take over time, also involve political compromises between the interests of development and conservation. But in this instance the opinions of Americans not resident in Alaska are reflected somewhat less directly—in part by decisions of the federal government agencies to fund or turn down the state's requests for federal supplementary support. If the ability and willingness of the federal government to invest or consume in Alaska is enhanced because it too shares significantly in the rents from Alaska's resources, then any additional federal expenditure may also be considered part of the direct benefits.

The key question concerns who in Alaska actually gains from increased state and federal expenditures in the state. The answer naturally depends on the composition of this spending and on procurement and contracting procedures. The point to be remembered is that expectations surrounding the distribution of future rents underlie the pressure for increased developmental use of Alaska's resources and that resource use and budgetary decisions are therefore wholly interrelated.

An additional source of direct benefits in principle is the use to which a private firm exploiting a natural resource puts its share of resource rents. Clearly the state may gain from taxing the firm's profits. If the firm is owned by non-Alaskans, the only remaining direct benefit to Alaska would stem from possible reinvestment of a portion of its earnings in Alaska's economy. The importance of such reinvestment, however, is reduced by the fact that Alaska is part of the economy of the United States. If any American firm wishes to invest in Alaska, it is free to do so. The same new investment opportunity that attracts the resource-based firm already operating in Alaska normally would be attractive to other firms not yet active in the state.

The economy of Alaska might gain additionally if the producing firm were owned wholly or in part by residents of the state. If local owners spend a portion of their return in Alaska, this spending will result directly in increased local incomes.[17] But the effects of saving and investing by local owners will differ little from those described above for non-Alaskans.[18] It is thus clear that the direct benefits from resource rents will come principally from the state government's share.

A second source of direct effects are gains from payments to Alaskan owners of factors of production. The choice of technology to employ in the production of resource-based commodities is a key determinant of the likely importance of these effects. This choice is never made solely on economic, engineering, or institutional grounds but on some combination of all three. The production technology adopted plus the input prices and quantities of outputs produced together determine the kinds of factors of production and materials that will be employed and the amounts of factor and material payments that will be made by the producing firm during the relevant production period.

It is, of course, necessary to identify the owners of the factors and materials as resident Alaskans or outsiders. Factor or material payments made by a producing firm to a non-Alaskan will have a positive impact on the economy of Alaska only to the extent that they are spent or taxed locally.[19] For example, if a pipeline welder employed by a petroleum company remits virtually all of his salary to Louisiana or if a salmon fisherman amortizes the loan on his gear in a Seattle bank, these actions have no positive effects on the economy of Alaska.

But even payments made to Alaskans do not necessarily represent a net benefit for Alaska's economy. A benefit equal to Alaskan factor payments arises only if the social opportunity costs of all employed local factors are zero, i.e., they would not have been employed at all in Alaska unless they were used in producing the particular resource-based commodity. This condition probably holds true for some unskilled labor and perhaps for certain categories of skilled labor in Alaska, but it is surely not met for other factors. It is likely that many unemployed Alaskans today are not just temporarily out of work but are technologically or culturally unemployable to a large degree. The answer to this serious problem is not more jobs, since new jobs would be outside the reach of the "hard core" unemployed just as existing jobs are, and would thus be largely filled by outsiders. A more appropriate response to chronic unemployment would be a program of long-term investment in education and training.

After allowing for any discrepancies caused by differences between social and private opportunity costs, one can arrive at a figure for gains attributable to local factor and material payments made by the resource-exploiting industry. If these payments to Alaskans are spent outside of Alaska, there is no further gain to the local economy. But if the payments (or payments to outsiders) are expended locally, this spending could initiate a multiple chain of incomes and expenditures. The ultimate impact of this multiplier effect would depend on the behavior of Alaskan income recipients. The large proportion of any additional income spent on imported products together with the proportions that are saved and paid as taxes probably amount on the average to over three-fourths of the total. Something less than one-fourth of additional income is spent on local goods and services. It is therefore unlikely that the income multiplier in the economy of Alaska is greater than about one and one-third; in other words, each additional dollar's worth of income in the state generates no more than perhaps 33 cents of further income elsewhere in Alaska.

Indirect Effects

Productive use of natural resources also involves indirect benefits and costs. These influences, comprising all economic effects other than those associated with resource rents and local factor incomes, are grouped into two categories—gains from additional industrial activity and gains or losses from externalities.

Additional economic activity generated by a resource-exploiting industry could involve backward linkages, that is, the purchase by the resource industry of local inputs of goods and services, and/or forward linkages, the furnishing by the resource industry of its own output as inputs for other local industries.[20] The mere existence of transactions involving the resource industry as purchaser or supplier does not in itself signify any gains for Alaska's economy. Benefits associated with linkages generally result from one or more of three phenomena—economies of scale, positive externalities in production, or use of unemployed or underemployed local factors.[21] Linkage costs, on the other hand, result from the existence of negative externalities or the creation of unemployment of local factors.

The concept of linkages must be applied carefully to avoid double counting. Assume, for example, that a resource-exploiting industry in Alaska purchases goods and services from a local construction firm. If this local firm would otherwise have been unemployed, that is, if its management, capital, and laborers all would have been idle, then the value added resulting from its work for the resource industry is a net gain for the economy of Alaska.[22] Alternatively, if the construction firm could achieve economies of scale in its operation because of its increased business, perhaps from spreading fixed overhead expenses over a larger volume of activity, then this too would bring gains to Alaska's economy. As a third alternative, the construction firm may benefit from positive externalities or generate negative externalities. An example of the latter would be harm caused to the commercial or sport fishing industries by the construction firm's use of river gravel. The point is that if none of these positive or negative effects is operative, there are no benefits or costs for Alaska's economy resulting from the fact that it is a local construction firm that happens to be employed by a resource-exploiting industry.

A second type of indirect effect results from externalities associated with the resource-exploiting industry. Externalities — costs imposed upon or benefits received by a producer or a consumer whenever the activity of some other producer or consumer imparts losses for which he cannot be charged or gains for which he need not pay — occur whenever relevant effects in production or consumption go wholly or partially unpriced. Such external effects in the use of natural resources are widespread and often very important. Because meaningful and correct statements about these effects can be made only on a case-by-case examination, generalization about them is not only difficult but often misleading.

Notwithstanding this fact, on one hand, proponents of development widely believe that significant positive externalities, such as free use of transportation facilities and creation of skills, often accompany the exploitation of a natural resource. And on the other hand, conservationists commonly argue that large and important negative external effects are imparted to the environment from the operation of most resource-based industries. Clearly both generalizations are valid in greatly varying degrees in actual situations in Alaska. In addition, conflicts generated by external costs arise not only between developmental and conservationist uses but also among various kinds of developmental uses. If, for example, petroleum development were to take place in certain parts of Bristol Bay, it might cause serious injury to the commercial salmon fishing industry, to big game guides, and to people who harvest the area's waterfowl.

There are several methods of controlling or eliminating externalities. The best method to adopt depends on the circumstances of each particular situation. As their name implies, externalities are costs or benefits that are external to the firm or consumer. One solution is to make these costs or benefits internal by pooling all interests, deciding the extent of such costs, and legislating a system of compensatory transfers within the newly created unit. A second method of adjustment involves governmental establishment of a quantitative limit, or quota, on the amount of any external cost that a producer or consumer can impose, for example by discharging a specific type of industrial waste into a particular river. A third procedure entails the imposition of taxes on gainers from externalities and/or the payment of subsidies to losers. A fourth suggestion is that a market be set up in which rights to create external costs, for example the right to pour effluents into or draw water from a stream, are traded among all affected parties. A fifth way of reducing external costs is through the right to invoke damage suits in the courts. Resolution of conflicts over external costs in the use of Alaska's natural resources will generally take one of these forms.

Perhaps brief mention should be made of one group of externalities that is popularly believed to have very strong positive effects—those associated with highway construction and surface transportation facilities in general. There seems to be a widespread belief in Alaska that resource uses which involve surface transportation networks are highly beneficial. If a private industry constructs and maintains a road or railroad that other producers and consumers can use at no cost, or at a smaller cost than would be incurred if the transportation system were built publicly or by other private industries, then positive externalities are generated. (There may also be negative external effects on the environment, but that is another issue.) This is an empirical question, not a logical one.

A Summing Up

Gains from the use of land and natural resources for conservationist purposes are usually very difficult to measure in dollar values. Depending on the extent and severity of resource conflicts and the ability of conflicting parties to resolve differences, this type of use may or may not impart important negative effects on economic development in Alaska. Conversely, the effects of developmental use of land and resources are quantifiable, at least in principle, but considerable analysis is required to sort out their ultimate importance for interested parties. Depending principally on the location of the resource, the production process employed in its extraction, and the profitability of the industry, exploitation of a resource may or may not make a significant contribution to economic development and/or bring about costly environmental damage.

In Alaska the developmental contribution of the state's share of rents is likely to be far greater than that of the combination of all other effects of resource exploitation. Local factor payments are significant in some resource industries but multiplier effects are small. Additional industrial activity brings little real gain to Alaska's economy. Positive externalities are of only marginal importance and negative external effects may sometimes be large. In order to make enlightened choices, public policy-makers must analyze each major type of use for Alaska's land and natural resources and compare the results with those for competing and complementary uses. This information must then be employed to decide optimal patterns of multiple land and resource use, except in those limited instances where single use is dictated by necessity.

Natural Resources in the Development of Alaska

The economic history of Alaska has been characterized by a series of booms and busts associated with outsiders' extraction of various land- and sea-based natural resources in Alaska. The exploitation of furs, gold, fish, copper, and to a lesser extent even military activities have all followed the same general pattern. Alaska had a natural resource available in limited supply. Outside capital, skilled and unskilled labor, and management moved in to exploit the natural resource. Rents attached to the resource were often very large, but there was no effective institutional mechanism to capture an important share of them for the permanent residents of the territory or state. Apart from those in a subsistence economy, the permanent population of Alaska lived off local factor payments, mainly wages, and indirect effects of the resource booms, including benefits from linked economic endeavors, mostly direct support activities and first-stage processing, and limited positive external effects, associated principally with transportation. As a result of this process, in 1969 more than three-fourths of income in Alaska originated in the government or services sectors and less than 7 per cent in extractive industries—mining, fisheries, and forestry.

Alaska is currently on the threshhold of a vast petroleum boom whose generation of rents is sure to surpass the importance of all earlier spurts several times over. There is another essential difference this time, in addition to the changed order of magnitude of the effects. There now exists a state government in a position, both as landowner and as sovereign, to capture a significant portion of the rents associated with the production of oil and gas. A large part of the direct effect of resource exploitation can thus be placed at the service of resident Alaskans. On the other hand, associated benefits—local factor payments and indirect effects—are likely to be proportionally much less important than they were in Alaska's earlier resource booms. Yet, ironically, many Alaskans seem to expect highly significant associated benefits from petroleum production and fail to realize that the important effects will result instead from the state government's spending of its share of resource rents.

This misplaced emphasis on associated benefits underlies much of the developmentalist opposition to conservation of Alaska's natural resources. But not all supporters of rapid development for Alaska misinterpret its likely effects. Some are much more concerned with the distribution of the gains—stated bluntly, their own piece of the action—than with the aggregate impact. Alaska's politically powerful construction industry has a concept of the process of economic development which may be rational from its own standpoint, but which is myopic from the point of view of the larger society. More and bigger buildings and roads are seen as good for the industry and thus for the state no matter what their longer run effects are on the economic and environmental development of Alaska.

Alaska's private land holders have a more subtle and continuing interest in an ever increasing level of economic activity in the state, whatever the benefits or costs to the existing residents of Alaska and to the environment. If migratory capital, labor, and other factors of production come into Alaska to exploit natural resources, the state government will not be the sole beneficiary of substantial rents. Those Alaskans, including speculators, holding well-sited, mostly urban, parcels of land will reap incremental rents from their private property as population and industrial activity grow. These groups stand to gain proportionately more if decisions regarding use of Alaska's natural resources and expenditure of the state's rental income are made to promote further industrial development and resource extraction rather than to provide services more directly valuable to the people currently residing in Alaska.

One of the fundamental issues for Alaska's development planners is whether Alaskans should bear the likely high costs of economic subsidies and environmental losses in order to industrialize or whether Alaska should instead develop primarily as a service economy living off rents from natural resources, including controlled tourism. In facing this type of decision on alternative ways of generating adequate incomes and employment opportunities for its residents, Alaska is nearly unique among contemporary regions and nations. Because of the expectation of large and growing resource rents, there seems to be no necessity for Alaska to progress gradually through the typical phases of development—primary products, consumer goods, capital goods, services—in order to raise the standard of living of Alaskans. So long as the population does not grow too rapidly through in-migration, extensive industrial activity might be superfluous in Alaska. Nevertheless, the state will surely want to make long run plans to allow for a possible decline in resource rents in the distant future.

The state's share of future resource rents can also reduce the importance of the related trade-off between income and employment. The issue itself does not disappear, but decisions are made easier in the presence of ample state revenues. In general, public policy decisions on economic issues should attempt to maximize incomes rather than employment opportunities because incomes can be taxed and then redistributed to create additional employment. This principle must, of course, be modified to allow for particular institutional arrangements and political realities. For example, there are some obvious sacrifices in direct incomes resulting from Alaska's current requirement that primary commodities produced in Alaska undergo first-stage processing in the state. Because rents from the state's natural resources are reduced by this regulation, the state has implicitly made a decision to subsidize processing industries for the purpose of creating employment.

Because this paper has focused mainly on the interactions between natural resource use and economic development in Alaska, relatively less attention has been paid to national interests in Alaska's future. Alaska contains about one-half of the publicly held land in the United States. American interest in the future use of Alaska's natural resources is thus every bit as legitimate and legally supported as that of resident Alaskans. The development versus conservation conflict, however, has been polarized in Alaska by archaic federal land laws which have forced a choice between single purpose reservations and uncontrolled development. Recent events that might importantly alter the federal government's posture toward Alaska include submission of the Public Land Law Review Commission's final report and passage of the National Environmental Policy Act. But even if Alaskans choose development policies that very carefully consider environmental effects, conflicts between national and state goals still may arise over questions of congestion and overcrowding. Large and growing numbers of Americans desiring to enjoy Alaska's natural assets first hand as tourists, for example, might quickly spoil certain frontier aspects of Alaska that are highly valued by its residents. Hence, no matter how much information and analysis is gathered and disseminated, conflicts will remain to be resolved through compromise.

This analytical discussion of the interactions between multiple resource use and economic development thus has important implications for policy decisions. The objectives of all interested parties must be identified. Policies to achieve these goals must be analyzed to ascertain whether each group's ends would in fact be served through enactment of the set of policies that it supports for this purpose. Conflicts arising from the rational pursuit of policies aimed correctly at achieving specific goals must be examined to discover the extent to which trade-offs between alternative goals actually exist. Analysis must be undertaken to measure the net economic and environmental benefits and costs over time and to determine the political and institutional support for alternative sets of policies. With this information in hand, policy-makers in the state and federal governments can make informed decisions on the proper use of Alaska's land and natural resources.

NOTES

[1]U.S. House of Representatives, *Alaska—Its Resources and Development* (75th Congress, Third Session, Document No. 485), January 20, 1938, p. 20.

[2]*Alaska — Its Resources and Development*, p. v.

[3]For discussion of the petroleum boom, see Richard Norgaard and Scott R. Pearson, "The Development versus Conservation Conflict: Petroleum in Alaska," Giannini Foundation, University of California, Berkeley, and Food Research Institute, Stanford University, 1971.

[4]For a summary of the principal considerations entering into this issue, see Arlon R. Tussing, "Issues of Land Use Determination in Alaska: For an Alaska Omnibus Land Act," in this volume.

[5]See U.S. Senate, Committee on Interior and Insular Affairs, *Alaska Native Settlement Act of 1970: Report* (91st Congress, Second Session, Report 91-925), June 11, 1970. In July 1970, this act passed the Senate by a vote of 76 to 8, but it was not considered by the House in the 91st Congress.

[6]Analytical discussions have tended to concentrate on the either/or choice rather than on multiple uses. See, for example, John V. Krutilla, "Conservation Reconsidered," *American Economic Review*, LVII, October 1967, pp. 777-786.

[7]In addition to political reasons for emphasizing the interests of Alaskans in the disposition of Alaska's land and natural resources, there are economic arguments for this emphasis, including equity considerations favoring special treatment for Alaskans, and, as explained below, differential indirect effects on local unemployed resources.

[8] See Tussing, *Op. Cit.*

[9]According to an alternative view of "wilderness," some placer mining, trapping, forestry, etc. might be compatible with some "wilderness" preservation.

[10]The framework developed in this section is similar in several respects to that employed by the author in a different context. See Scott R. Pearson, *Petroleum and the Nigerian Economy* (Stanford, California: Stanford University Press, 1970), pp. 39-54.

[11]One or more of these four effects could, of course, be zero.

[12]This statement must be qualified to the extent that individuals or groups attach additional value to benefits associated with long run development that is anchored in Alaska. For example, some Alaskans might prefer an annual cash flow of benefits payable to residents of Alaska in perpetuity over a lump sum payment with an equal present value.

[13]In the face of both uncertainty and irreversibility, it is generally correct to postpone all decisions that can possibly be postponed. Note also that irreversibility can result from either natural factors or institutional considerations.

[14]Persons and groups who have little confidence in their ability to capture future benefits of an economic activity are likely to have a particularly strong preference for present income and consumption. Accordingly, the implicit discount rates of transient workers, of entrepreneurs in highly speculative lines of business, and of members of marginal social groupings tend to be particularly high.

[15]This approach can be used to evaluate situations of single or multiple uses of land, but the measurement problems become more complex when the land area is under multiple use.

[16]The state also shares directly in rents generated by production on lands not owned by the state—through severance taxes, for instance, and through its ninety per cent share of federal mineral leasing revenue and its twenty-five per cent share of federal timber sale revenues.

[17]It might also initiate a multiple chain of expenditures and incomes. The immediate gain to Alaska would be confined to the merchandising mark-up on a non-Alaskan good, but additional incomes for Alaskans could result if expenditure is on goods and services produced locally. As argued below, the multiplier effect in Alaska, however, is likely to be small.

[18]There could conceivably be dynamic differences in the saving and investing behavior of local and outside owners.

[19]This impact is discussed below.

[20]These familiar concepts were initially suggested by Hirschman in a somewhat different context. See Albert O. Hirschman, *The Strategy of Economic Development* (New Haven: Yale University Press, 1958), pp. 98-119.

[21]Economies of scale arise when an industry experiences additional demand for its output which allows it to reduce its unit cost of production. Externalities in production are non-appropriated benefits or costs that appear when the resource industry furnishes free inputs or imposes uncompensated costs to other industries. Gains from the use of unemployed or underemployed factors are analogous to those from factor payments considered above and thus must be considered net of social opportunity costs.

[22]Clearly, if the firm would otherwise have been employed but less productively, then the gain is equal to the additional income derived from working for the resource industry.

[23]Several recent advances have been made in the theory of externalities. See especially J.M. Buchanan and W.C. Stubblebine, "Externality," *Economica,* Vol. XXIX (November 1962), pp. 371-84; E.J. Mishan, "Reflections on Recent Developments in the Concept of External Effects," *Canadian Journal of Economics and Political Science,* Vol. XXXI (February 1965), pp. 3-34; F.T. Dolbear, Jr., "On the Theory of Optimum Externality," *The American Economic Review,* Vol. LVII (March 1967), pp. 90-103; and R.U. Ayres and A.V. Kneese, "Production, Consumption, and Externalities," *The American Economic Review,* Vol. LIX (June 1969), pp. 282-97.

This article appeared as an issue of the *Alaska Review of Business and Economic Conditions*, Vol. VII no. 6. (College, Alaska: Institute of Social, Economic and Government Research) December 1970.

ALASKA'S ECONOMY IN THE 1960'S

George W. Rogers

It is traditional at the close of a decade that there is an outpouring of review and commentary covering the events of the past ten years, accompanied by speculation on the course of future developments. The exercise is interesting and worthwhile as a taking of stock and a re-examination of goals, but it has the arbitrariness of the bookkeeper's fiscal year. It is only by chance that a particular decade embraces something unique or marks a true watershed in history. However, in Alaska's case, the decade of the 60's includes major periods of basic change, the most spectacular of which occurred in 1969.

Only ten years earlier, in January 1959, Alaska's first state legislature convened and took its first steps as a newly created "sovereign state" of the union. The political context of the economy was basically changed, as were the values and goals it was to serve. Alaska during the 1940's and 1950's had emerged from the former colonial-resource economy based on outside exploitation of the salmon, gold and fur resources. The transition began with the frantic defense build-up of World War II in the early 1940's. Fiscal year 1947-48 launched a further boom as the outmoded World War II defense establishment was replaced by one based on the new technology of long-range bombers and electronic warning systems. A third boom began in 1959-60 with the introduction of missile technology and improved distant early warning systems. Thus, although the value of Alaska's fisheries, oil and gas, minerals, and forest products industries steadily increased, the major "industry" of the state was based on the activities of the Department of Defense and, to a lesser extent, other federal government agencies, rather than on any internal natural resources.

As a result of the 1968 discovery of oil in commercial quantities on Alaska's North Slope, the state was presented the opportunity to enter the "big-time" of international resource development. The magnitude of this was demonstrated when, in September of 1969, representatives of the domestic and international petroleum industry made bonus payments of $900 million on leases of state land on the North Slope, the richest lease sale thus far in the history of the United States. As further evidence of the prospects — and challenges — facing the state, route and design work commenced on the formidable task of constructing an 800-mile, 48-inch, pipeline from the Arctic Ocean to the Gulf of Alaska, and the Northwest Passage was explored by the giant ice-breaking tanker, *Manhattan,* the first commercial vessel ever to make that passage. The shape of the next ten years will be determined by how these events progress and by the responses of Alaskans to them.[1]

That 1969 actually was a watershed in Alaska's history requires that we provide the traditional decade-end review and commentary. Thus, the year 1969 will be considered, not for itself, but as a vantage point from which to look back to 1960 (with an occasional sighting on 1950) and forward to 1980. What can be seen will be evaluated from two levels of interest: the national-international (the Outside) and the resident Alaskan interest.

Alaska's National and International
Economic Significance

Geographic location was Secretary of State Seward's primary concern in purchasing Alaska, with the possibility of acquiring valuable natural resources as a further consideration. There has been a natural resource yield in Alaska, but for the most part it was specialized and spasmodic (i.e., the Gold Rush at the turn of the century and the brief revival of gold production on the eve of World War II, a couple of decades of major copper production, and others). On the other hand, Alaska has remained in the forefront of United States' fisheries production, despite initial and continuing mismanagement. Still, on balance, a look at Alaska's resource and development potentials and needs as late as 1937 was justifiably negative. One contributing agency then characterized our northern territory simply as a difficult-to-defend outpost of possible value in time of war and a high cost course of a few strategically important raw materials. In spite of this, the events of the last three decades were to demonstrate Alaska's importance in the terms that prompted "Seward's Folly."

Alaska's first and continuing major significance to the nation is its strategic northern location. Situated on the marine transport great northern circle route between the continental land masses of the east and west, and at the crossroads of the North polar air routes between Europe and the Far East, Alaska has become the United States' northern territorial foothold—a Stefansson's "Mediterranean" of the twentieth century.

The 1942 invasion of the Aleutian Islands by the Japanese indicated the importance of Alaska to national defense. The federal government subsequently developed the defense potential, so that by the 50's and 60's Alaska had become primarily an "exporter" of military defense, from the national point of view. Between 1951 and 1954 (construction of the DEW Line), spending by the Department of Defense in Alaska averaged $412.9 million annually. This declined from a peak of $512.9 million in 1953 to annual amounts fluctuating between $264.6 million and $352.0 million (reflecting the intermittent funding of radar installations in the interior) during the decade of the 1960's (Table 1). If these expenditures could be adjusted to eliminate monetary inflation, the drop would be even more dramatic. The number of military personnel stationed in Alaska stabilized at about 33,000 persons and civilian employees of the department between 6,800 and 6,500 for the decade.

The late 50's had witnessed the end of developmental build-up of the defense establishment, followed by a plateau of maintenance and periodic renewal. Although Alaska's strategic location is of continued importance to hemisphere defense, national attention during the decade of the 60's has steadily shifted to its natural resources (Table 2). Gold and furs are no longer significant, but fish continue to give Alaska top ranking among the nation's fisheries, and there has been rapid growth in outputs of forestry products and petroleum. Total natural resource production rose from a value of $130.6 million in 1950 to about $500 million by the end of the 60's. These values are projected to exceed two billion dollars by the last half of the 70's.

This trend started with forest products, the annual cut rising from 72.4 million board feet (MBF) in 1950 to 581.1 MBF in 1969. The maximum sustainable yield of the resource will probably level off at about 800 MBF by the end of the decade (Table 3). The development of the Cook Inlet-Kenai petroleum and natural gas fields reached its peak, or soon will, with production rising from about half a million barrels in 1960 to 74.7 million in 1969 (Table 4). These fields will continue as major producers throughout the decade and beyond, but the annual outputs soon will begin a downward trend.

The 1968 discoveries at Prudhoe Bay added an estimated five to ten billion barrels of crude oil to the nation's reserves, and it is anticipated that the total North Slope province will contain at least two more major fields and possibly add as much as fifty billion barrels of oil and three hundred trillion cubic feet of natural gas to national reserves. Exploration and development work will continue into the opening years of the decade, with production commencing near the mid-1970's. There will be other major discoveries elsewhere

TABLE 1.

Department of Defense Expenditures in Alaska

Year Ending June 30	Wages and Salaries		Prime Contract Awards		
	Military	Civilian	Construction	Procurement	Total
	(Millions of dollars)[1]				
1951	111.0	n. a.	n. a.	n. a.	455.9
1953	148.0	n. a.	n. a.	n. a.	512.9
1960	127.8	44.1	56.9	78.6	307.5
1961	124.1	44.7	40.4	91.8	301.0
1962	128.8	47.8	24.7	63.3	264.6
1963	129.5	46.2	22.8	103.5	302.0
1964	132.7	42.1	51.6	101.5	327.9
1965	149.5	47.9	32.0	74.2	303.7
1966	163.0	50.6	27.1	71.7	312.4
1967	164.1	51.7	32.5	76.7	325.0
1968	154.8	54.9	40.0	107.0	352.0
1969[2]	146.7	65.4	39.0	100.0	337.4

n. a. = comparable data not available

[1] Current unadjusted dollars

[2] Payroll and contracts from Alaska Command. Procurement estimated.

SOURCES: 1951 and 1953 totals and 1960-1968 totals and detail from Executive Office of the President's Bureau of the Budget. 1969 preliminary estimate, Alaska Command data.

TABLE 2.
Value[1] of Major Alaska Natural Resources Production

Calendar Year	Crude Petroleum & Natural Gas	Fisheries Products	Other Minerals	Forest Products	Furs	Commercial Agri. Products	Total Natural Resource Production
		Dollar Value[2] (Millions)					
1950	——	100.2	17.7	6.1	4.4	2.2	130.6
1955	——	69.7	23.6	29.5	4.6	3.4	130.8
1960	1.5	96.7	20.4	47.3	4.8	5.4	176.1
1961	17.8	128.7	16.9	48.0	4.2	5.5	221.1
1962	31.7	131.9	22.5	52.3	4.3	5.8	248.5
1963	33.8	109.0	34.0	54.1	4.4	5.5	240.8
1964	35.5	140.9	30.6	61.0	4.4	5.5	278.0
1965	35.6	166.6	47.6	57.5	5.8	5.2	318.3
1966	50.4	197.3	35.9	73.7	7.0	5.5	369.8
1967	95.5	126.7	39.2	81.5	5.5	5.5	353.9
1968	191.1	191.7	30.6	94.8	6.0	5.3	519.5
1969	218.7	137.7	25.9	106.0	6.0	4.5	498.8
1970	250.0	150.0	30.0	108.0	6.0	5.0	549.0
1975	900.0	200.0	50.0	150.0	6.0	7.0	1,313.0
1980	2,200.0	200.0	80.0	160.0	6.0	8.0	2,654.0

---

[1]*Fisheries products:* Wholesale market value, final stage of processing within Alaska.

Petroleum and natural gas: Crude oil and natural gas at well-heads price. Does *not* include estimate of value by manufacturing.

Other minerals: Average selling price of refined metals as computed by U.S. Bureau of Mines; land, gravel, stone at estimated value to construction industry.

Forest products: Value of pulp and lumber f.o.b. mill.

Furs: Raw fur value, includes U.S. share of sales of Pribilof furs at auction.

Commercial agricultural products: Wholesale market values.

[2]*All dollar values:* In unadjusted current dollars. 1970-80 estimates computed at 1968 unit values.

SOURCES: U.S. Department of the Interior agencies, Alaska Department of Natural Resources, Alaska Department of Fish and Game estimates by G. W. Rogers.

TABLE 3.

Volume of Timber Cut from Government Managed Lands,[1]
and Estimated Value of Wood Products, Alaska, 1950-1980

Calendar Year	U.S. Forest Service	U.S. Bureau of Land Management	Alaska Division of Lands	Bureau of Indian Affairs	Total	(Millions $) Estimated Value of Wood Products[2]
		(Thousands of board feet)				
1950	59,961	12,396	——	——	72,357	36.1
1955	218,766	12,348	——	——	231,114	29.5
1960	351,109	14,913	210	——	366,232	47.3
1965	404,444	3,263	24,161	——	431,868	57.5
1966	476,000	848	31,220	7,132	515,200	73.7
1967	476,816	100[3]	45,816[3]	9,067	531,799	81.5
1968	533,303	100[3]	47,974[3]	8,192	589,569	94.8
1969	523,341	50[3]	49,018[3]	8,684	581,093	106.0
1970	550,000	100	50,000	9,000	609,100	108.0
1975	745,000	10,000	55,000	10,000	820,000	150.0
1980	805,000	15,000	60,000	10,000	890,000	160.0

[1]Timber volumes cut from private lands in Alaska are negligible except in 1969 when an estimated 15.3 million board feet of logs were cut and exported as round logs to Japan at a declared value of $1,800,000.

[2]Value of products f.o.b. mills.

[3]Estimated figure based on timber sales.

SOURCES: U.S. Forest Service, Regional Office, Juneau, Alaska; State Division of Lands, Annual Report; U.S. Bureau of Indian Affairs.

TABLE 4.
Crude Oil Production, By Regions
1960 - 1985

Calendar Year	Cook Inlet-Kenai Fields	North Slope Fields	
		Moderate Development	Rapid Development
	(Thousands of bbls. annually)		
1960	559	—	—
1961	6,327	—	—
1962	10,259	—	—
1963	10,740	—	—
1964	11,059	—	—
1965	11,128	—	—
1966	14,358	—	—
1967	28,917	—	—
1968	66,145	—	—
1969	74,698	—	—
1970	70,000	—	—
1972	66,000	—	180,000
1975	60,000	219,000	292,000
1980	36,000	365,000	730,000
1985	20,000	730,000	1,460,000

SOURCE: 1960-69: Alaska Department of Natural Resources, 1970-85: Stanford Research Institute, *Planning Guidelines for the State of Alaska*, (Menlo Park: 1969), p. 5.

in Alaska, Bristol Bay being a likely candidate for the next development installment, probably after 1980. The actual scheduling will depend heavily on the outcome of the present massive programs for moving the North Slope production to market. Other minerals will be developed, both as a result of the external economies related to petroleum and forest products and in response to national and international demands.

Prior to World War II, Alaska's foreign trade was almost negligible, consisting of goods moving through Alaska to and from Canada's northern territories. It remained insignificant until the 1960's, when exports directly to foreign countries tripled in value from about $20 million to $60 million, most of this in shipments of forest products to Japan. Imports of pipe and industrial supplies and equipment from Japan also rose as resource development expanded (Table 5). Projections for total foreign trade in the future are based on amounts identified in existing or planned contracts for continuing major deliveries of wood products and petrochemicals to Japan. Interest is being shown in the entire range of Alaska's natural resources, including the purchase of fish and fish products from Alaska fishermen and shore plants.

There is now significant international investment in most phases of Alaska's recent developments in oil, forest products, minerals, and fisheries. The subsequent growth of Alaska's foreign trade that has accompanied this shift in investment points toward a growing international orientation.

Alaska's Resident Economy

Statistics on federal spending in Alaska and total wholesale value of resource production do not give a true picture of the Alaska economy. Much of the construction and procurement expenditures never enter the resident economy because the equipment and supplies must be imported. Some local resources may be converted into construction materials and local resale activities may be generated, but only a fraction of the money actually enters the state

TABLE 5.

Alaska's Foreign Trade[1]

Annual Average for Periods:	Exports		Imports	
	Total	Japan	Total	Japan
		(millions of dollars[2])		
1931 - 1940	0.4	——	0.3	——
1948 - 1953	2.8	——	1.4	——
1954 - 1959	7.3	——	2.9	——
Calendar Year				
1960	19.5	——	5.7	——
1961	25.2	——	6.5	——
1962	24.4	18.6	8.1	——
1963	32.1	26.3	8.1	0.8
1964	36.0	30.4	6.9	0.9
1965	36.7	29.1	7.9	2.2
1966	43.3	38.9	10.1	2.2
1967	47.4	41.5	11.7	5.2
1968	55.3	47.3	23.7	5.5
1969 (est.)	60.0	50.0	70.0	50.0[3]
1970	70.0	60.0	300.0	260.0[3]
1975	120.0	100.0	80.0	50.0
1980	350.0	200.0	100.0	50.0

[1]Direct shipments to and from Alaska. Does not show foreign products shipped via the continental U.S. or Alaska products shipped to the continental U.S. destined for foreign markets.

[2]Current unadjusted dollars.

[3]Includes TAPS pipe from Japan.

SOURCE: U.S. Department of Commerce, Bureau of the Census. Estimates by G. W. Rogers.

and the multiplier effect in the Alaska economy is low. The construction work force has a strong nonresident bias, and a great deal of the total value of natural resources likewise escapes the resident economy in the form of profits, interest, equipment and supplies purchases, transport, and seasonal wages paid to nonresidents.

The Alaska economy can be better represented and analyzed in terms of standard statistical series on population, employed work force, and personal income received by resident Alaskans. The total figures for each series give a composite impression of the relative size of the total economy and its trends (Table 6). Although growth has been continuous, rates of increase were highest during the 1950's. The work force declined as a percentage of total population during that decade, reflecting an increase in the number of families (dependent-worker ratios). Increases in income have done better than just keep up with inflation during the 60's.

Table 7 summarizes the annual estimates by the U.S. Bureau of the Census (1950-70)[2] for military personnel and resident civilians and presents the major components of change. This series indicates that the spectacular upsurge in population between the 1940 and 1950 census enumerations continued into the early 50's, after which the rate of increase began to decline (in two years there was an absolute decline). Military movements played the dominant role in generating marked immigrations between 1950 and 1953 and out-migrations between 1956 and 1960. The Alaska earthquake of 1964 and its reconstruction aftermath account for much of the fluctuation in migration between 1964 and 1967, and the North Slope oil boom and related activities account for the final upsurge of in-migration in 1969. Natural net increase rose sharply during the first half of the 1950's, in part because of the growing population base, but primarily as a reflection of the increasing effectiveness of public health programs in reducing the tragically high Native death rates. Subsequent declines reflect a leveling off of reduced death rates and a decline in birth rates.

TABLE 6.

Estimated Total Population, Employed Workforce,
Participation Rates, and Personal Income Received
By Residents, 1950-1980

Calendar Year	Total Population[1]	Total Employed Workforce[2]	Participation Rate[3]	Total Personal Income
	(12 month average, thou. persons)		(%)	(Millions $)[4]
1950	138.0	78.5	56.9	322
1955	221.0	108.8	49.2	505
1960	228.0	100.1	43.9	649
1961	235.0	106.8	45.4	635
1962	243.0	108.7	44.7	666
1963	251.0	113.1	45.1	704
1964	256.0	117.5	45.9	791
1965	267.0	114.0	42.7	858
1966	272.0	116.5	42.8	915
1967	278.0	121.7	43.8	1,017
1968	285.0	123.6	43.4	1,136
1969	295.0	131.0	44.4	1,272
1970	305.0	137.0	44.9	1,350
1975	365.0	160.0	43.9	1,600
1980	407.0	178.0	43.7	1,800

[1]Population:　12 month moving average. Centered on July.

[2]Includes members of the armed forces and other Department of Defense employees.

[3]Employed workforce a percentage of total population.

[4]Personal income in current dollars. Projections for 1969-1980 in 1968 dollars.

SOURCES: Population from U.S. Bureau of the Census, *Current Population Reports.* Series P-25 and Alaska Department of Labor.

Workforce from Alaska Department of Labor, *Workforce Estimates, Alaska By Industry* (annual summary), plus estimates military personnel from population estimates.

Personal income estimates by Office of Business and Economics, U.S. Department of Commerce.

1970 and 1980 estimates:　G.W. Rogers worksheets for Alaska Department of Labor, *Alaska's Manpower Outlook—1970's.*

TABLE 7.

Estimates of Total Alaska Resident Population and
Components of Change, 1950-1969

July 1	Total Population	Population Composition[1] Military	Civilian	Total	Components of Change[2] Natural Increase	Net Migration Military	Civilian
			(thousands of persons)				
1950	138.0	26.0	112.0	8.0	2.5	(4.0)	9.5
1951	164.0	38.0	126.0	26.0	2.8	12.0	11.2
1952	196.0	50.0	146.0	32.0	3.8	12.0	16.2
1953	212.0	50.0	162.0	16.0	5.0	——	11.0
1954	218.0	49.0	169.0	6.0	6.1	(1.0)	0.9
1955	221.0	50.0	171.0	3.0	6.4	1.0	(4.4)
1956	220.0	45.0	175.0	(1.0)	6.5	(5.0)	(2.5)
1957	228.0	48.0	180.0	8.0	6.7	3.0	(1.7)
1958	213.0	35.0	178.0	(15.0)	6.5	(13.0)	(8.5)
1959	220.0	34.0	186.0	7.0	6.5	(1.0)	1.5
1960	228.0	33.0	195.0	8.0	6.3	(1.0)	2.7
1961	235.0	33.0	202.0	7.0	6.3	——	0.7
1962	243.0	33.0	210.0	8.0	6.4	——	1.6
1963	251.0	34.0	217.0	8.0	6.5	1.0	0.5
1964	256.0	35.0	221.0	5.0	6.5	1.0	(2.5)[3]
1965	267.0	33.0	234.0	11.0	6.3	(2.0)	6.7[3]
1966	272.0	32.0	241.0	5.0	5.8	(1.0)	0.2
1967	278.0	33.0	245.0	6.0	5.5	2.0	(1.5)
1968	285.0	33.0	252.0	7.0	5.4	——	1.6
1969	295.0	32.0	263.0	10.0	5.3	(1.0)	5.7

[1]Estimates are 12 month moving averages centered on July 1.
[2]Decreases are net out-migrations shown in parentheses.
[3]Reflects effects of 1964 earthquake and 1965 reconstruction.

SOURCES: 1950-1966: U.S. Bureau of the Census, *Current Population Reports*, Series
P-25; 1967-1969: Alaska Department of Labor *Current Population Estimates,
Alaska.*

The total impact of the Department of Defense on the economy requires special accounting and analysis, but the impact on the resident population is obvious and directly recorded in the summing up of military personnel, civilian employees, and their dependents (Table 8). Even these partial data (workers and dependents of private contractors with the department are not included) indicate that military-associated population accounted for 32 per cent of total resident population in 1964 and 25 per cent in 1969.

Annual data on employed work force by industrial classification give a good representation of the structure of the Alaska economy and its shifts over time (Table 9). Trends in both the defense and commodity producing components of the economy were discussed in the previous section. By translating these components from dollar expenditures and product values into employment, we have illustrated the degree to which they are shared between the Alaska and "outside" economies. The rise in employment in commodity producing industries between 1950 and 1969 has been modest for two decades of development. The 1950 level of 13,900 was not exceeded until 1967. Contributions to the significant rises since and those projected to 1980 come from the oil and gas and the construction industries, but the employment growth rates fall far below those for the corresponding value data because much of the petroleum industry is capital-intensive. Distributive industries and nondefense government employment grew most dynamically and caused continual change in the structure of the total economy from 1959 to 1969. These components require further analysis and comment.

Distributive industries (transportation, communication, public utilities, wholesale and retail trade, finance, insurance, real estate and services) are generally considered support activities for commodity producing industries and serve the total population. In a developed and stable economy it can be assumed that the relative position of these industries in the total employment pattern is fairly constant. During past periods of slow growth or stagnation, this was also true of Alaska's employment patterns (see data for 1950 and 1955, Table 9, for example). Since 1958, however, the Alaska economy has been

TABLE 8.

Department of Defense Military, Civilian Employees, and
Dependents in the State of Alaska, 1964-1969

YEAR	MILITARY	CIVILIAN EMPLOYEES[1]	MILITARY DEPENDENTS	CIVILIAN DEPENDENTS	TOTAL MILITARY ASSOCIATED POPULATION
1964	35,000	5,700	37,100	3,500	81,300
1965	33,000	6,200	34,700	7,700	81,600
1966	32,000	6,200	32,900	7,600	78,700
1967	33,000	6,200	32,400	7,700	79,300
1968	33,000	6,300	31,800	8,000	79,100
1969	32,000	5,860	30,360	4,990	73,210

[1]These data do not check exactly with Alaska Department of Labor data because of different reporting bases.

SOURCE: Alaskan Command records.

TABLE 9.

TOTAL EMPLOYED WORKFORCE—STATE OF ALASKA, 1950-1980

	1950	1955	1960	1965	1966	1967	1968	1969	1975	1980
	(12 month average—thousands of persons)									
TOTAL EMPLOYED WORKFORCE	78.5	108.8	100.1	114.0	116.5	121.7	123.6	130.9	160.0	178.0
DEPARTMENT OF DEFENSE	31.0	59.0	41.5	39.5	39.7	40.4	39.4	39.0	38.5	38.5
Military Personnel	26.0	50.0	33.0	33.0	33.2	33.7	32.6	32.4	31.7	31.7
Civilian Employees	5.0	9.0	8.5	6.5	6.5	6.7	6.8	6.6	6.8	6.8
COMMODITY PRODUCING INDUSTRIES	13.9	12.7	12.8	13.8	13.9	14.6	15.4	17.2	25.8	27.6
Oil and Natural Gas	0.5	0.1	0.4	0.7	1.0	1.6	2.2	3.2	4.5	4.3
Other Mining	1.4	1.2	0.7	0.4	0.4.	0.4	0.3	0.3	1.7	2.4
Construction	6.3	6.4	5.9	6.4	5.9	6.0	6.0	6.7	9.3	8.9
Manufacturing										
Food Processing	4.7	2.9	2.8	3.0	3.4	3.1	3.3	2.7	2.7	2.8
Wood Products[1]	0.6	1.5	2.2	2.3	2.3	2.6	2.5	2.5	4.1	4.8
Other	0.4	0.6	0.8	1.0	0.9	0.9	1.1	1.8	3.5	4.4
DISTRIBUTIVE INDUSTRIES	12.2	16.8	21.4	27.0	28.4	30.5	32.2	36.0	46.5	54.7
Transportation, Communications, and Public Utilities	3.7	5.0	6.8	7.2	7.3	7.5	7.8	8.8	10.9	13.0
Trade,										
Wholesale	0.4	0.9	1.4	1.9	2.1	2.4	2.5	2.8	4.5	5.3
Retail	4.5	5.5	6.3	8.1	8.7	9.4	10.0	11.2	13.5	15.7
Finance, Insurance, etc.	0.4	0.9	1.4	2.2	2.3	2.3	2.5	2.6	4.2	5.4
Services and Miscellaneous	3.2	4.5	5.5	7.6	8.0	8.9	9.4	10.6	13.4	15.3
GOVERNMENT (NONDEFENSE)	10.7	10.4	14.2	23.2	24.3	25.1	25.4	26.8	34.7	40.7
Federal (other than Defense)	8.6	8.7	7.1	10.9	11.0	10.7	10.1	9.9	10.1	11.2
State (Territory)	0.9	1.8	3.9	7.0	7.6	8.1	8.7	9.3	14.0	17.0
Local	1.2	1.9	3.2	5.3	5.7	6.3	6.6	7.6	10.6	12.5
NONWAGE & NONSALARY EMPLOYMENT	10.7	9.9	10.2	10.5	10.2	12.0	11.2	11.9	14.5	16.5

[1]Logging, lumber, pulp.

SOURCE: Alaska Department of Labor, *Workforce Estimates*. Military from 1950 and 1960 Census and 1960-1969 annual *Current Population Estimates*. 1975 and 1980 projection from Alaska Department of Labor, *Alaska's Manpower Outlook—1970's*, worksheets.

in a period of growth and change in industrial composition, with distributive industries' employment increasing both absolutely and relative to population and total employment (Table 10). During this period, the establishment of the Department of Defense early warning and communications systems were completed and substantial staffing was assumed by private contractors. Since the mid-1950's, the urbanization of Alaska's population has continued at accelerating rates, accompanied by declines in rural populations. Growth in tourism is evidenced by continuous and significant increase in travel to and from Alaska and the high demand for space on cruise ships, the Alaska ferry system, and airlines during the summer. This impact was also registered in distributive industries. Finally, since the early 1950's there has been a continuous shifting of headquarters functions in Alaska's private industry from Seattle and other outside places to Anchorage and other urban centers in Alaska. This was first noticed immediately after World War II in the increase in wholesale trade employment relative to retail trade employment. It is now most evident in the evolution of the Alaska petroleum industry, which has a larger administrative and support service work force based in the state than have any of Alaska's past major industries. For the future, it is assumed that these trends will continue, but at a declining rate, and will level off by the end of the decade.

Federal government employment in Alaska has always been abnormally high relative to population and total employment. In part, this is because of a number of special programs associated with managing the huge acreage of public domain lands in Alaska (approximately half of all lands owned by the federal government are located in Alaska), the relatively large number of indigenous peoples who are nominally wards of the federal government (approximately one-fifth of Alaska's total population), and the basic transportation and communications functions performed by federal agencies that are private responsibilities elsewhere (Alaska Communications System, Alaska Railroad, etc.). The largest single factor contributing to the high level of federal employment, however, is Alaska's importance to national defense. Besides its obvious direct effect on employment, the defense establishment also increases federal involvement in transportation, communications and public works.

TABLE 10

Shifts in Distributive Industries Employment
Relative to Total Population and Total Employment,
State of Alaska

Calendar Year	Total Population	Total Employment[1]	Distributive Industries
1950			
Thousand persons[2]	138.0	78.5	12.2
% of total population	100.0	56.9	8.9
% of total employment	——	100.0	15.5
1955			
Thousand persons	221.0	108.8	16.8
% of total population	100.0	49.2	7.6
% of total employment	——	100.0	15.4
1960			
Thousand persons	228.0	101.1	21.4
% of total population	100.0	43.9	9.4
% of total employment	——	100.0	21.2
1965			
Thousand persons	267.0	114.0	27.0
% of total population	100.0	42.7	10.1
% of total employment	——	100.0	23.7
1969			
Thousand persons	291.0	130.5	35.9
% of total population	100.0	35.6	12.3
% of total employment	——	100.0	27.5

[1]Includes military personnel

[2]Population: 12 month moving average centered on July 1.

Employment: 12 month average for calendar year

SOURCE: Table 9.

Since the mid-1960's, a modest but continuing decline in federal nondefense employment (from 10,900 in 1965 to 9,900 in 1969) has accompanied the final phases of transfer of certain functions to the new state government (Table 11). For the future, it is assumed that federal programs in Alaska will share the same expansionist forces operating elsewhere in the nation, but there will be deflating forces in the form of continuing transfer of land management functions to the State of Alaska and the implications of provisions included in pending Native lands legislation, which would make the future of Native education, health, and social services a state responsibility.

Changes in the levels of employment in state and local government should reflect population change and development requirements. Alaska's experience has clearly demonstrated, however, that the most dynamic influence has been changes in revenue availability. Shortly after statehood, for example, the formula for calculating federal funds for highway construction in Alaska was changed to acquire generous federal funding for a token state participation (approximately five cents state money for every dollar of highway construction funds). This resulted in a dramatic increase in state government employment caused by the expansion of the Department of Highways. Since the growth of the petroleum industry has provided an expanding source of state revenues, which has more than kept pace with the rate of state government expenditures and employment growth, the growth of state and local government employment has been at a greater rate than that of population or total employment (Table 11).

By the mid-1960's, the State of Alaska had substantially accomplished the transfer of functions performed by the federal government during the territorial period. The establishment of an adequate local government system, however, is still in process. On the state level, it is assumed that the expenditure and/or investment of the September 1969 oil lease sales bonuses and anticipated production revenues will exert an upward influence beyond that required to meet the bare necessities of population growth and development requirements. In the rural north and west there will be further growth factors created by shifting Native health and

TABLE 11.

Shifts in Nondefense Government Employment
Relative to Total Population
and Total Employment

Calendar Year	Total Population	Total Employment[1]	Nondefense Federal Government[2]	State (Territory)- Local Government
1950				
Thousand persons	138.0	78.5	8.6	2.1
% of total population	100.0	56.9	6.2	1.5
% of total employment	——	100.0	10.9	2.7
1955				
Thousand persons	221.0	108.8	6.7	3.7
% of total population	100.0	49.2	3.0	1.7
% of total employment	——	100.0	6.3	3.4
1960				
Thousand persons	228.0	101.1	7.1	7.1
% of total population	100.0	43.9	3.1	3.1
% of total employment	——	100.0	7.0	7.0
1965				
Thousand persons	267.0	114.0	10.9[3]	12.3
% of total population	100.0	42.7	4.1	4.6
% of total employment	——	100.0	9.5	10.8
1969				
Thousand persons	291.0	130.5	9.9	16.9
% of total population	100.0	35.6	3.4	5.8
total employment	——	100.0	7.6	13.0

[1]Includes military personnel.

[2]Excludes all military personnel and civilian employees of the Department of Defense.

[3]Includes some temporary expansion associated with Alaska's 1964 earthquake recovery and new poverty and development programs.

SOURCE: Table 9.

education programs from the federal to the state and local levels in the aftermath of a Native lands settlement, and by establishing local government units in the present "unorganized borough" areas through legislation and funding.

Coming to Alaska to make a quick fortune appears to be an enduring American myth. Much of this has its basis in reports of high wages made on emergency construction projects, an unusually large salmon harvest, or the gold and oil bonanzas. The rest of the facts of life are conveniently omitted: too many Alaskans in the rural villages live at or close to a bare subsistence survival level; high earnings realized in a brief summer season must be made to carry others over the lean off-season months, and the high cost of living drastically deflates the U.S. dollar in Alaska.

A truer picture of income in Alaska can be gained from published statistics on average incomes and living costs. Table 12 summarizes the U.S. Department of Commerce's annual estimates of per capita income for Alaska, the far west, and the United States. Although generally above the national average, the trend toward increase in Alaska's per capita income has slowed in relation to both national and far west trends. In 1957 through 1959, Alaska actually dropped below the far west averages and has since remained near that level. From a 1950 high of 1.59 times the national per capita income, Alaska's personal income fell to about 1.21 of national averages. Because Alaska's much higher cost of living has not been considered in these comparisons (they are all expressed in current unadjusted United States dollars), the magnitude of this relative decline in per capita income is not fully revealed (Table 13).

Again, population data give additional insight into the economic and geographic dimensions of change in Alaska during the 1960's (Table 14). The 30.2 per cent increase between April 1, 1960 and July 1, 1969 was not evenly shared throughout the state. Five of the original twenty-four election districts of the state actually experienced significant loss of population (because of migration and declining birth rates) and four had net increases by 1969 of less than 10 per cent of their 1960 population. At the other end of the scale, eleven districts exceeded the state's relative growth, the highest being

TABLE 12.

Per Capita Personal Income
Alaska, Far West, and United States
1950-1969

Calendar Year	Alaska	Far West[1]	United States	Ratio: Alaska to United States
		(current unadjusted dollars)		
1950	$2,385	$1,788	$1,496	1.59
1951	2,835	1,975	1,653	1.72
1952	2,614	2,068	1,734	1.51
1953	2,493	2,103	1,805	1.38
1954	2,302	2,089	1,785	1.29
1955	2,275	2,210	1,876	1.21
1956	2,446	2,326	1,976	1.24
1957	2,325	2,397	2,045	1.14
1958	2,357	2,430	2,068	1.14
1959	2,509	2,572	2,161	1.16
1960	2,835	2,621	2,215	1.28
1961	2,681	2,691	2,264	1.18
1962	2,731	2,808	2,368	1.15
1963	2,785	2,906	2,455	1.13
1964	3,052	3,043	2,586	1.18
1965	3,226	3,182	2,765	1.17
1966	3,473	3,410	2,980	1.17
1967	3,798	3,602	3,162	1.20
1968	4,116	3,895	3,421	1.20
1969	4,513	4,158	3,680	1.23

[1]California, Washington, Oregon, Nevada.

SOURCE: Office of Business Economics, U.S. Department of Commerce. 1960-69 revised estimates; *Survey of Current Business*, April 1970.

TABLE 13.

Indexes of Intercity Differences in the Cost of Equivalent Goods and Services

Anchorage, Fairbanks, Juneau, and Ketchikan Alaska, Compared with Seattle Washington[1]

Autumn 1964, 1965, 1966, 1967, and 1968 (Costs in Seattle = 100)

City and Year		All Items	Food[2]	Housing Total[3]	Housing Rental[4]	Apparel and Upkeep	Other Goods and Services[5]	All Items Less Housing
Anchorage	1964	123	121	132	162	110	120	119
	1965	122	123	130	157	110	117	118
	1966	122	123	130	152	112	116	118
	1967	121	122	130	146	108	116	117
	1968	119	119	127	142	110	115	115
Fairbanks	1964	134	138	143	188	124	127	130
	1965	133	140	141	187	124	123	129
	1966	132	139	141	180	122	122	127
	1967	132	142	140	179	120	121	127
	1968	132	139	141	176	126	120	127
Juneau	1964	124	123	133	150	118	119	120
	1965	124	126	134	151	116	116	119
	1966	125	127	135	147	115	117	120
	1967	127	132	137	147	115	119	122
	1968	126	130	135	146	117	117	121
Ketchikan	1964	119	118	121	126	117	117	117
	1965	117	119	121	127	116	113	116
	1966	118	122	122	127	114	113	116
	1967	118	123	122	126	117	113	117
	1968	119	121	122	124	118	115	117

[1]Based on the average pattern of expenditures of Alaskan wage and clerical-worker families of two or more persons who were full-year residents in the state during 1959 or 1960. (Average expenditures of families living in Anchorage, Fairbanks, Juneau, or Ketchikan were combined with a system of weights based on the estimated number of consumer units in each city as derived from the 1960 Census of Population).

[2]Includes food at home and away from home.

[3]Includes rent, hotel and motel rates, homeownership costs (mortgage principal and interest payments, taxes, insurance, maintenance, and repairs), fuel and utilities, household furnishings and operation. (Intercity indexes measure differences in the costs of maintaining a home as reflected in principal payments and mortgage interest charges. These indexes cannot be used to measure changes in acquisition costs, i.e., interest rates and the prices of owned homes purchased in current markets.)

[4]Average contract rent for tenant-occupied, 2-, 3-, 4-, and 5-room dwellings meeting defined standards, plus cost of heating fuel, utilities, and specified equipment when the cost of these items is not included in the monthly rent.

[5]Includes transportation, medical care, personal care, recreation, reading and education, tobacco, beverages, and miscellaneous expenses.

SOURCE: U.S. Department of Labor, Bureau of Labor Statistics.

TABLE 14.

Estimates[1] of Total Resident Population of Alaska
By Election District, July 1, 1969 and April 1, 1960

		July 1	April 1	NET CHANGE		Military
	ELECTION DISTRICT[2]	1969	1960	Number	Per cent	Personnel
	ALASKA	294,560	226,170	68,390	30.2	32,360
1	Ketchikan-Prince of Wales, Total	14,910	11,840	3,070	25.9	330
	Ketchikan (2)	12,810	10,070	2,740	27.2	330
	Prince of Wales (1)	2,100	1,770	330	18.6	——
2	Wrangell-Petersburg (3)	5,970	4,180	1,790	42.8	20
3	Sitka (4)	7,770	6,690	1,080	16.1	70
4	Juneau (5)	13,330[3]	9,750	3,580	36.7	230
5	Lynn Canal-Icy Straits (6)	3,620	2,950	670	22.7	20
6	Cordova-Valdez, Total	4,540	4,600	-60	-1.3	70
	Cordova-McCarthy (7)	2,240	1,760	480	27.3	70
	Valdez-Chitina-Whittier (8)	2,300	2,840	-540	-19.0	——
7	Palmer-Wasilla-Talkeetna (9)	7,000	5,190	1,810	34.9	——
8	Anchorage (10)	114,150[4]	82,830	31,320	37.8	14,460
9	Seward (11)	2,700	2,960	-260	-8.8	50
10	Kenai-Cook Inlet (12)	13,550	6,100	7,450	122.1	450
11	Kodiak (13)	9,870	7,170	2,700	37.7	1,670
12	Aleutian Islands (14)	8,660	6,010	2,650	44.1	3,660
13	Bristol Bay (15)	5,040	4,020	1,020	25.4	470
14	Bethel (16)	7,750	5,540	2,210	39.9	100
15	Yukon-Kuskokwim, Total	6,780	6,400	380	5.9	1,000
	Kuskokwim (17)	2,850	2,300	550	23.9	270
	Yukon-Koyukuk (18)	3,930	4,100	-170	-4.1	730
16	Fairbanks-Fort Yukon, Total	48,900	45,030	3,870	8.6	9,170
	Fairbanks (19)	47,320	43,410	3,910	9.0	5,920
	Upper Yukon (20)	1,580	1,620	-40	-2.5	250
17	Barrow-Kobuk, Total	9,060	5,690	3,370	59.2	240
	Barrow (21)	4,480	2,130	2,350	110.3	100
	Kobuk (22)	4,580	3,560	1,020	28.7	100
18	Nome (23)	6,390	6,090	300	4.9	290
19	Wade Hampton (24)	4,570	3,130	1,440	46.0	100

[1]All data including 1960 Census data have been rounded to the nearest ten.

[2]1960 Election (Census) district indicated in parentheses.

[3]Special Census taken December 1968 tabulated 12,853.

[4]Special Census taken October 1968 tabulated 113,522.

SOURCE: Alaska Department of Labor, *Current Population Estimates by Election District Alaska, 1969.*

the Kenai-Cook Inlet district with a 122.1 per cent increase and the Barrow district with 110.3 per cent, almost all of which occurred between 1967 and 1969.

NOTES

[1]Humble Oil and Refining Co. has suspended research on Northwest Passage transportation of oil by ice-breaking tankers announcing that "ice-breaking tankers are economically feasible but pipeline transportation appears to have an economic edge at present." *Fairbanks Daily News-Miner*, October 21, 1970.

[2]Final 1970 census figures released in November 1970 indicated the state's population at 302,173.

ADDITIONAL READING

"Alaska's $50 - Billion Boom." *Forbes.* November 15, 1969.

Armstrong, Terence. "Soviet Northern Development, with Some Alaskan Parallels and Contrasts." *ISEGR Occasional Paper.* No. 2. College, Alaska: Institute of Social, Economic and Government Research, October 1970.

Boll, Heinrick. "Northwest Passage to What?" *Saturday Review.* November 1, 1969.

Chasan, Daniel Jack. "On this side, nothing but Virgin Wilderness . . . On that side, nothing but Virgin Wilderness . . . Down the middle, the Trans Alaska Pipeline." *Esquire.* June 1970.

Cooley, Richard A. *Politics and Conservation: The Decline of the Alaska Salmon.* New York: Harper and Row, 1963.

Frederick, Robert A., editor. *Frontier Alaska: Historical Interpretation and Opportunity.* Anchorage: Alaska Methodist University Press, 1967.

Gruening, Ernest. *The Battle for Alaska Statehood.* College, Alaska: University of Alaska Press, 1967.

Gruening, Ernest. *The State of Alaska.* New York: Random House, 1968.

Hulley, Clarence C. *Alaska: Past and Present.* Portland, Oregon: Binfords and Mort, 1970.

Lapham, Lewis. "Alaska: Politicians and Natives, Money and Oil." *Harpers Magazine.* May, 1970.

Nichols, Jeannette P. "Alaska's Search for a Usable Past." *Pacific Northwest Quarterly.* April, 1968.

Rogers, George W. *Alaska in Transition.* Baltimore: Johns Hopkins Press, 1960.

Rogers, George W. "Avenues to Alaska Development." *Alaska Review.* Vol. II, No. 4, 1967.

Rogers, George W. (ed.) *Change in Alaska: People, Petroleum and Politics.* Seattle: University of Washington Press, 1970.

Rogers, George W. "Current Political Trends in Alaska." *Polar Record* Vol. XIV, No. 91, 1969.

Rogers, George W. *The Future of Alaska.* Baltimore: Johns Hopkins Press, 1962.

Wilson, William H. "Alaska's Past; Alaska's Future." *Alaska Review.* Vol. IV, No. 1, 1970.

SECTION II: LAND

This article was prepared for presentation at the Battelle Memorial Institute Conference, "Land Management in the 70's: Concepts and Models," Seattle, Washington, September 11, 1970.

ISSUES OF LAND USE DETERMINATION IN ALASKA
For an Alaska Omnibus Land Act

Arlon R. Tussing

In principle, effective land use planning should be much easier in Alaska than in other states because virtually all the land is still empty of intensive economic activity or of vested private rights; more than 98 per cent of the land remains in government ownership, federal or state, and more than two-thirds of the land remains unreserved federal public domain. The two governments as landlords can directly determine present and future land use patterns, the patterns of settlement and industry, and the quality of environmental protection. Nevertheless, the question of proprietorship, that is, the question who shall own and control what are presently the public lands in Alaska, is still the key issue in land use determination in the forty-ninth state; almost every other question of land or environmental policy depends upon the resolution of this issue. Yet the interaction of the public land laws, aboriginal rights of the Indians and Eskimos, and the policies of the state and federal government, have made the ultimate ownership of most of the land in Alaska subject to extreme uncertainty, and moves either to develop or to protect Alaska's lands and resources have been brought to a general standstill.

The Federal Land Laws: First Come-First Served

The main source of this stalemate is the philosophy implicit in most of the federal land laws that land and resources are extremely abundant compared to the demands on them, and that the public interest in these lands and resources is in disposing of them rapidly. Almost all the laws applicable to the unreserved public domain, and a substantial number of the laws which apply to other kinds of federal property, dispose of land or resources on a first come-first served basis and are self-executing. A miner simply stakes a claim and automatically acquires an equitable right in the land staked. He may do anything to that land he thinks is necessary to prove or develop a mine, without regard to the impact on wildlife, on the watershed, or scenery, or any of the other values of the surface or of adjacent lands. Likewise the homesteader chooses his land anywhere on the unreserved and unclassified public domain, whether or not it is suitable for agriculture, clears a portion of it, and plants a crop. Whether or not that crop is ever harvested, the homesteader now has a legally defensible right to the land. There are almost no restrictions upon geological and geophysical exploration for oil and gas on the public domain, although these activities may significantly affect surface resources. On most of the public lands oil and gas rights are leased to the first applicant regardless of their probable value. The pre-emptive and self-executing features of the law are not confined to private appropriation. Any federal agency may reserve land for its exclusive use simply by filing a withdrawal order with the Secretary of the Interior. Unilateral withdrawals of public land are made for administrative sites, defense reservations, hydro power sites, protection of wildlife, protection of antiquities, for public roads, and for a host of other purposes. All of these are legitimate public purposes, but many withdrawals are much larger or more restrictive than any public interest would justify, and they typically survive long after their original purposes have been discharged. In few instances is there adequate provision for public hearings, for the weighing of alternative uses, or for review and reversion of the withdrawal.

States also have pre-emptive rights in the land. An 1866 law allows any state an unrestricted right to build a road across federal public domain. More important here, Alaska is entitled under its Statehood Act to select more than a hundred million acres of unreserved public domain generally without review and without weighing of the national interest in this land.[1] Rather, the state is entitled to select land provided no one else gets it first. That is, the state's selection right, which is in many respects the heart of the statehood act and the guarantee of the state's economic and fiscal viability, is limited to whatever the homesteaders, miners, mineral lease speculators and the various federal agencies have not first pre-empted.[2]

Native Land Claims: A Total Stalemate

In this system of first come-first served land disposal, the first users were, of course, the aboriginal occupants of Alaska: the Eskimos, Indians and Aleuts. Their claims cloud almost every other land claim or title, private or governmental. But no administrative or legal machinery and no clearly applicable body of case law exists to reconcile aboriginal rights in Alaska with the public land laws and the Alaska Statehood Act.[3] The legal and political relationship between aboriginal occupancy and other land uses in Alaska is basically unchanged from the indeterminate situation set out in the Alaska Organic Act of 1884, which provided that ". . . the Indians or other persons in said district shall not be disturbed in the possession of any lands actually in their use or occupation or now claimed by them but the terms under which such persons may acquire title to such lands is reserved for future legislation by Congress."[4]

The Alaska "Land Freeze"

The protests of Native groups against the disposed of lands claimed by them have brought to a halt state selections and most other kinds of land and resource transfers under the public land laws. Shortly before and shortly after he became Secretary of the Interior, Walter J. Hickel made a number of remarks about "lifting" this land freeze.[5] But the Senate Committee on Interior and Insular Affairs went to great pains to convince the secretary that things were not that simple, and that resolution of the problem required affirmative action by Congress.[6] More recently, the Ninth Circuit Court of Appeals—and implicitly the Supreme Court, by denying review—has held that a Native protest cannot be summarily overridden; that is, that the state's selection rights take second place to aboriginal rights which are as yet undefined.[7]

The lands of Alaska were not completely fragmented in the past only because of their remoteness and the general lack of interest in them. Now, settlement of the Native claims and an abrupt end to the land freeze would lead to new land use conflicts, administrative confusion, and litigation; the discovery of a multi-billion dollar oil province has given new life to every old device for getting free or cheap land. The roads and air strips associated with oil development and with the proposed pipeline will rapidly open public access to literally millions of acres which can now be drawn into the scramble.[8]

Political Conditions of a Settlement

In the remainder of my time I shall outline a possible resolution of these problems. My main propositions are

(1) that the issues of Native claims, environmental protection, resource development, and land administration are intertwined enough and urgent enough to justify their simultaneous resolution by Congress;

(2) that the principal contending groups—the Natives, the oil and gas industry, the conservation interests and the state—would all benefit from such a settlement; that each of them is in practice willing to compromise; and finally

(3) that the elements of such a resolution are already at hand for action in this Congress—in the form of a Native claims settlement already passed by the Senate, together with some of the recommendations of the Public Land Law Review Commission.

Alaska's Native claims, together with the land freeze, have imposed some costs or delays in widely scattered parts of Alaska's economy. But above all, they have been a major contribution to delaying construction of the trans-Alaska pipeline. Hundreds of millions of dollars annually in industry profits and state royalties and taxes wait upon the pipeline project; construction activity alone will be in the order of a billion dollars. This stake has given a settlement special urgency to the oil and gas industry, to the state government and to all those who expect a share either of the construction boom or of the state's royalty income. In this way the Natives have been given a powerful lever to influence when and how their claims shall be settled.

The initial obstacle to a pipeline—that its route must cross Native-claimed land—coincided with the mushrooming of concern for ecology, pollution and wilderness in Alaska and nationally, and with passage of the National Environmental Policy Act. This timing has given the environmental protection interests a significant bargaining position, if not a veto power, on the conditions under which a trans-Alaska pipeline may be built. In the same way, the advocates of wilderness and wildlife will have an important influence on Congress' dispostion of the Native land claims.

The new influence of Alaska Natives and of the conservation forces have drawn an understandably negative reaction from the state government and from the development factions. The public discourse among the various groups has tended to emphasize slogans like, "The Rape of Alaska," or, on the other side, "The Plot to Strangle Alaska." But the real aims of each of the contending parties may be less extravagant than its slogans, and there is evidence that each one of them is in fact willing to compromise. The behavior and thinking of the oil companies operating on the North Slope have undergone amazing transformations since it became clear that the American people cared about what happened to that remote tundra and to its wildlife. The land scars and the garbage of oil exploration twenty years, five years, and two years ago are still conspicuous, but their contrast with most of today's practices can be ignored only by those who are determined to see the worst. And the preparations for building the trans-Alaska pipeline have become continually more scrupulous through the constant pressure of world publicity and of the National Environmental Policy Act.

The past speeches of Alaska politicians like Secretary Hickel, Senator Ted Stevens, or Tom Kelly, the state's Commissioner of Natural Resources, are rich with belligerent statements about conservationists and about ecology. But you can find few such statements made by these three gentlemen over the last year, and Wally Hickel's utterances are mainly on the other side these days. I am also impressed by the firm support that Secretary Hickel and Senator Stevens have given to settlement of the Native land claims. And the view that the business and political establishment of Alaska has the support of the overwhelming majority of the state's voters for a policy of development at any cost is not consistent with the fact that almost every statewide candidate in this year's primary election made environmental protection one of his top campaign slogans.[9]

On the other side, listen carefully to Dr. Edgar Wayburn of the Sierra Club, to Dr. Robert Weeden, who was the conservation lobbyist at the Alaska legislature, or to Art Davidson, the Alaska representative of the Friends of the Earth. Their aims are not to lock up all of Alaska in an absolute wilderness, but their seeming inflexibility comes from the fact that wilderness is about the only interest which has no right to pre-empt land under the public land laws, so that no block of wilderness will be preserved in Alaska so long as there is anyone at all who has another use for it.

The continuation of the land deadlock in Alaska will impose new costs on all sides. It is an obstacle to construction to pipelines for the North Slope, and to the state's land selection program. Without the flow of royalties and severance taxes from Prudhoe Bay production, the expectations generated by the state's $900 million windfall in 1969 will probably leave the state fiscally over-extended. While the land freeze is sufficient to block or postpone a vast and complex construction project like the trans-Alaska pipeline or like a North Slope highway, it will not prevent the steady incursion of mining claims, squatters and other large and small violations of the areas which would be most desirable for public recreation or for the preservation of wilderness. A continued impasse over Native claims will deepen the bitterness of Alaska Natives over the majority's indifference to their rights and their welfare; it will also deepen the bitterness of entrepreneurs, construction workers and other Alaskans against Natives and conservationists for seemingly standing in the way of economic progress. Failure of the federal government to move ahead with the reservation of wilderness areas or the establishment of new parks will reinforce the impression of conservationists and of Americans generally that the oil industry and most Alaskans have nothing in mind but the destruction of the environment for the sake of short run dollar gains.

Elements of a Settlement: The Senate Land Claims Bill

An essential condition of any accommodation and the key element in ending the deadlock over the public lands of Alaska is the settlment of the Native claims by congress. In this session the Senate passed by a vote of 76 to 8 a settlement bill which is a new departure in America's treatment of its aboriginal peoples.[10] Comparison of this legislation with past treatment of American Indians is a huge topic which I cannot possibly deal with in a few moments.[11] The overwhelming vote in the Senate is a tribute to Scoop Jackson's ability to put together a viable compromise. If anything proves this point it is the unconditional support for this bill by both of Alaska's senators, who stand at opposite ends of the political spectrum on almost every other conceivable issue. Senate bill 1830 grants to the Natives $500 million from the federal treasury to compensate them for lands taken from them by the federal government, a two per cent royalty up to a total of $500 million on mineral revenues from public lands in Alaska in compensation for the Native interest in these lands, and approximately ten million acres of land associated with their homes, villages, hunting ranges and fishing camps.

The bill passed by the Senate also tries to deal with speculative and developmental demands which have built up since the land freeze because of the discovery of oil at Prudhoe Bay. Section 23, which was requested by the state, temporarily withdraws the unreserved public lands of Alaska from private disposition under the Mineral Leasing Act, the mining laws, and the general land laws except where they have been classified by the Department of the Interior to allow these dispositions. [12] The section is intended to allow the state to complete its land selection program ahead of private claimants and to preserve the *status quo* with respect to land tenure, other than Native grants and state selections, until congress has had an opportunity to consider the Public Land Law Review Commission's recommendations on Alaska and on federal land laws generally.

The Public Land Law Review Commission Report

The Public Land Law Review Commission, inspired by Wayne Aspinall and under his chairmanship, has worked five years examining all aspects of public land law in the United States; its report was published in June of this year.[13] In many places the Commission's report directly reflects the position of the State of Alaska. The Commission urged the lifting of administrative and technical obstacles to the state's receipt of the land to which it was entitled by the terms of the statehood act, including 400,000 acres of national forest land.[14] It recommended repeal of the federal Homestead Act, which now applies only to Alaska, on the ground that classification and disposition of land for intensive agriculture ought to be the responsibility of the state.[15] For the United States as a whole, it urged that leasable minerals be leased competitively wherever there is competitive interest in them—the same standard used by the State of Alaska.[16] It recommended that withdrawals or reservations of land by federal agencies and land classifications by the Bureau of Land Management be made only on the basis of carefully defined congressional guidelines,[17] and that state selection should have precedence over such classification.[18] Machinery was urged to review existing withdrawals or reservations and to revoke them or modify them if they are no longer appropriate.[19] On the other hand, the Commission placed the primary responsibility on the federal government to identify, withdraw, and recommend to Congress as soon as possible, the truly unique areas considered to have national significance warranting retention by the federal government.[20] The Commission also proposed "a joint federal-state natural resources and regional planning commission . . . for Alaska."[21] Finally, it strongly recommended " . . . the early enactment of legislation to resolve the problem of Native claims and end the current impasse."[22]

For an Alaska Omnibus Land Act

Senate bill 1830 and the Public Land Law Review Commission recommendations on Alaska agree on several key points and disagree upon none. On the whole they are also consistent with positions taken by the Secretary of the Interior. Together with a congressional determination regarding some park and wilderness areas, and regarding the trans-Alaska pipeline, the two packages provide the framework for an Alaska Omnibus Land Act. I cannot and should not spell out every item in such an act but the elements needed to come to grips with the problems, and to muster enough political support for a solution, might include the following:

1. The provisions of the bill passed by the United States Senate to resolve Native land claims in Alaska; and

2. The retention of the provision in that same bill expanding the competitive leasing of oil and gas. This item and the next five stem from the recommendations of the Public Land Law Review Commission;

3. Establishment of the machinery for joint state and federal land use planning and land classification in Alaska;

4. A grant of authority to this planning body to review all existing federal withdrawals including Naval Petroleum Reserve No. 4 and to recommend to Congress their disposition; together with a provision that all withdrawals or reservations greater than 5,000 acres not established by Congress will in five years automatically be revoked;

5. A repeal of the federal Homestead Act in Alaska;

6. The essential features of Section 23 of the Senate Land Claims Bill providing for a partial moratorium on appropriation of public lands under the public land laws pending their classification. In line with the recommendations of the Public Land Law Review Commission, however, the legislation should specify carefully the standards and procedures under which classifications shall be made by the Department of the Interior. Also the Act would;

7. Clarify Congress' intention that the Department of the Interior and the Department of Agriculture speedily process   without administrative or technical obstructions, state land selections under the Statehood Act.

The remaining features are in addition to, but not inconsistent with the provisions of Senate bill 1830 and the final report of the Public Land Law Review Commission. For the conservation interests, the law would provide:

8. Dedication of the Katmai and Glacier Bay National Monuments as National Parks and an end to mining in National Parks and Monuments in Alaska; legislative confirmation of the Arctic Wildlife Range and with one exception its designation as a wilderness area; and

9. Withdrawal by Congress from all forms of appropriation for five years those areas identified as of unique national significance for parks or wilderness, including but not limited to, the proposed Gates of the Arctic National Park and the proposed Wrangell   Mountains   National   Scenic   Area,

pending recommendation to Congress by the Department of the Interior on the future of these lands.

For the oil industry and for Alaska's economic development, the law would grant:

10.

Legislative designation of a system of oil and gas pipeline easements, including the proposed trans Alaska pipeline route from Prudhoe Bay to Valdez and its major alternatives. This would include the one exception to the wilderness status of the Arctic Wildlife Range: a pipeline easement east across the coastal plain from Prudhoe Bay area to the Canadian border to facilitate a possible mid-continent pipeline. These reservations would be coupled with a Congressional commitment to federal authorization of pipeline construction, including construction of the Prudhoe Bay to Valdez project, subject to proper engineering and Congressionally defined environmental standards.

The elements I have outlined here are only the suggestion of a framework for bargaining and compromise. Like the senate land claims bill and like the Public Land Law Review Commission report, they will not satisfy everyone nor will they satisfy anyone completely. They resolve some of the uncertainty about land ownership and control, but do not settle the important issues of administrative policy. Yet a settlement along these lines would clearly be an enormous advance beyond the *status quo* for each of the main interests involved: for the Natives of Alaska, for the defenders of wilderness and wildlife, for the oil and gas industry, and for the sound economic development of Alaska. The elements of such legislation are immediately at hand for action by Congress this fall. The need for a resolution is urgent, and agreement may become more difficult as time goes by.

This article was prepared for presentation at the Institute of Governmental Studies, University of California conference on "Public Lands — One Third of a Nation," San Francisco, December 7-8, 1970.

ALASKA—THE FEDERALLY OWNED STATE

George W. Rogers

The specific assignment given to each panel speaker was to "deal with the key recommendations of the commission's report which relate to the topic in question." In my case the topic in question is Alaska. The commission has made a number of recommendations relating specifically to Alaska, and others of general application which have special application or meaning in Alaska. In terms of the specific recommendations, it could be said that the State of Alaska fared extremely well at the hands of the commission. Some of the deadwood in existing laws and regulations would be cleared away, basic policy of federal and state governments on the public land issues would be brought closer together, the critically important matters of determination of Native land claims and state land selections would be given top priority, and institutional arrangements established for the continued coordination of Alaska and federal public land policies and programs.

On a laundry list basis we got from the commission virtually anything any reasonable Alaskan could hope for. It is not out of any sense of ingratitude, therefore, that I will address myself to what has been left out of the report in its treatment of Alaska as a whole based upon an understanding of the meaning of the creation of a new state from the public lands. Looking beyond Alaska, I would expand these observations to conclude that what the commission has left out has been the community and human aspects of public land management. This implies a major shortcoming, but it was inevitable given the analytical system and assumptions they subscribed to for arriving at decisions. Although the commission may have believed it was entitled to overlook these factors, a critique cannot.

I could have saved myself and this audience considerable trouble by simply identifying, describing and evaluating the clearly Alaska-related recommendations of the report. These might be identified as being the "key recommendations" intended by the assignment, but beyond giving footnote references I will pass them over here to be taken up in the discussion following as appropriate.[1] Rather than making a selection of key recommendations, I will relate what appears to be the basic pattern which underlies all of the 137 recommendations of the report to the idea of Alaska as a new and still-developing state.

Alaska—the Federally Owned State

According to the report of the Public Land Law Review Commission before us, public lands under the jurisdiction of federal agencies in 1968 comprised 95.3 per cent of Alaska's total land area, in effect making it a federally owned state.[2] Also in 1968, forty-six per cent of the United States' public lands were in Alaska, which makes our state of special importance to this conference or any other consideration of the recommendations of the Public Land Law Review Commission. (It should be noted that sixty-four per cent of the United States' continental shelf area is off our shores, the implications of this fact being overlooked or ignored in the Commission's report on the management of the outer continental shelf.) As the State of Alaska makes its selections under the land grant provisions of the Alaska Statehood Act these percentages will decline, but even if we succeed in completing the process by the 1984 deadline the federal government will still own sixty-seven per cent of the state's land area, and thirty-eight per cent of all public lands of the nation will be located within Alaska. If this represents a significant reduction in the relative areas involved, it does not, however, alter the generalization drawn from the 1968 statistics that on the one hand Alaska is important in any consideration of the nation's public lands, and on the other hand public lands play a key role in any consideration of Alaska.

Furthermore, twenty-four to twenty-six per cent of the federally managed public lands in Alaska have been reserved or withdrawn from entry by past executive and congressional actions. With the exception of limited areas within the national forest reserves to allow for community expansion, these lands are excluded from selection by the state and represent an important restriction on what can be accomplished by the state in reducing the continued dominance of federal land management on future developments. The two largest urban centers in Alaska, Anchorage and Fairbanks, in which reside approximately 57 per cent of the state's total current population, and the next-ranking centers in southeast Alaska, containing an additional 14 per cent of the total population, are almost totally dependent upon activities related to or taking place on the large federal reserves adjacent to or surrounding them. The future of these communities, therefore, will continue to reflect how the federal government manages public lands under its jurisdiction no matter how much land is selected by the state. For the most part, state selections have been made opportunistically on strictly real estate grounds or in order to bring the emerging petroleum provinces under state ownership. This will provide enlargement of "living room" and sources of funds to finance state and local government programs, but the primary employment of most Alaskans will still depend heavily upon how the federally retained lands are used.

The commission clearly recognized this. In discussing the need to set up a joint federal-state natural resources and regional planning commission for Alaska under recommendation 15, it notes that although "a significant part of that land base will belong to the state in the future . . . the state's desires and needs underscores the federal responsibility to plan for the retention and management or disposition of the lands that it will have after the selection process is completed, in a manner not to thwart the state's effort to chart its own destiny."[3]

In addition to the importance of these continuing Alaska-federal public lands relationships, Alaska is caught in cross currents: the claims of the descendants of the aboriginal inhabitants of Alaska to title to most of the land (and the attendant "land freeze" of Public Land Order 4582, U.S. Department of the Interior, January 17, 1969), the private development and transportation land and right-of-way requirements following the discovery of a major petroleum province on our arctic slope, the sale of timber from large tracts of our southeastern forest lands, and the concern of many Alaskan and outside conservation groups over the threat of environmental degradation implied in major land developments. All of these are of vital concern to us, but given the manner in which my topic is to be developed, time would not permit even a cursory treatment. Furthermore, we have on our panel able representatives of the principal "contending groups" (the state legislature, the petroleum industry, and Alaska Natives, and conservation interests) and they will be presenting their special views of current public land issues in Alaska, which I could here only anticipate or duplicate.[4] Here I will deal with what lies behind or beyond current Alaskan land issues.

There is not one Alaska, but a compound of many "Alaskas." There are several quite distinct and different regional Alaskas. There also have been several distinct socio-economic Alaskas defined by quite different objectives and patterns of development (Native Alaska, colonial Alaska, military Alaska), each having dominated a discreet historical period and all continuing to exert some influence in the whole that is contemporary Alaska.[5] Each of these regional and historical Alaskas would relate differently to the commission's report, but for this discussion we will focus on the essential meaning of Alaska as a state in process of development. For more than twenty-five years I have been a resident of Alaska and have been deeply and continuously involved in the process, so I cannot be objective. What is perhaps even worse is that over time my very subjective views also have fluctuated widely because the involvement has been a long one.

The State of Alaska as an Anachronism

The idea of Alaska as a state has appeared at times as a hopeless anachronism in an age of increasing urbanization and specialization. This mood comes over me following certain happenings—exposure to a chamber of commerce or tourist industry refurbishing of the "last frontier" image, hearing a speech or reading of a report urging construction of a railroad into the arctic as a means of "opening the country," or hearing plans to resettle unemployed urban workers on Alaska's "vast and empty lands." All of this is an attempt to replay the nineteenth century "winning of the West" in a northern frontier setting. When Alaska became a state just past the mid-twentieth century mark, this was the final act in a process designed in the eighteenth and nineteenth centuries and here set in motion late in the nineteenth century when Alaska was created as a district of the United States. Statements justifying or explaining the creation of a new state out of the raw materials of the public lands have a stirring ring to them, but they also sound like an echo from another time, a long-gone heroic age. The following by a congressman two years after Alaska was organized as a territory, the last step in the process before becoming a state, is typical.

> When the United States acquires extensive domain over extensive tracts of territory, the duty devolves upon it not so much to exploit the natural resources for the benefit of the people of the States as to build there a civilization, to induce immigration and settlement . . . that homes may spring up and that that territory may contribute to the general strength and happiness of the whole Union.[6]

But aren't we in the wrong century to carry out such a program? According to a 1937 report by the National Resources Committee on the value of Alaska to the nation:

> In the past, the empty spaces of the earth were peopled gradually over a long period of time. Immigrants were at first predominantly subsistence farmers. They expected to hew down forests, to work

> from dawn to dark, to do without any luxuries, to live in isolation,
> to do without schools, police protection and doctors—they were
> ready to live at a very low level of subsistence provided they could
> look forward to ownership of a piece of land that in the second or
> third generation might yield a competence and a reasonable degree
> of comfort. Migrants of this type are becoming fewer and fewer in
> the world, and it is doubtful if the United States has even its
> proportionate share . . . The modern "pioneer" thinks in terms of
> government and what it will do for him. If settlement is not made
> easy for him, the present-day pioneer will seek more sheltered
> spaces or call upon his government to discharge its social
> responsibility toward him.[7]

Based upon this line of reasoning, the 1937 report recommended
against federal investment in programs to "force-feed" settlement
and, indirectly, against the creation of a state.

   Looked at realistically, it appears that the development of
whatever economic values Alaska held for the nation could best be
done without the encumbrance of settlement and the political
development represented by statehood. This was substantially the
pattern that had been followed from the period of Russian
ownership to the date Alaska actually became a state. Hundreds of
millions of dollars of products were drawn from Alaska's resources
by seasonal or temporarily imported labor, with virtually no change
in the levels of population from the turn of the century until the
construction and manning of the military establishment in World War
II and after. Elsewhere in the polar lands a similar pattern was being
followed. After an initial drive to settle its north in the 1920's and
1930's, the Soviet Union substantially abandoned this approach to
northern development in the 1940's and 1950's. The approach to
development in the forest and tundra zones of the northern regions,
according to studies of official policy available to me was by the
"selective method of developing lands by separate cases and areas"
and with

> periodic importation (for definite terms) of labor force from other,
> more southerly regions of the country. The principal aim of creating
> a complex is the working of especially valuable mineral resources,
> forests, and the wealth of fish and other sea animals. Modern
> technology and economics permit the development of this northern
> wealth through especially high mechanization and the shifting of the
> process to such forms of energy as water and oil power, which make
> it possible to reduce sharply the expenditure of live labor.[8]

This approach has a sound twentieth century ring to it and, if intelligently implemented, would maximize the net economic contribution of these regions to the gross national product of their nation owners—the United States, the U.S.S.R., Denmark, and Canada. In terms of the stereotype of frontier development going through a set series of stages or being based upon agricultural settlement of the land, the idea of Alaska's attempting to recreate the process is not only an anachronism but, given the limited agricultural lands, the climate and other factors, either a grossly expensive undertaking or an impossibility.

The State of Alaska as a Possible Model of the Future

Having gone to this limit, anyone who is a resident of Alaska or who has visited it will immediately recognize that the potential of Alaska's public lands offers more than merely being a supply depot to be drawn upon for certain economic goods when the price is right according to the calculations of the analytical system devised to maximize these values. Richard Cooley sums this up for most of us in his classic work on Alaska's public lands, a basic work which surprisingly I found neither mentioned nor reflected in the commission's report.

In years past, Alaska was thought of primarily as a place to go to work, to acquire money, and to leave. The population was highly transient. In the last decade, however, more and more people are coming to Alaska with an altogether different purpose in mind. They have become dissatisfied with their hurly-burly, complex, and often meaningless existence that offers comfort, entertainment and security but little real satisfaction. They are well enough off financially, but happiness seems to be absent from their lives, and they come to Alaska seeking a new environment that will fulfill this need ... What happens in Alaska could prove to be a kind of reformation; a discarding of the old mythology and a creative adventure in shaping new approaches to land and resource policy adjusted both to nature and to man's needs and values in the modern world.[9]

Not all that is happening in Alaska fits into this ideal presentation of what could be realized. As a resident, I would say that the majority of those who have come in during the last decade are still motivated by the old drive of acquiring money quickly and leaving as soon as possible. Many of the mistakes made to the south also are being repeated in the development of our communities and industries. But there is a shift in public opinion and a growing concern about what happens to the land and the environment, and a comparison of the characteristics of the last three decennial census reports reveals a growing balance and stability in the total population which was absent from previous reports. Even if Alaska is hardly more than a state in name only, the fact that it is so considered has put a definite pattern on what has happened over the last decade tending to direct development toward realization of the ideal of creation of a real human community.

At other times, therefore, the idea of Alaska as a state appeared to me not as an anachronism, but as a model of the future. This mood comes over me most strongly following a trip "outside." Many of us who are long-term Alaskan residents have been able to sense and see, on periodic trips "outside," the progressive destruction of the physical conditions essential for life more clearly than those who have acquired a protective immunity by reason of living with daily increments of environmental degeneration and social decay. In our efforts to prevent these things happening here we are finding allies in new Alaskans who represent a growing body of contemporary refugees seeking a new life in a frontier not yet totally lost. But more than escape for a fortunate few is involved.

At the heart of the multiple crises facing our society are the excessive concentrations of population until they go beyond the scale which the natural environment can carry without destruction and beyond the scale in which the individual can survive as a human being. Over the last twenty-five years I have made regular visits to several of the great metropolitan centers of the United States and Canada and have seen them grow steadily bigger and at the same time more chaotic, shoddy and dehumanized. They now face either being dismantled and reconstructed in an attempt to make them fit places for human habitation or being burned down by their inmates. Over the past decade combinations of both alternatives have been taking place.

The commission report recognizes the need for models for something better and has recommended that steps be taken to make some public land available for a prototype "new city" on an experimental basis to provide information and guides for rebuilding a better future.[10] The discussion in the report is limited to narrow real estate considerations and would appear to view the problem as primarily one of passively responding to population and industrial growth. It also points out that such experiments are complex and costly and, hence, would be limited. In attempting to develop a new state in Alaska we are using the public lands in a similar but broader, more complex and costly experiment in attempting to create a model for an entire new society.

The public lands must do more than provide space on which to build towns and cities in this experiment. They must be used in such a manner as to provide local employment to support the population of these communities. It was these goals which caused the U.S. Forest Service management programs in Alaska to include not only the principles of multiple use and perpetual yield, but also the requirement that "logs, cord wood, bolts, and other similar products not be transported for primary manufacture outside the State of Alaska." The working circles which form the basis of the timber management programs are based upon both inventories of forest resources and plans for establishment of new industrial enterprises at each of the major existing population centers within the forest reserve. There is an economic cost involved in that the return to the U.S. Treasury on the stumpage is not maximized by the primary processing requirement (the purchaser will reduce his bid by a factor representing the cost to him of constructing and operating a plant in Alaska), but the primary object of this policy is to realize other values from the commercial use of the forest resources.

The experiment involves other departures from policies which an adherence to limited systems of economic development would dictate. Additional economic costs must be assumed by developers to protect the physical environment and other necessities and amenities for the "good life." Certain lands and resources must be withheld from use and harvesting for commercial values in the interest of preserving higher environmental values for the enjoyment and benefit of non-resident visitors as well as residents of Alaska.

None of these departures from traditional development and land management goals would pass muster with the analytical systems of traditional liberal economics, but the discipline itself is in a period of change reflecting the underlying ferment in contemporary society. As in all such periods of ferment, it is not certain whether the process is one of chaos or creation, although the latter at one time came from the former. What is needed is a laboratory for the testing of new approaches and hypothesis as well as demonstrations of new models. Alaska, in carrying out its experiment, can serve as such a laboratory for the nation and could make a contribution toward the "general strength and happiness of the whole Union" which goes far beyond what the Congressman quoted in the previous section could ever have envisaged in his less-developed and less-threatened time.

The State of Alaska and the Native People

It is no chance occurrence that the emergence of Alaska's Native people (Indian, Eskimo and Aleut) as a potent political force coincided with the opening decade of Alaska's experiment with statehood. This movement deserves more than the quick look afforded it here, because a full understanding of its meaning leads to an understanding of the ultimate meaning of Alaska as a state—a political means of attempting to re-establish in our society a positive relationship between people and place. More is involved than simply getting an answer to the question of who owns Alaska's lands, although this is the only avenue which conveniently presents itself.

The approximately 55,000 people of aboriginal ancestry living in Alaska today are descendants of an estimated 75,000 population in this region at the time of the first Euro-American contacts in the mid-eighteenth century. They lived under several distinct social, economic and cultural systems reflecting the adaptations made to the limitations imposed and the opportunities offered by the physical environment and the harvestable natural resources in each area. These sensitive and durable human adaptations to the various natural environments of Alaska were disrupted, and in many areas completely destroyed, by invasions of outside economic forces which looked upon Alaska not as a home but as a short-term supply depot from which to ruthlessly extract, while they lasted, a specialized list of raw materials of high value in distant markets. The true cost of these outside economic developments were not paid by the outside exploiters (or "spoilers" in the old Alaskan idiom), but by the Native people who only participated in a marginal way in the related activities and benefits. Survival was achieved by maintaining a greatly degraded semi-subsistance way of life (resulting in a decline in numbers to 26,500 by 1920) more recently combined with "benefits" from the welfare state branch of the dominant non-Native society (resulting in a rise to 43,000 by 1960).

The non-Native society was neither heartless nor unaware of its inability to assist the Native people in coping with their tragic situation. Attempts were made to provide escape routes. From the beginning some form of educational program was provided with the object of assimilating the Native people into the new dominant culture and wage labor economic system. Where the traditional aboriginal pursuits had some affinity for the new commercial enterprises as in salmon fishing and canning there appeared to be some progress toward these goals, but subsequent developments (i.e., the crash of the salmon resource in the late 1940's and 1950's and the failure of Indian fishermen to move into new jobs created in forest products) have proved even these cases to be illusory. A comparison of vital statistics and census data have revealed that each decade several thousand Alaska Natives "disappear." Allowing for statistical errors, this is an indication that a significant number who migrate from the villages or from Alaska do cease to be "Natives." But the majority stubbornly rejected the route of assimilation as a means of escape from the poverty in which they are caught.

Other alternatives were suggested by the statehood movement of the 1940's and 1950's. The basic objective was to obtain more local control over or ownership of Alaska's natural resources and to substitute resident for non-resident interests as the guide in their utilization and management. Self-determination and other political values were also involved, but these were means toward the economic and social development aims of the majority of Alaskans who supported the movement. As they found their ancestral lands threatened in the post World War II period by a formidable array of federal giants—the Atomic Energy Commission with its plans to convert the Alaska arctic into a nuclear testing grounds and the Corps of Engineer's giant Rampart power development, and then the invasion of the international petroleum industry, regional Native groups set up organizations to protect their interest in their land and their way of life. These were transformed into the statewide Native land claims movement and the development of a unified political force in the Alaska Federation of Natives. The Native movement is more than a parallel to the statehood movement which preceded it and goes much deeper.

Land is more than a convenient economic symbol or a commodity for the Alaska Native. He finds his whole identity as a human being tied up with it, whether he still lives in the village of his people or is making his way in the white man's world at Anchorage or elsewhere. It has become an effective political tool or weapon in dealing with the white community. Depending upon the terms of the settlement arrived at, it will provide in itself or through revenues derived from its use a set of meaningful alternatives for the Native to choose from in selecting his future. No longer will he face the alternative of continued poverty in a subsistence village life with a depleted resource base or one of making a full assimilation into a foreign culture. As in the case of the broader experiment of creating a state, this will also require programs for its realization which will be justified on values other than purely economic.

The Commission's Public Benefit—
A Case of Misplaced Concreteness

Developing a state has basic implications for ownership and use of public lands. It looks at land as a place to live as well as the source of making a living, as a home as well as a supply depot. The benefits to be promoted appears to be primarily regional and local, but as I have indicated they could have significant national benefits implied in the whole legal process of advancement to this status. The commission's concept of maximizing public benefits must be related to Alaska as a state in the making, given the dominance of federal public lands in Alaska and the dominance of Alaska in the total public lands of the nation.

The Organic Act under which the commission was created and functioned sets forth specific duties to be performed and the general charge to report to the President and Congress the legal and administrative actions needed to assure that the "public lands of the United States shall be (a) retained and managed or (b) disposed of, all in a manner to provide the maximum benefit for the general public." A study of the efforts of the Commission as reflected in the discussions of the 137 recommendations, the preface, the program for the future, and chapter two and chapter three of the resulting report is of critical importance in relating the recommendations to the topic of this panel. At the heart of the report is the determination of the meaning of the "general public" and the "maximum benefit" which will guide continuing decisions as to disposal of public lands and management of those retained. In approaching these two objectives, the report follows two different and sometimes conflicting routes.

Public benefit is an evolutionary and highly subjective and relative concept. It cannot be determined by reference to absolutes. This is properly the objective to be served by the political process of a democratic society, in which divergent opinions and interests come into contact and conflict and resolve themselves into a consensus approximating what the "general public" believes to be its "maximum benefit." The commission has recognized this and gives recommendations which could make existing political institutions and machinery more effective in discharging this essential task in relation to public land issues. The first basic premise of the commission's program for the future, for example, is that "Congress, elected by and responsive to the will of the people, makes policy; the executive branch administers the policy." Some of its recommendations would enlarge the role of state and local governments, provide for public discussion and participate in all major decisions, create regional commissions for land use planning, etc.

The commission (or its members and staff), however, is only human, and as such has an underlying split personality which would support a more certain, objective and "scientific" means of achieving these aims. Throughout there is a strong urge to discover or create some order in the subject, to make the definition of public good objective and the measurement of the maximizing effects of existing or proposed policy as scientific as possible. From the outset we are told that there are to be "controlling standards, guidelines, and criteria," although it is noted that "judgment would be required." We are told in the preface that in considering its talk, the commission used a check list of "justifiable interests" that led it to its subsequent recommendations and conclusions which met "the test of providing the maximum benefit for the general public." We are also informed in the preface that "the Commission considered all the resources and uses of the public lands to be *commodities*," which would lead us to anticipate an analytical system drawing from the academic discipline of economics rather than politics. In fact there is strong evidence that economic factors alone are to be the primary measure of public benefit. This approach reaches its most complete statement in the discussion of recommendation 2.

Maximum public benefit in planning for public land use will be obtained, according to the recommendation, when the Congress specifies the factors to be considered in making the decision and an "analytical system" determines the application of these factors to the specific decision by the executive agency involved. Having made this recommendation, however, the commission immediately deprives Congress of its role by going on to list the several general categories of factors which "can serve all of the agencies equally." In order to assure consistency of results and effort among the several agencies, "this process should be standardized with common units of measurement and a system for the comprehensive analysis of the factors considered." After considering benefits-costs analysis, the executive branch's PPBS (Planning, Programming, and Budgeting Systems) and the techniques used by the Department of Commerce in its national income measurements, the commission concludes that a regional input-output analysis is "the only approach that provides a reliable basis for making comparisons of economic impacts for different land uses." Although the commission intends "the factors and procedures suggested above to be the primary basis for land use decisions generally ... *for those limited situations where choices among conflicting uses cannot clearly be made after application of this system*, Congress should attempt to provide guidelines that could be used to resolve such conflicts." [italics added] [11] In other words, even those factors and goals which at present do not fit the "common units of measurement" are not to escape what will eventually be an all-embracing machine system or possibly an alliance of systems covering economic, social and other factors and goals.

The other half of the commission's personality, however, asserts itself repeatedly throughout the report and even in this crucial section. When the system personality of the commission asserts in recommendation 30, for example, that "dominant timber production units should be managed primarily on the basis of economic factors so as to maximize net returns to the federal treasury," its non-system personality counters in recommendation 34 by asserting that the "Federal Government has an obligation to those who depend on public lands for their livelihood" and that they "should be given consideration in the management and disposal of public land timber" even to the extent of continuing such un-economic practices as the ban on export of logs from public lands and setting "the size limit for this industry in terms of qualifying for Small Business Administration assistance. [12]

This see-sawing is continued from the beginning to the end of the report, but it is in no sense a real debate between opposite views. The most the non-system side of the commission does is seek recognition that some minor exceptions must be made as we go along. Ultimately the analytical system should determine the correct decision in each public land issue. Full realization of this only awaits further refinements of the system to embrace those "limited situations" that at present do not fit in and the generation of appropriate data.

The Commission's Analytical System— The Wrong Tool Kit

It could be argued that I am in error in seeing the commission as split into system and non-system personalities. The true split may be between accepting only economic factors and analysis as determinants of all decisions or allowing exceptions only until companion systems can be devised to take care of all general categories of factors. Limiting our observations only to the forms of economic analysis considered by the commission and implied in its assumptions and approach, however, we find a further narrowing of scope and vision. With the exception of the chapter dealing with the environment and passing references to it elsewhere in the report, I had the impression of reading a report of the 1940's or 1950's when the national crises focused on the natural resource base and progress was still defined in terms of economic output of goods and services. Now economists are recognizing such additional values as the "quality of life" and the environment as something embracing the resource base and transcending it in terms of economic welfare.

The commission gave no evidence of being aware of these changes, or possibly the evidence was that they choose to ignore them. In the consideration of goals and systems of analysis, they showed no awareness that we are finally freeing our choices of futures for our society from the tyranny of economic growth and traditional analysis. The sacred Gross National Product is being treated with diminishing awe by a new generation of economists. As defined by Edward J. Mishan,

> This index, as economists know, is an artless though effective device which can be counted on to register some economic gain for almost any country from one year to the next. For the principle employed

is simply that of toting up the values of all man-made goods while assiduously ignoring all the man-made bads that are produced simultaneously. These bads (or "spillovers" as they are commonly called) include development blight, the erosion of the countryside, the accumulation of oil and sewage on our coasts, contamination of lakes and rivers, air pollution, traffic congestion and shrieking aircraft.[13]

Professor Mishan has proposed a number of approaches to including these "bads" or social costs in the economist's calculus, among them the recognition of "amenity rights" on the same basis as the traditional economists have recognized property rights. Regional economists have for some years included "amenity resources" (i.e., natural resources that do not enter directly into the production process, but condition the manner in which economic decisions are made) in a region's natural resources endowment.

Professor Mishan is not alone in pointing out that the contempt that the so-called hard-boiled economists heap upon the "soft" or "sentimental" economists is based upon a "misplaced concreteness which, despite occasional disclaimers in our more civilized moments, tends to associate utility, or value, with market prices. But if all that is priced has value, the reverse is certainly not true." Among economists interested in welfare he is not alone in putting a "price" on those things that escape the market mechanism. Inspired by the teachings of Galbraith, Ayres, Myrdal and others, for example, there has emerged the first steps toward an institutionalization of the search for new approaches in the recent establishment of the Association for Evolutionary Economics.

Addressing himself primarily to young economists in underdeveloped countries in the 1950's, Gunnar Myrdal urged them to "have the courage to throw away large structures of meaningless, irrelevant and sometimes blatantly inadequate doctrines and theoretical approaches and to start their thinking afresh from a study of their own needs and problems. This would take them far beyond the realm of both outmoded Western liberal economics and Marxism."[14] His advice of over a decade ago has application to the young economists of the so-called developed nations and we have had an upsurge of unorthodoxy within the profession in response to recognition of the failures of traditional approaches to meet the critical needs of our times. Unfortunately none of this is reflected in the report.

The Public Benefit Revealed—Over and Over Again

It is not my intention to belabor this point beyond noting that the evaluation of any system of analysis is not in terms of its elegance and appearance of precision, but in the identification of what the system takes as given (i.e., not problematical). Ideas and factors that would disrupt or cannot be conveniently assimilated into the system are consciously or unconsciously discarded and what is left in does not necessarily reflect what is strategically important in the real world or the objectives and aspirations of real people. The regional input-output systems favorably considered by the commission as a means of establishing benefit maximization, or any of the other systems considered, can only treat those factors which are set to common units of measurement and included within the framework of the system. In short, they are capable of treating in only a limited way a narrow range of economic values, factors and goals. Virtually everything I have discussed as representing the values, factors and goals inherent in the experiment of creating a state from the public lands of Alaska, and the more basic Native land issue, therefore, would be off limits in any analytical system of the sort considered. The commission's view that all resources and use of the public lands are to be considered as commodities, for example, is incompatible with the land ethic of the Native Alaskan which treats it as home. This relation of the underlying pattern of the recommendations to Alaska raises the question of their relevance in the determination of any other version of the public benefit.

I repeat that the public benefit is an evolutionary, highly subjective and relative concept. It is not an absolute and it cannot be discovered and measured and weighed and described by application of a set of absolute principles, standards, criteria and analytical systems. Granting all of the truly great accomplishments of the commission in performing this tremendously important and difficult task, one basic flaw is the search for concreteness and stability, when it could or should never be found, in the concept of the public benefit.

In preparing for this conference, I found in my files a form letter from the director of the commission dated 13 October 1966 inviting me to provide suggestions of "identifying and structuring criteria" for determination of the maximum benefit for the general public which would "put decision-making within the commission on a plane above reliance on divergent opinions arrived at without reference to a common base." At the time this letter was received I was reading a journal article by my friend and former colleague Harvey Berlott on "New Directions in Social Planning." The original source and reference is lost, but I had written the following quote on the bottom of the letter, "Voluntary and democratic processes have been built into social planning operations; broad citizen involvement has been sought; a pluralistic approach to the definition and solution of social problems has been accepted." This was the only reliable formula I could offer to the commission for the determination of public benefit and the only approach toward maximization. The comments of Director Pearl this morning were of considerable interest and concern to me in this regard. To paraphrase, he concluded that policy *must* be established in advance in accordance with a "public interest test" so we would "know the rules of the road" in arriving at the correct decisions. If we are to follow this approach, there will be no voluntary and democratic process or broad citizen involvement and with a hygienically predetermined test, no pluralistic approach to the definition of the benefits to be maximized, the determination of policies of maximization and the solution of problems. Goals and objectives will all be determined by the system.

NOTES

[1]Public Land Law Review Commission, *One Third of the Nation's Lands*, Washington, D.C., June 1970 (hereinafter referred to as PLLRC). Recommendation 8, pp. 54-56; recommendation 15, pp. 64-65; recommendation 34, pp. 99-101; recommendation 49, pp. 132-133; recommendation 68, pp. 177-178; recommendation 70, pp. 180-182; recommendation 78, pp. 198-199; recommendation 107, pp. 248-249; and an unnumbered but strong recommendation for " . . . the early enactment of legislation to resolve the problem of Native claims and end the current impasse," pp. 248-249.

[2]PLLRC, p. 327.

[3]PLLRC, p. 65.

[4]I am having duplicated for distribution with my paper a current treatment of these matters by my colleague, Professor Arlon R. Tussing, "Issues of Land Use Determination in Alaska," September 11, 1970. One of the best treatments of Alaska land administration and the implications of statehood is contained in R.A. Cooley, *Alaska, A Challenge in Conservation* (Madison, The University of Wisconsin Press, Second Printing 1967). A comprehensive background analysis of the Native claims issue is contained in the Federal Field Committee for Development Planning in Alaska, *Alaska Natives and the Land* (Washington, D.C., U.S.G.P.O. 1968) and U.S. Senate, Committee on Interior and Insular Affairs, *Alaska Native Settlement Act of 1970: Report* (91st Congress, Second Session, Report 91-925), June 11, 1970. G.W. Rogers, editor, *Change in Alaska: People, Petroleum and Politics* (Seattle, University of Washington Press, 1970) presents an anthology of essays treating the petroleum and environment issues.

[5]G.W. Rogers, *The Future of Alaska, The Economic Consequences of Statehood* (Baltimore: The Johns Hopkins Press, 1962), pp. 60-104.

[6]Representative Halvor Steenerson, Minnesota, February 5, 1915. Quoted in E. Gruening, *The State of Alaska* (New York, Random House, 1968) p. 191.

[7]National Resources Committee, *Alaska—Its Resources and Development* (Washington: U.S. Government Printing Office, 1938), p. 16.

[8]N.N. Kolosovsky, "The Territorial-Production Combination in Soviet Economic Geography," *Osnovy Ekonomicheskogo Rayonirovaniya* (Moscow, 1958). Quoted in Rogers, *op. cit.*, p. 286. For a full historical treatment see T. Armstrong, *Russian Settlement in the North*, (Cambridge, 1965); also T. Armstrong, "Soviet Northern Development, With Some Alaskan Parallels and Contrasts," *ISEGR Occasional Papers*, No. 2, October 1970, (College: University of Alaska).

[9]Richard A. Cooley, *Alaska, A Challenge in Conservation*, (Madison: The University of Wisconsin Press, 1966), pp. 129-130.

[10]PLLRC, p. 227.

[11]PLLRC, pp. 45-47.

[12]PLLRC, pp. 96-97, 99-101.

[13]E.J. Mishan, "The Spillover Enemy, the Coming Struggle for Amenity Rights," *Encounter*, December 1969.

[14]Gunnar Myrdal, *Rich Lands and Poor*, (New York: Harper & Bros., 1957), p. 104.

This article was prepared for presentation at the Institute of Governmental Studies, University of California conference on "Public Lands — One Third of a Nation," San Francisco, December 7-8, 1970.

THE REPORT OF
THE PUBLIC LAND LAW REVIEW COMMISSION:
AN ALASKAN CONSERVATIONIST'S VIEW

Robert B. Weeden

The public land laws are among the most important of the institutions that have made Alaska what it is and are likely to direct its future. Discussing the influence of this set of laws on how natural resources are being used, how and where people have settled, and on the appearance and social usefulness of the landscape as a whole, obviously is too big a job to accomplish in ten minutes. I have selected six topics that are of paramount interest to Alaskans: disposal policy, state land grants, joint federal-state land planning, environmental quality, mineral and petroleum law, and timber policy.

The major difficulty in fulfilling this task, aside from the sheer number of items to discuss, is that so often the force of initial generalizations by the commission is deflected and dissipated later on. Like New Year's resolutions, the good beginnings are nibbled and hedged by afterthoughts, leaving uncertainty about the true meaning of the initial statement.

Disposal of Federal Lands

The outstanding example is the first general recommendation in the introductory summary [1] that

> The policy of large-scale disposal of public lands reflected by the majority of statutes in force today be revised and that future disposal should be of only those lands that will achieve maximum benefit for the general public in non-federal ownership . . .

This seems to be a bold stand in favor of retention of public lands. On reading further, one realizes that although the commission is against wholesale disposal of federal public lands, it envisions a rather brisk retail business. The best of many statements in evidence of this is the proposal[2] that public lands chiefly valuable for grazing, intensive agriculture, mining, some occupancy uses, and provision of outdoor recreation by state and local governments should "be made available for disposition on certain conditions and to a limited extent" in fee simple.

The commission often refers to situations where the general public interest may be best served through disposal of public lands to individuals, but never defines them or describes criteria for such a decision. My own view is that there are too many millions of Americans who can never become landowners to countenance abdication of national control of the remaining federal acreage. When private profit can be made on public lands without harm to public values, a variety of permit and leasing systems can be employed to assure investment security while retaining ultimate control in public hands.

Alaskan State Land Grants and Joint Planning

Even in Alaska the practice of disposal of federal lands to private interests should be severely curtailed, although massive disposals of public lands will be and should be made to the State of Alaska in accordance with the Statehood Act. In fact the right of the state to select 104 million acres of unreserved public domain makes it unnecessary for the federal government to dispose of land directly to private individuals. The state is better able than the federal bureaucracy to judge the need for land for community growth and private enterprise, and its land classification system and land use regulations are considerably more modern than their federal counterparts. The State of Alaska should thus be an active intermediary in the planned transfer of lands from public to private ownership when this is in the public interest.

The PLLRC report dwells at some length[3] on the subject of land selection by the State of Alaska, since this process will involve transfer of more than one acre out of seven now in federal ownership throughout the nation. The meaning of this huge land grant to the emerging Alaska was explored carefully by Dr. Cooley in 1966,[4] and critical new developments were described in recent reports.[5] I will attempt only a brief summary of the subject here.

The present landholder is the federal government, controlling 98 per cent of Alaska. The contenders for proprietorship are federal agencies, the state, and Alaska Natives. As Dr. Rogers pointed out earlier, if the state obeys current political (if not economic or social) necessity and does select 104 million acres by 1984, it will control 28 per cent of the uplands of Alaska, plus the tidelands to the three-mile limit. It is too early to predict the nature of congressional settlement of Native land claims, but bills introduced so far have entailed transfer of no more than 60 million acres of public land to Native corporations. This would mean Native ownership of 17 per cent of the state, leaving the federal government with a residual of about 55 per cent.

Federal agencies wanting Alaskan real estate for purposes ranging from military games to national wildlife refuges have used withdrawal and classification regulations to obtain control. All of these except certain Bureau of Land Management classifications have eliminated future state selection. Thus the state has viewed federal withdrawals with a good deal of disfavor.

The state, which has only 14 years left in which to select its lands, is in a dilemma. It wants to select lands as soon as possible to make sure of state control, but would like to select as late as possible to take advantage of new knowledge of population growth patterns and the location of commercially profitable natural resources.[6]

The Natives' position is that no federal public land should be further committed to state, private, or federal agency tenure until their aboriginal title is defined and satisfied.

The logical solution to the three-way impasse requires three actions. The first, both chronologically and in priority, is to settle Native claims in such a way as to foster mutual respect between Natives and non-Natives. The second is to suspend the operation of federal land disposal laws pending broad policy decisions about ownership and management of regional and sub-regional land units. The third is to create a mechanism for joint state-federal participation in these broad decisions.

The PLLRC report seems to have recognized this solution,[7] or at least two-thirds of it (I could find no reference to sustaining "the freeze" after settlement of Native claims).

Settlement of Native claims first is a matter of long overdue justice. It would also give a slight economic boost to precisely that group of Alaskans least prepared to benefit from the "good times" following recent massive oil discoveries. And in the context of the present three-cats-in-a-bag situation, claims settlement would satisfy one contender and greatly reduce the chance for prolonged court intervention.

The second step is not likely to be popular in Alaska because many people think that private, fee-simple tenure of the federally-controlled hinterland is an essential step in economic progress. A continuation of a land freeze for a year or two in reality will have very little economic effect, especially if, as seems to be assumed by most people, the "freeze" would be lifted when the trans-Alaska pipeline can be authorized. It is crucial, however, to the effectiveness of joint land planning between the federal and state governments.

Joint participation of the two governments obviously is necessary for sensible resolution of differences and orderly achievement of goals. Both parties have said they would participate. What remains to be done is to create a mechanism for the process.

In my opinion the immediate and most important task for a state-federal Alaska Land Commission is to agree on areas which present knowledge indicates have dominant national values.[8] In view of the extensive federal withdrawals to date, I do not think these areas will comprise much of the remaining Alaska public domain. Following this the state would indicate the areas in which it has a present interest, and would immediately begin the selection process expedited by federal help. Finally, the state would define areas of probable future interest. These areas could be classified as soon as possible by BLM, retaining the option of state selection.

Environmental Quality

Before addressing aspects of commercial resource utilization discussed in the report, I would like to give an impression of the commission's treatment of the subject "environment."The extensive discussion of this all-pervading question is, to me, one of the most interesting and valuable parts of the report. The discussion[9] of a technique for classifying existing levels of environmental quality (that is, air, water, quality of experience, and biosystem) on public lands is especially useful. In addition, one cannot argue with the several recommendations[10] that elevate environmental quality to high status in land policy decisions, and propose means to maintain environmental quality as it is and try to keep it from getting worse, instead of defining it as it could be and trying to make it better. This is an important difference on lands already subjected to degradation of quality.)

The analytic orientation of the report surfaces in the chapter on environmental quality where the commission states[11] that

> The desired level of environmental quality and specific use constraints that are necessary for each area of public lands will be determined by topography, soils, vegetative cover, climate, and the whole calculus of variables peculiar to different public and locations.

Certainly land capability and characteristics are important, but shouldn't the public also have something to say about "desired levels of environment quality?" On this very important question, the commission recommends[12] mandatory hearings at the request of states or the Council on Environmental Quality, and discretionary hearings when the plea comes from anyone else (even another federal agency). Assuming that state governments will not often see the need for environmental impact hearings with respect to economic development projects, the overworked council will have to assume the burden.

Mineral and Petroleum Policy

Mining, petroleum extraction, and logging are the three most important extractive resource activities in Alaska. Land laws affect how and where these activities occur. Therefore the commission's approach to these industries is of great interest to Alaskans.

Turning first to mining, I read the report for answers to three questions: first, did the commission express itself on the matter of priorities to be given to mining and mineral exploration on public lands? Second, did the commission discuss criteria by which preferences could be expressed in given cases? Third, did the commission reduce the pre-emptive, first-come, first-served implications of existing mining laws?

With considerable uneasiness I read in the report that[13]

> Mineral exploration and development should have a preference over some or all other uses on much of our public lands . . . development of a productive mineral deposit is ordinarily the highest economic use of land.

The first part of the statement is at least debatable and is not even defensible if meant as a blanket statement of national priorities (I wonder what the commission would have done if the Atomic Energy Commission had struck oil on Amchitka Island?). The second part is simply untrue unless one uses only the narrowest of short-term economic evaluations, excluding all social costs or "externalities." To illustrate my contention another way, there is no conceivable cinnabar (mercury) deposit important enough to give mining preference over preservation of a park containing the continent's highest mountain, yet this is exactly what is happening at Slippery Creek in Mount McKinley National Park. My opinion is that there should be no expression of general priority with respect to mining in comparison with other activities that compete for space, water, and so on. The preference among conflicting potential uses must be in the context of a particular situation.

The commission does suggest the outlines of a system for allocating resources in general, including mineral resources.[14] This system is an example of misplaced concreteness, treating land values and uses as commodities regardless of whether they are emotional or economic in nature.

The answer to my third question is much more satisfying. The commission recommends major changes in existing laws[15] to streamline and modernize the existing archaic non-system. In effect the recommendations amount to a substitution of leasing for location and patenting, although the name and certain aspects of the leasing system were not adopted. Furthermore, the commission balked at giving administrators any power to withhold a mining or exploration permit on lands generally open to mining.

All Alaskans are by now familiar with the arguments for and against competitive bidding for petroleum leases outside of known producing fields. Under Alaskan conditions, where oil and gas reserves will be developed by a few large companies, whether or not land is leased competitively may have little bearing on environmental standards set in field operations. Nevertheless, it is of considerable interest whether the state (or nation) gets bonus and lease monies or whether they go to private investors, because of the difference in potential utilization of the revenue. Conservationists generally, and I for one, are gratified that the commission favors enlarging the conditions under which competitive sales are mandatory.[16]

Timber Policy

Alaska's timber resources are mainly in southeast Alaska within North and South Tongass National Forests. As brought out in Dr. Roger's speech, Forest Service programs have long been geared to the goals of maximizing timber production and increasing local employment in the forest products industry. Conservationists have become increasingly worried about the imbalance in Alaska Forest Service policy; specifically, we argue that there has been too much of the accessible commercial timber (which occurs along shorelines where people live) committed to logging, and that in fact there may have been an overcommitment in terms of sustained production capacity. A suit by conservation groups against the Forest Service, now being heard in Alaska courts, has brought this disagreement to a head.

One of the arguments of Alaskan conservationists is that "no cut" management programs should be established on some forest lands—lands with unusually high scenic characteristics, natural science research areas, recreation areas, and so on. In recommending a statutory requirement that highly productive timber lands be classified for dominant use as timber production areas,[17] the commission apparently views big trees as no more than stores of cellulose. As with mining, the basic problem is the commission's attempt to state a blanket preference.

Where forests in southeast Alaska are protected from logging at all they are protected mainly by the marketplace: that is, by the diseconomies of logging all but the easiest places. But, as we all know, markets change and harvesting techniques improve. Forests now "inaccessible and non-commercial" will succumb to helium-filled balloons, Japanese demands for pulp, and governmental road building. The only satisfactory solution, to me, is to establish effective spatial limits to timber production in Alaska's national forests which say "so far, and no farther."

I am convinced that these spatial limits can be set so that present-day industrial demands and work forces can be sustained, with every opportunity for healthy growth through intensified forestry; and so that the fantastically beautiful timberlands of southeast Alaska can play their part in meeting burgeoning national demands for wild places. The way to do this is not contained in the PLLRC report.

Summary

And now by way of summary I will stand back and evaluate the report as it expresses or implies the broadest objectives for federal lands, and as it relates to Alaskan development.

My biggest disappointment is that the commission did not state and hew to the most important fact of all: that the nation should retain responsibility for the management of all but a tiny fraction of today's public lands (land grants to states excepted). The public has, after all, only one-third of the nation's land.

The second most important criticism is that the commission embraced inappropriate or partially appropriate systems for deciding who should use public lands in specific cases. These systems express the failure of American culture to recognize basic human values apart from economic survival. The result is the rejection of unpriceable values in cost-benefit analyses.

On the positive side the commission clearly understood the new role of comprehensive planning in public land management. The commission's report is replete with valuable recommendations for new policies, techniques, and mechanisms for planning.

In addition the report at least occasionally recognizes that America has rejected technocracy. The public and the political process are the courts of judgment of land use issues, to which we must refer time and time again.

Finally, the commission tried very hard to meet the undeniably different land situation in Alaska. Its positions on Native land claims, state selection, and joint federal-state planning are generally excellent.

The work of the Public Land Law Review Commission reflects the deep interest of the commission and the whole nation in Alaskans' struggle to find themselves. Still, it is plain that the commission worked only with a few (very important) pieces of the puzzle that is Alaska. We could not expect anything else: the mark was not missed, it simply was not attempted. The commission worked by analysis, but Alaska can be built only by synthesis. It is up to Alaskans to take what pieces of the report they can use and fashion new ways of life for themselves out of respect for and understanding of both man and nature together.

NOTES

[1] Public Land Law Review Commission Report, p. 1.

[2] *Ibid.*, p. 48.

[3] *Ibid.*, pp. 248-249.

[4] Richard A. Cooley, 1966. *Alaska: A Challenge in Conservation.* University of Wisconsin Press.

[5]Notably the report of the Federal Field Committee for Development Planning in Alaska, *Alaska Natives and the Land*, 1969.

[6]If we can assume that a sizable share of the 104 million acres will not be selected by the state until 1980 or later, the state will continue for over a decade to oppose steps by the federal government to secure tenure over any public domain. This would seriously stultify federal investments in resource management on lands likely to be "lost" to the state.

One possible mitigation of this problem might be through a new federal law granting the state the opportunity to exchange previously selected lands (up to some stated limit) for new ones during the remaining years until 1984. Congress would need to give its approval for each specific exchange. This would permit expeditious land selection by the state while at the same time encouraging BLM to classify lands and begin essential management programs.

[7]PLLRC, p. 248-249; recommendation 15, pp. 64-65.

[8]The national values I refer to are primarily the values of wild places. It must be clear to everyone that Alaska is now the only American state with extensive opportunity to preserve the rare and precious feelings of solitude, unity with nature, physical challenge, and mental recreation that are intrinsic in wilderness experience. Because these values are diffuse, general, long-term, and non-commercial they tend to fare badly in the cost-benefit approach advocated by the Public Land Law Review Commission.

[9]PLLRC, pp. 75-79.

[10]PLLRC, recommendations No. 16, 24, 25, 26.

[11]PLLRC, p. 77.

[12]PLLRC, recommendation 22, p. 81.

[13]PLLRC, p. 122.

[14]PLLRC, recommendation 2, p. 45 *et seq.*

[15]PLLRC, pp. 124-134.

[16]PLLRC, pp. 132-133.

[17]PLLRC, p. 92.

This article was prepared in November, 1969, in response to a request from the Regional Coordinator for Alaska, Office of the Secretary, U.S. Department of the Interior. The conclusions do not necessarily reflect the policy of any federal agency.

WHEN THE ALASKA "LAND FREEZE" ENDS:
Issues of Policy and Administration Associated With the Expiration of Public Land Order 4582

Arlon R. Tussing

In November 1966 Secretary of the Interior Stewart Udall announced the suspension of mineral leasing on public lands in Alaska claimed by Native groups. By August 1967 the Department of the Interior had suspended almost all proceedings to dispose of disputed lands or rights in resources on them under the public land laws and the Alaska Statehood Act. This administrative action was superseded on January 20, 1969, by Public Land Order 4582, which withdrew all unreserved public lands in Alaska from disposition. Both the original suspension of land disposition and the withdrawal order have come to be known popularly as the "land freeze"; the term is used here to include both actions.[1]

This paper was prepared in response to a request from the Regional Coordinator for Alaska, Office of the Secretary, U.S. Department of the Interior, for an independent evaluation of administrative and policy problems which might be anticipated upon the end of the land freeze. The conclusions here do not necessarily reflect the policy of any federal agency.

Federal Land Laws

Federal land laws, including the Mineral Leasing Act and mining and homestead laws, generally provide for disposal of public lands or rights in public lands on a first-come, first-served basis. Land selection authority under the Alaska Statehood Act, and the ability of the government to withdraw land for various federal purposes operate on the same principle. In most cases these laws and procedures automatically give control of the land or of specific resources to the first claimant and provide no means of determining what use of the land would be the most productive or which ownership status would be most in the public interest.[2]

None of the above is new or unique to Alaska; the land laws have come under great criticism in recent years, and the Public Land Law Review Commission has examined possible reforms in all areas of land law and administration. But the existing laws will contribute to a particularly critical situation in Alaska upon expiration of the Native protests withdrawal. At that time there will have been a three-year period in which filings and applications were not processed. Even under normal circumstances the Bureau of Land Management would have legal and administrative difficulties in sorting out and processing the backlog of applications and filings. But during the freeze Alaska entered a spectacular oil boom and the demands upon the public lands for development and for speculation have increased enormously. In addition, the winter haul road, the pipeline road, and new airstrips and roads assocation with oil exploration and development will have opened millions of additional acres to access by the general public or by selected private interests. This set of circumstances raises the possibility of administrative chaos and years of litigation.

Expiration of Segregation Authority
Under the Multiple Use and Classification Act

An aggravating factor is the imminent expiration of the Multiple Use and Classification Act, which temporarily allows the Department of the Interior to segregate from disposal some of the public lands to classify them for priority uses after public hearings. The segregation authority expires six months after the Public Land Law Review Commission presents its final report to Congress. Under the present calendar, the end of this authority will coincide exactly with the end of the land freeze.[3]

National Parks, Wilderness and Wildlife

Another critical issue sharpened by public attention on Alaska—particularly northern Alaska—during the period of the land freeze is the demand for new national parks and monuments, wilderness areas, and wildlife reserves. The failure to meet this demand will (with some justification) encourage opposition from conservationists and public sentiment generally to any further natural resource development on public lands in Alaska.

The Secretary of the Interior has limited authority under the Pickett Act and the Antiquities Act to make protective withdrawals of lands for preservation purposes. Although several secretaries have asserted and exercised this authority, the chairman of the Interior and Insular Affairs Committee of the House of Representatives and other members of Congress vehemently insist that these actions have been violations of the intention of the law. Unilateral executive order or administrative preservation withdrawals would be strongly resented and opposed within Alaska, and could force a confrontation between the Department of the Interior and the House Committee.

State Selections

The Alaska Statehood Act authorizes the state to select within 25 years of statehood up to 103.5 million acres from the unreserved public domain. The state was authorized to select land under federal mineral lease for a period of ten years, which authority has now expired. The state was not to obtain land belonging to Alaska

Natives—hence the Native protests and the present freeze. All land selected by the state was "subject to valid existing rights"—mining claims, homestead entries, etc.

The rationale of the State of Alaska's own land laws and administrative practices is somewhat different from those of federal law. The state requires classification and development planning before disposal of land—it generally provides for disposal of resources competitively or otherwise at fair market value. It requires prospectors to obtain permits and requires protection of, or payment for, surface resources affected by exploration or mining activity. The state, therefore, has strong grounds for selecting land in order to control development and to avoid dissipation of potential mineral revenues. Just as important, the state must select land defensively before the issuance of federal mineral leases or location of mining claims in order to protect its right ever to select the land.

Native Claims Settlement

It is not possible now to predict whether legislation settling Alaska Native claims will be passed prior to the revocation of the land freeze, nor to predict the character of that settlement, if any. The absence of a settlement would probably result in litigation over each individual parcel of land selected by the state or entered under the public land laws, but even a complete legislative settlement would leave behind many difficulties. Pending bills provide for land withdrawals, land selection rights for Native groups or individuals, and/or shares of revenues from public lands. Any or all of these features would add further complications to the legal and administrative situation, unless the land claims legislation resolves some of the existing conflicts, irrationalities, and ambiguities. Such provisions would also place on the Bureau of Land Management further responsibilities which it is not now organized, staffed, nor funded to perform.

Preemption, Confrontation, Administrative Chaos

Regardless of the nature of any Native claims settlement, upon lifting of the land freeze, the factors listed above will cause:

1. a rush by developers and speculators to obtain mineral leases and control of public lands under the more "liberal" federal land laws;

2. defensive selection of lands by the state[4] to prevent loss of potential mineral lease bonuses and loss of the state's option ever to select the land in question, and to prevent haphazard and scattered private enclaves and unwise land use; and

3. demands from within the government, from conservationists, and from certain classes of resource users for unilateral executive order or administrative withdrawals of public land in Alaska.

At present neither the Bureau of Land Management, the State of Alaska Division of Lands nor the Congress is prepared to deal with these issues. The situation is an invitation to administrative chaos and to confrontations among the Department of the Interior, the State of Alaska, private interests, and perhaps Alaska Natives and/or Congress. It suggests years of delay in the consummation of legitimate public land entries, leases, and transfers, including state selections, and suggests the possibility of years of litigation. It is unlikely that the outcome will be a wise pattern of land ownership and land use.

Some Approaches to Resolution

There are a number of ways in which a resolution of these problems might be approached. For instance, one study[5] has suggested placing unreserved federal lands under state land laws and establishment of a joint state-federal commission with authority (1) to determine which lands would be retained by the federal government and which would be transferred to the state; (2) to develop a statewide land use plan and classification system fro both state and federal lands; and (3) to review existing federal withdrawals.

A less radical program would include some or all of the following:

1. Extension of life of the Multiple Use and Classification Act until all public lands are classified;

2. an increase in funds and personnal of the Bureau of Land Management to enable it to carry out with reasonable dispatch its responsibilities under the public land laws, the extended Multiple Use and Classification Act, the Statehood Act, and the anticipated Alaska Native claims settlement;

3. an increase in funds and personnel of the Geological Survey to permit acceleration of geological mapping and resource inventory for intelligent land classification;

4. reform of the mining and homestead laws (e.g., replacement of the existing claims system with a uniform leasing system for all minerals, separation of minerals from the surface estate, replacement of the Homestead Act with sale at fair market value of land classified for agriculture, etc.);

5. authority for competitive leasing of all Leasing Act minerals wherever there is competitive interest in them; and

6. temporary withdrawal from disposal of land under consideration for inclusion in the federal preservation system (National Parks and Monuments, wilderness areas and wildlife reserves, and wild rivers) and appointment of a commission to make an early recommendation to Congress for additions to this system within Alaska.

Emergency State-Federal Planning

All the measures suggested above, and most alternatives of a similar kind, would require some action by Congress. Few if any are likely to be accomplished before the end of the land freeze. There are some important steps, however, which can be taken without new legislation.

Before the end of the land freeze, the Department of the Interior and the State of Alaska should agree upon the lands which need immediate protection from entry under the public land laws.[6] Lands which are obviously candidates for provisional protection are substantial corridors along the rights of way of the Walter J. Hickel Highway and the trans-Alaska pipeline, and the area of the proposed Gates of the Arctic National Park. This protection might come either from state selection or from administrative withdrawals. Yet in the absence of planning and cooperation, the two governments will almost certainly use these measures *against each other*; i.e., federal withdrawals may be made, at least in part, to frustrate state selection and state selections may be made to preclude federal withdrawal. There have been instances of both kinds in the past; the pressures for them will be much stronger under the new circumstances.

The administrative complications of preemptive selection of withdrawals are easy to see; in some cases they will amount to a new *de facto* land freeze. Possible political repercussions also deserve attention. Selection by the state, for instance, of the Gates of the Arctic area as it selected the Wood River-Tikchik Lakes area in order to prevent establishment of a National Park, could now cause a serious national backlash against Alaska and its entire land selection program. Public and congressional acceptance of further state selections north of the Yukon-Porcupine line (which selections require secretarial approval) is already questionable; a confrontation over a potential national park would not be in the state's interest. On the other hand, an administrative or executive order withdrawal in the same area in the face of state protests could also generate a furor in Congress from which neither the state nor the Department of the Interior would benefit. Failure of either to act would leave the area open to fragmetation by speculators and reduce the ultimate value of any national or state park.

A similar dilemma can be foreseen for the areas adjoining the pipeline and winter haul road rights of way.

Prior to expiration of the land freeze, the Governor of Alaska and the Secretary of the Interior should at minimum come to an agreement regarding:

1. federal land to be selected by the state and to be processed promptly (without opposition by the department) at least to the stage of tentative approval;

2. federal lands to be temporarily withdrawn or segregated from entry under the public land laws (without opposition by the state) pending resource inventory, classification, consideration for park and wilderness status, or consideration by the state for selection; and

3. federal lands to be closed to noncompetitive mineral leasing pending either amendment of the Mineral Leasing Act, determination of existence of a "known geological structure," or a decision on state selection.

Clearly, no agreement of this sort will be able to satisfy both state and federal interests completely, but both interests—and the interest of the public at large—will be much better served under such an agreement than in its absence. The secretary and the governor

ought to be prepared to support both the contents of their
agreement and the means by which it was achieved before the
relevant committees of the Congress.

Conclusion

Calling things by their right names, the proposals here amount
to another temporary land freeze. There will surely be strong
protests in Alaska against any new land withdrawals, however
temporary or partial they are. It is repeatedly said that the present
land freeze is strangling the state's economic development. This is the
official stance of the state government and the nearly unanimous
voice of Alaska's newspapers and business leaders. Alaskans need to
realize just how ludicrous this complaint looks to non-Alaskans,
including influential members of Congress, in the context of the
state's unprecedented growth and in the face of the state's assured
revenues from oil and gas leases.[7] Alaska's big economic problem
over the next few years will *not* be a rate of mineral development
and industrial development which is too slow. Because Arctic oil
the state is entering a boom which is already outstripping its supply
of skilled labor and of housing, its public utilities and service
industries, and the administrative capacities of state and local
governments. The critical economic issue in Alaska in the near future
will be inflation rether than stagnation. In this situation neither the
national interest nor the state's interest demands an immediate and
irreversible commitment of the newly accessible lands to
uncontrolled speculation and unplanned development.

The purpose of the proposed agreements would not be to lock
up forever the resources of northern Alaska but to allow the state,
the Department of the Interior, and the Congress time to take a hard
look at the development and conservation needs of this huge and
neglected region.

NOTES

[1]When this paper was written the land freeze was due to expire December 31, 1970. On December 11, 1970 the Acting Secretary of Interior issued Public Land Order 4962 (FR 35 No. 240) extending the freeze until June 30, 1971 or until a law concerning Native claims is signed. Ed.

[2]With a few exceptions, the public land laws do not provide for payment of a fair market price no matter how valuable are the rights conveyed, and they require no test of *bona fides* or development intentions. Homesteads can be filed where there is no possibility of commercial agriculture. The mining laws provide no protection for surface resources; claims do not even have to be recorded, and there is no way the government can contest a fraudulent claim or void an abandoned claim.

The vast majority of homestead entries in recent years have never been farmed; only a very small proportion of mining claims is actually ever explored for minerals, and the great majority of noncompetitive mineral leases have never been drilled. Many of these archaic laws now seem to be made to order for purely speculative raids on the public domain rather than for development.

[3]The Classification and Multiple Use Act did expire December 31, 1970. The public land order was extended, as already noted. Ed.

[4]Public Land Order 4582 and its December 11, 1970 extension allow the state a selection priority over other applicants for three months after temination of the withdrawal.

[5]Tussing and Erickson, *Mining and Public Policy in Alaska*, prepared for the Federal Field Committee for Development Planning in Alaska and the Public Land Law Review Commission, Fairbanks: University of Alaska, 1969, pp. 19-24.

[6]An especially urgent need is for suspension of, or control of, claims on locatable minerals in critical areas. Prospecting activity, whether *bona fide* or otherwise, and claims location are not affected by the present withdrawal order, but they represent the single most

serious threat to the integrity of future national or state parks or to any classification program, through the easy creation of nonconforming inholdings. Next to noncompetitive mineral leasing, they are the second most serious obstacle to completion of the state's land selection program. Open entry and uncontrolled activity on mining claims in the vicinity of the trans-Alaska pipeline may threaten the structural security of the pipeline itself because of erosion and solifluction.

[7] A study by the Federal Field Committee staff in 1968 found no clear instance in which the land freeze in effect at the time had stood in the way of any contemplated economic development. (Federal Field Committee for Development Planning in Alaska, *Alaska Natives and the Land*, Anchorage, 1968, pp. 522-527.) As has been pointed out above, neither the original administrative "land freeze." which was in effect from November 1966 to January 1969, nor Public Land Order 4582 stands in the way of exploration for locatable minerals or location of claims anywhere in Alaska.

ADDITIONAL READING

Cooley, Richard A. *Alaska: A Challenge in Conservation.* Madison, Wisconsin: University of Wisconsin Press. 1967.

Cooley, Richard A. *Land Policy and the Future of Alaska.* Alaska Research Center. Juneau, Alaska, June, 1965.

Federal Field Committee for Development Planning in Alaska. *Alaska Natives and the Land.* Anchorage, Alaska, 1968.

Johnson, Hugh A. and Jorgenson, Harold T. *The Land Resources of Alaska.* New York: The University Publishers, 1963.

One Third of the Nation's Land. A Report to the Congress by the Public Land Law Review Commission. Washington: U.S. Government Printing Office, June, 1970.

United States Senate, Committee on Interior and Insular Affairs, *Alaska Native Claims Settlement Act of 1970: Report.* 91st Congress Second Session, Senate Report No. 91-925. 1970.

SECTION III: PETROLEUM DEVELOPMENT

A somewhat different version of this article appeared as a chapter of *Alaska Survey and Report, 1970-71* (Anchorage: Research Institute of Alaska, 1971), entitled "The Economy: An Alaskan View."

OIL AND ALASKA'S ECONOMY

Arlon R. Tussing

In September 1969, the state of Alaska sold the oil and gas exploration rights in a small corner of the state for more than $900 million. This cash windfall — amounting to about three thousand dollars for each resident — has helped to cement Alaska's reputation as a land of rich natural resources and booming resource industries. The 1969 oil lease sale was indeed an indication of the potential wealth of one of Alaska's resources, but surprisingly, Alaska's economy is still proportionally less grounded on extractive industries than are most states or the United States as a whole.

It is not widely appreciated how much Alaska is still a colony of the military establishment and of other specialized federal agencies. In fiscal year 1969, the Department of Defense and related agencies spent $349 million and the Atomic Energy Commission spent $49 million in Alaska. Together these outlays amounted to more than half of total federal spending — which was just about three-quarters of a billion dollars — in the state. This total has to be compared in turn with a level of all economic activity — technically the gross domestic product — of about one and a half billion dollars in the same year. These 1969 defense expenditures total equalled eighty per cent of total value produced from Alaska's natural resources (including crude oil and natural gas). There were almost twice as many military personnel in Alaska as the total of all workers in farming, forestry, fishing, mining including oil and gas, construction, and manufacturing combined. (The average number of military personnel was 32,360, and average monthly employment in all commodity producing industries was 17,200.) All levels of government employed twenty-one times the number of workers employed in oil and gas and related industries. Federal outlays and their indirect impact through government purchasing, construction and contracting and the spending of government employees, ultimately account for at least three-fourths of all employment and income in the state.

This preponderance of government in Alaska's economy is in addition to the fact that almost all the land and all the natural resources are owned and managed either by the state or by the federal government. These two features are unique among the states of the United States and explain many of Alaska's political and economic peculiarities. It resolves the seeming paradox of universal lip service to free enterprise fundamentalism together with a remarkable combination of federal, state and municipal "socialism." Precise measurement is difficult but Alaska has the highest proportion of its non-governmental services produced by government, and the highest levels of business subsidies, of any state. There is also a unique love-hate relationship of Alaskans with the federal government, an attitude which at one minute says, "Yankee go home" and the next minute says, "let Uncle Sam do it," asking the federal government to pay for some project in Alaska that other states pay for themselves or get private enterprise to do. This attitude, typical of dependent colonials, is not surprising considering how much Alaska really is still a federal colony.

The large role of the federal government over the last generation has also been a prominent reason for Alaska's notorious high prices and living costs. Defense construction has been an especially powerful inflationary factor. For a number of years after World War II, defense construction was on an explicitly cost-plus basis, and in general federal outlays have been rather insensitive —

in economic language "inelastic" — to the prices of the goods involved. Construction was at the heart of the problem: in one recent year heavy construction contractors in Alaska made a median net profit on tangible net worth of 76.4 per cent compared to a national average of 11.5 per cent. Heavy construction contracting, which was almost all done for government, was by far the most profitable activity, but all categories of contract construction had profit rates far above national averages and above other industries in Alaska. The difference in construction wages over their national counterparts is also much higher than in other Alaska industries and occupations. Together with environmental conditions and a small market, these circumstances have produced a cost of shelter in Anchorage calculated by the Bureau of Labor Statistics as 59 to 118 per cent higher than the national average, depending on the level of family income. This differential contrasts with cost of all items in the family budget except shelter only 18 to 26 per cent above national levels. The high money wages, the high profits in government contracting activity, and the inefficiency which prevails there, seem to have become the norms for the entire construction industry, and indirectly for the entire Alaska economy. An interesting issue in 1970 is whether the oil industry with its heavy and urgent construction demands will be an additional source of regional inflation.

Despite the main place of government in supporting most of Alaska's present economy, there is no doubt that oil is the industry where the action is. In 1969 oil and gas passed the fisheries as Alaska's number two industry in gross value of product. There are still many more workers attached to the fisheries, and this will continue to be the case for many years. But the oil is where the spectacular growth is taking place and it is oil which is generating a boom in Alaska, not only in petroleum exploration but in exploration for hard minerals, in retail trade, and in residential real estate. Because of the psychological impact of the oil boom Alaska has suddenly occurred to investors as a promising place to put money.

Oil exports from Alaska are still very modest today by national standards. By the end of 1970 the state was producing an average of 240,000 barrels of oil and 601 million cubic feet of gas per day. This was about two and one half per cent of the rate of oil production for the United States as a whole and an insignificant proportion of the gas. The value of this output in 1970 was still only about $257 million, but this needs to be put beside the industry's 1969 spending of over $900 million on exploration rights alone, against a probable 1970 investment in exploration and development of around $200 million, and against a planned annual investment of $300 to $500 million in pipeline construction beginning in 1971. Production from only the three pools so far defined in the Prudhoe Bay field can be expected to pour $200 to $300 million per year into the state's treasury in royalties and severance taxes after the pipeline is completed; additional discoveries might make the actual revenue flow much greater.

In spite of the big streams of crude oil, profits, and state revenues expected from Alaska's petroleum industry, it may not produce many permanent jobs or — directly at least — much business for Alaska firms. Alaska's oil fields discovered so far could be developed and produced with a permanent labor force of fewer than three thousand workers, the 1969 average in the industry. If other fields comparable to the Prudhoe Bay field were found nearby, five thousand permanent workers in drilling, production, pipeline and harbor services could deliver as much as one-third of North America's energy requirements for two or three decades. The purpose of pointing out these remarkable comparisons is to indicate that petroleum's long-run contribution to the state's economic development will not depend mainly on oil industry jobs nor upon the business it generates directly for Alaska enterprise. Oil's contribution to both the pace and shape of economic development in Alaska will be determined largely by the amount of revenue the state receives from its oil and gas leases and the way in which it spends this revenue.

Rural poverty and unemployment are among Alaska's most troublesome problems. The state has both the highest unemployment rates and some of the poorest communities in the United States. These problems have been completely unresponsive to industrial growth in the state, and they probably will not be directly affected much by the growth of the oil industry. Alaska's unemployment is not really caused by a lack of jobs in the ordinary sense, but by two peculiarities of the state: the existence of seasonal industries such as salmon fishing and construction, and a serious mismatch between the education, lifestyle and location of most Alaska Natives, and those required by the modern industries including government. Neither of these factors will be changed by the kind of economic growth that oil and gas will stimulate. The oil industry itself may be less seasonal than the older industries of Alaska, but so long as these other industries require many more workers in the summer than in the winter, there will be severe winter unemployment. And petroleum is singularly unpromising for a direct solution to Native unemployment problems — far less promising than government, for instance, because of oil's relatively small but highly specialized manpower requirements. The petrochemical plants which have followed oil and gas discoveries on the Kenai Peninsula and the pulp and lumber mills at Sitka, Ketchikan, Wrangell and Haines, made no inroads on the unemployment of workers who lived there before the plants were built.

The recent petroleum discoveries are much more promising for dealing with seasonal or hard-core unemployment than other industrial development in Alaska only because they generate stable revenues that might be devoted to direct attacks upon unemployment and poverty. Indeed, the income from investing 1969's bonus revenue alone, distributed equally among the state's permanent residents would virtually eliminate poverty in Alaska. If there were 215,000 eligible recipients, investing $900 million to yield a current income plus realized capital gains of ten per cent could raise the income of each family of five persons in Alaska by more than two thousand dollars. This situation contrasts with that of the wood products industry, for instance, which has not produced large government revenues, but has required big subsidies in the form of tax exemptions and credits, and in the form of fifty year timber sale contracts at prices below the competitive value of the timber. Hardrock mining is now dormant, but its expansion might cost the people of Alaska more in direct and indirect subsidies than it would benefit them in net gains of employment and income.

It is unlikely that 1969's bonus revenues, or the forthcoming royalties, will be distributed directly to Alaska's citizens, or be devoted mainly to providing jobs or incomes for the poor. But these examples do point out how much more the impact of oil on Alaska depends upon the spending of oil revenues than upon the allocation of jobs or of contracts by the industry. Ironically, therefore, the replacement of government by petroleum as the state's leading industry would only increase the importance of government in determining the shape of the new Alaska, only this time it will be the state government in one way or another under the control of the people of Alaska.

This article appeared in September 1970... appeared in F... Reprinted in ... the Math. Colloq. ... Institute, Cambridge... Bulletin, Vol. ... no. 47, 1971, pp. 165-171.

This article, prepared in September 1970, appears in *Polar Record* (published by the Scott Polar Research Institute, Cambridge, England), Vol. 15, No. 97, 1971, pp. 463-478.

INTERNATIONAL PETROLEUM AND THE ECONOMIC FUTURE OF ALASKA

George W. Rogers

The year 1969 was a major watershed in Alaska's history. This was the year when the full extent of the international petroleum industry's invasion became apparent to all Alaskans. Most viewed it as a cause for rejoicing and optimism. Overnight the State of Alaska had become rich when the industry made bonus payments of over $900 million for leases on oil and gas lands on the North Slope and the prospects of literally hundreds of millions of dollars of annual royalty and tax payments loomed for the decade ahead. The state no longer had to worry about where the money was coming from and could concentrate on spending. Private employment climbed and all the gold rush legends of quick wealth resumed currency. The magnitude of what was being done by the oil developers and promoters and what was being proposed went beyond anything dreamed of by the wildest "boomers" of a few years back. No physical barrier and no financial cost seemed too great to hinder a prolonged boom. All Alaskans had to worry about was how to cash in on it.

The Petroleum Industry

The story of petroleum in Alaska goes back at least 50 years when systematic investigations were made of the oil seepages along the arctic coast reported by Eskimos and early traders. In 1921 the Standard Oil Company explored and made an effort to stake claims to potential oil lands at Cape Simpson. These efforts were abandoned when discoveries in Oklahoma and Texas turned private developers away from the then remote Arctic. President Harding in 1923 set aside 37,000 square miles of the North Slope as Naval Petroleum Reserve No. 4, however, and over the years exploration has been carried out by the Geological Survey and the Navy, the program being recessed in 1953 when sufficient evidence had been developed to conclude that a major petroleum province existed in northern Alaska.[1] Favorable geologic conditions existed elsewhere in Alaska, and for a period during the 1930's there was a small commercial production and crude refinery operation in the Katalla district on the southcentral coast. But it was not until the discovery of oil in July 1957 on the Kenai Peninsula that the Alaska petroleum industry could be said to have truly come on stream. Exploration, development and production activities continued in this province throughout the 1960's, and by the end of 1969 production of crude oil was coming from five fields in the province and of natural gas from nine fields.[2] Wildcat activities were scattered throughout Alaska, Japanese interests were looking into the Bristol Bay area, and Australian interests were rumored to be interested in the Alaska Peninsula. But after a few false starts, most development interest was building up in Alaska's Arctic, its North Slope province.

The growth of these activities can be traced in statistics on annual exploration and development drilling footages and annual crude oil and natural gas production. Annual crude oil production rose from a token 187,000 barrels in 1959 to 74 million barrels in 1969 and natural gas from 310 million cubic feet to 149 billion cubic feet. Wellhead value of this production rose from $1.5 million in 1960 to $219 million in 1969 and petroleum was easily Alaska's first industry on the basis of raw material production alone. Further value was added by processing. A natural gas pipeline was constructed to transport gas to the city of Anchorage, and by the end of 1969 a refinery-petrochemical complex was well established on the Kenai Peninsula—two petroleum refineries producing jet, diesel, and heating fuels, a plant producing 530,000 tons of ammonia and 350,000 tons of prilled urea, and a plant liquifying 135 million cubic feet of natural gas per day for shipment by special refrigerated tankers to Tokyo.

Alaska's Economy

During the decades of the 1950's and 1960's, Alaska served primarily as an "exporter" of military defense, but it was increasing in importance as an exporter of natural resource products. During the five-year period 1951-54, spending by the Department of Defense in Alaska averaged $412.9 million annually. By the end of the 1950's the defense establishment had passed the stages of developmental build-up and achieved the plateau of simply maintaining and periodically renewing itself. The number of military personnel stationed in Alaska stabilized at about 33,000 men and the civilian employees of the department at between 6,800 and 6,500. From a peak of $512.9 million in 1953, defense expenditures declined to annual amounts fluctuating between $264.6 million to $352.0 million.

The shift of the economic base from dominance by the military to natural resource production was clear during these two decades. From a total 1950 value of $130.6 million, the value of natural resource products rose rapidly to half a billion dollars by the end of the 1960's. The outlook is that these values probably will exceed two billion dollars by the last half of the 1970's. This trend started with forest products, the annual cut rising from 72.4 million board feet in 1950 to 581.1 million board feet in 1969. The maximum sustainable yield of the resource will probably level off at about eight hundred million board feet by the end of this decade. The development of the Cook Inlet-Kenai petroleum and natural gas fields reached its peak, or soon will, with production rising from about half a million barrels in 1960 to 74.7 million in 1969. These fields will continue as major producers throughout the decade and beyond, but the annual outputs soon will begin a down trend. The North Slope province will not hit its peak, on the other hand, until well into the 1980's.

Annual data on employed workforce by industrial classification gives a representation of the structure of the Alaska economy and its shifts over time. In spite of the marked shift from defense to commodity production, employment analysis indicates that commodity producing industries remained almost constant during most of the 1950's and 1960's, and that past and projected increases in direct employment in oil and gas has not significantly altered this situation. Distributive industries and non-defense government employment experienced the most dynamic growth and caused the structure of the economy to be in continuous change. In part this reflects the inter-relationship between the defense programs and the supporting industries. Much of the transportation and communications employment, for example, comes from private contractors performing these services for the Department of Defense. Government growth in part reflects the development of the State of Alaska since its creation in 1959.

The Alaska petroleum industry has also contributed directly to the growth of these sectors of the economy. As it has been emerging over the past ten years, the petroleum industry clearly differs from any other commodity producing industries in Alaska's experience. The petroleum industry is establishing within the state an executive and administrative component which will give its main operations and planning functions an Alaskan base. Furthermore, it relies heavily upon contracting for its various supporting services. This overhead component of the Alaska salmon industry was represented within Alaska only by seasonally imported lobbyists and resident legal representatives, and the minerals and forest products industries simply comprised the Alaskan production extensions of a multitude of individual firm operations headquartered elsewhere. Stated in other terms, employment in these other Alaskan industries has been dominantly productive with a nominal overhead element, while in the emerging Alaska petroleum industry the "overhead" element far overshadows the productive.

The expansion of government programs and employment in part reflects a response to expressed need, but more basically it is a function of resources available to the government for spending. With the growth of the petroleum industry, the revenues received by the state and in part passed on to local governments has steadily increased without signficant raises in tax rates or the creation of new taxes. The amount received from the industry in 1969 ($936.2 million) is enough to pay for the entire state budget at 1968 levels for four and a half years. This will not be repeated, but the anticipated annual oil industry revenues are such that future expansion of state and local government employment need not be hindered because of money.

However, there is a further economic impact of the petroleum industry which will cause the future Alaskan economy to differ from that of the past. This is the cyclical nature of industry activities as has been dramatically and painfully experienced in the period 1968-1970.

The 1969 Boom and 1970 Bust

The July 1968 announcements of Atlantic Richfield Company (ARCO) and Humble Oil and Refining Company that they had completed two spectacularly successful wildcat wells at Prudhoe Bay on Alaska's North Slope touched off one of the biggest resource rushes in the history of the North. The first estimates were that the new field might hold reserves of up to ten billion barrels of crude, compared with Canada's known eight billion barrels and Texas' fifteen billion barrels. Furthermore, on the basis of three competitive oil and gas lease sales by the State of Alaska in 1964, 1965 and 1967, only one other oil company, British Petroleum (BP), had a stake in this bonanza.[3] The state had scheduled for September 10, 1969 a fourth sale covering another 450,000 acres of its North Slope land, and the oil rush by those companies not already in was on.

In a straight line the two discovery wells were some 290 miles from the nearest spur of the state's road system and 340 miles from the head of the Alaska Railroad. Ocean transport was possible by barge, but only for a brief one or two months, depending upon sea ice conditions. In an unsuccessful attempt to provide land access, the state in the winter of 1968-69 pushed through a rough cat road some 360 miles from Livengood to Sagwon, too late to move more than a token amount of equipment before the spring breakup reduced the project to a useless and impassable mud and water canal. Most of the 1968-69 supplies were airlifted by C-130 Hercules transports carrying average loads of 22 tons each from the Fairbanks and Nenana airfields on an around-the-clock basis. Fairbanks took on all the characteristics of an oil boom town.

While the exploration activities of other firms were going on, the establishment Big Three of the slope (ARCO, Humble, and BP) were busy with plans to spend $900 million to build a 48-inch pipeline to move oil 800 miles south to the ice free port of Valdez on the Gulf of Alaska. Initial capacity projected for 1972 was 500,000 barrels daily with an ultimate capacity of 2,000,000 barrels daily. The Trans Alaska Pipeline System was organized and route survey and procurement activities launched.[4] The same firms also launched a forty-million-dollar tanker test of the Northwest Passage. The largest merchant ship under the American flag, the 115,000 ton S.S. MANHATTAN, was converted into an ice-breaking tanker and, in the company of one United States and two Canadian ice breakers, explored the passage. If the 4,500-mile tanker route to the east coast of the United States proved economically feasible, there would be launched a program to construct over the next ten years thirty 25,000-ton ice-breaking tankers at a cost of $1.5 billion. The result would increase the present U.S. flag tanker fleet 2.5 times.[5]

The search for information by the oil companies was carried out under the tightest security conditions, but excitement was kept at a boil by periodic upward revisions of estimated reserves by "reliable sources." The Prudhoe Bay field reserves rose from ten to twenty billion barrels of crude[6] and the ultimate recoverable reserves of the North Slope province were estimated at fifty billion barrels of oil and three hundred trillion cubic feet of natural gas.[7] Clearly the tanker route and TAPS would not have the capacity to accommodate this. The Alberta Gas Trunk Line Co., Ltd., of Canada proposed a

1,550-mile natural gas pipeline from Prudhoe Bay through the Yukon Territory to connect with its system in Alberta. The project would cost as estimated $1.5 billion and could be operational by 1974. Another pipeline was under study by a group of United States and Canadian interests which would run 2,500 miles to Emerson, Manitoba, and would cost $2.5 billion.[8]

The Alaska boom psychology reached fever pitch with the September 10, 1969 competitive oil and gas lease sale. An Alaskan boom-bust fever chart could be represented by the monthly employment reports for the industrial classification "mining; oil and gas." From a 1961 monthly average of 500 employees, the level rose steadily to 1,000 by 1966, and afterwards more rapidly to 1,600 in 1967 and on to 2,200 and 3,200 in 1968 and 1969, the peak months being August and September 1969 with 3,700 each.[9] In the broader context of the excitement generated by the 1969 announcements of pipelines and Northwest Passage development and the bonuses received by the state at the September 1969 lease sales, a continued increase in direct employment in the petroleum industry with related expansion throughout the economy was confidently predicted. Most of this increase was taking place within the North Slope (in fact, there were offsetting mining employment declines within the developed Cook Inlet-Kenai province). Anticipating that it would be the staging area for these developments, the business community of Fairbanks went heavily into debt to gear up for the 1970 boom. While frozen ground permitted movement, several construction firms moved an estimated $45 million worth of heavy equipment into camps strategically located along what appeared to be the route of the TAPS line in order to get a jump on capturing contracts for construction of the $120 million access road.

The peak of the boom passed by September 1969, but the boomer spirit of Alaskans persisted well into 1970 before giving way to the despair of a bust psychology. The initial drop in oil and gas "mining" employment from 3,700 in September to 3,000 in October 1969 was dismissed as a temporary readjustment, but concern increased as a continuing downtrend developed, oil and gas employment falling by June 1970 to 2,300. Although what was described as "the largest single ocean shipment ever to Alaska"

(187,000 tons including 117,000 tons of pipe for TAPS) moved by barges 3,200 miles from Seattle to Prudhoe Bay during the brief summer of 1970, the Fairbanks-North Slope air lift of 1969 dwindled, with a resulting 22 percent drop in local employment in air transportation. Unease increased as it became evident that TAPS was uncertain as to what the actual route of the pipeline should be and how much would have to be elevated above ground to prevent permafrost thawing. By April it was apparent to all that there would be no construction during 1970 due to lack of data and design, and an organizational change within the consortium.

In the Fairbanks area unemployment in June 1970 rose to 13.8% as compared with 8.5% in June 1969[10] and the state put up booths in outside airports to warn job seekers to stay away from Alaska.

Delay, Uncertainty and Cycles in Petroleum

The oil and gas employment drop on the North Slope and the rise in unemployment throughout the northern economy was popularly attributed to the postponement of the pipeline construction. This in turn was blamed upon the alarmist outcry of environmentalists both inside and outside Alaska, the Department of the Interior's delay in granting right-of-way permits until design was completed, and Native groups who objected to invasion of their hunting and trapping areas. Actually, the subject of these demands and requirements was already a matter of concern to the industry which did not wish to add further fuel to national protest over the succession of oil spills in the Santa Barbara Channel and Gulf of Mexico. A public statement by a senior vice president of Philips Petroleum Company in August 1970 suggested that furthermore, given the magnitude of the undertaking and the lack of basic geologic data, delays in construction of the pipeline or even its abandonment were part of the industry's long-range planning. "Scientists have determined that about 20 per cent of the line needs to be elevated, but some disagree and insist that 80 per cent or more needs to be above the permafrost. Even with 20 per cent above ground, new cost figures project to $1.3 billion for the cost for building the pipeline today as compared to the original $900 million estimate. (This has been based upon preliminary advice that ninety per cent could be buried.) Certainly, if it is decided that more of the line must be above ground, that figure would be even higher. To venture a personal opinion, I believe that regardless of what is decided concerning the ecology, the final cost of the complete project is now most likely to be very near to $2 billion. If more problems are encountered with the pipeline and tanker alternatives, the economics of huge submarines may well become more attractive. In any case, you can easily see that the lead time for brining any of these alternatives into reality is quite long."[11]

In addition to lack of data sufficient to select a route and produce an adequate design and plan, the August 28, 1970 announcement of the creation of the Alyeska Pipeline Service Company to replace TAPS revealed that the loosely structured consortium of eight firms was proving unequal to the task of planning and launching construction of the pipeline. An Alaskan editorial commented, "Few, if any, will mourn the demise of the old Trans Alaska Pipeline System. The oil companies which created it recognized its failings; realized that as organized it could not accomplish the monumental task assigned it. A consortium of oil companies, it was operated by committee. The official announcement of the new Alyeska company states that 'within general policy guidelines' the new president will have 'broad responsibilities and authority for the service corporation to build and operate the pipeline' . . . The Alyeska company 'will also provide a single contact point for various governmental representatives and agencies.' "[12]

Beyond the problems of planning and securing permits for the construction of the pipeline, there were other causes of the 1970 employment slump. In April 1970 the state Department of Labor noted, "Also figuring in the decline are negotiations concerning unitization of the Prudhoe Bay oil field. Although it has been agreed to unitize the field, specifics of the plan have yet to be worked out. Because of this, even if a pipeline completion date were known, many companies would be unable to proceed with development plans."[13] By mid-year it appeared that the field would be developed in two sectors with BP Alaska, Inc., serving as operating company for all leaseholders in the western half and Atlantic Richfield Company as operator of the eastern sector. Under this system, the leaseholders would receive shares of oil produced from each sector of the field based upon the extent of their holdings.

Although preliminary plans for development of Prudhoe Bay finally were made public in September 1970, significantly the news releases gave no indication of when a decision would be made to proceed.[14] This final delay and uncertainty could be attributed to the size of the contemplated developments alone and the uncertainty of the industry as to the potential impacts upon national and world petroleum supplies, costs and regulation. Petroleum economics experts in August 1969 at the Alaska Science Conference had discussed whether or not a rapid rate of development of the North Slope might even break up the regulatory systems of the other oil producing states, completely disrupt United States oil import policies, and cause basic reorganization of the corporate and institutional relationships within the industry.[15] Although these discussions and the continuous flow of speculation that followed were inconclusive and contradictory, by mid-1970 it was apparent that the urgency of industry action and intensity of interest in 1968 and 1969 was one of competition to accumulate information as a means of securing a share in the anticipated bonanza. After September 10, 1970 the need was for thoughtful weighing of the consequences of any further course of action or inaction and analysis of the options which were now available to the international petroleum industry. Too much was at stake for precipitous action.

In addition to the more apparent delay and uncertainty in the decision making process, Alaskans were to learn that employment and economic decline had other causes inherent within the petroleum industry itself. As the development plan for the Prudhoe Bay field emerged, it became clear that the process of exploration, development, and finally production was a cyclical one unlike any other resource development pattern Alaskans had experienced before. In other resources the generalized pattern was one of small beginnings building up to a peak and then declining as the resource

was depleted (as in the case of other minerals and fishing) or
dropping off with market decline (as in the case of furs). Watching
employment and economic levels ascend rapidly during the final
years of the 1960's, Alaskans anticipated that they would continue a
climb paralleling that of projected petroleum output. In a meeting on
the possibility of development of new arctic communities held in
July 1970, for example, one Alaska resource development expert
predicted that the North Slope population would rise from its
estimated level of 5,900 persons in 1969 to 15,000 persons.[16] At
the same meeting a representative of BP put forward a completely
opposite forecast, pointing out that the peak of employment on
the Prudhoe Bay field had been achieved in the period
May-September 1969, would continue tapering off during this final
period of exploration and development and would drop to 300 to
400 persons during the productive phase. There would be no new
communities beyond temporary camps due to the nature of the
cyclical process and the highly automated nature of production.[17]

The basic nature of the temporary peak of employment and
activity during the exploration and development phases is reflected
in the practice of the petroleum producers of contracting for most of
their drilling, geophysical, supply and support services rather than
building up their own direct labor force beyond a level needed for
the longer-run production periods. For example, an industry report
of direct employment in Alaska gave the 1965 employment by the
oil companies as 414 persons and by service companies under
contract to the oil companies as 749. In 1969 the report was that oil
company employment had risen to 775 persons (an 87.2% increase)
and contractor employment to 2,400 persons (a 220.4% increase).[18]
The contracted services during the development phase are further
increased by construction contracts, the building of field systems,
the trans-Alaska pipeline, etc. The major objective of the oil
companies appears to be to maintain as nearly as possible a constant
rate of production and a relatively constant level of company
employees. The contracting firms, on the other hand, seek to
maintain their employment levels by moving freely throughout the
petroleum world in response to development forces. These practices
have important implications for Alaskan efforts to implement their
local hire preference policies. If Alaska Natives were trained for these

jobs, they must then be geographically mobile in order to continue in these employments. The Alaska based jobs in production, on the other hand, will be extremely limited in number.

The Future Impact

The essence of the announced development plans for the Prudhoe Bay field are maximum co-ordination of all production (the objective of unitization) and minimum labor input per unit of output (the objective of automation of production and maintenance of high levels of output). The BP plan for the western sector of the field calls for twelve drilling islands (gravel pads raised above the tundra, which is subject to thawing and flooding) of four wells each, three crude oil gathering and treating centers and a system of thirty miles of gathering and transit pipelines connecting the producing wells, the centers and the final transmission line. Both sectors of the field will share common utility, transport and support systems. The production process will be automatic and managed primarily from outside the North Slope region, probably from Anchorage. Oil will flow from the ground under natural pressure into the three gathering and treating centers where gaseous matter will be separated and a certain amount of skimming will take place before the oil enters into the main transmission system. This gathering and treating system will be provided with electronic monitoring devices, automatic safety locks and diversion systems, standby capacity, etc. In addition to promptly detecting leaks and failures, the system will be programmed to take immediate corrective action. As a further safeguard, the operation of each unit will be covered by close-circuit TV to permit frequent check by trained human observers from the field control center. The limited number of field personnel required will be housed and work in a central headquarters complex on a two weeks on and one week off basis. Frequent rotation will eliminate need for construction of family units or elaborate community, recreation and other social services in the field.[19]

Employment projections have been made on the assumption that over the next twenty years there will be continuing exploration and development work on the North Slope and that final commercial production will come from the present Prudhoe Bay field and two somewhat smaller fields. Exploration employment will recover and build up between 1970 and 1980 and drop off rapidly during the 1990's. Most of the basic construction and development work will take place during the 1970's, reaching its peak about midway through the decade. These activities account for most of the employment projected for oil and gas mining and much of contract construction for 1970, 1975 and 1980. Primary production employment will reach its peak about 1980 and will fall off during a longer secondary recovery production period probably extending to the end of the century. At most, however, this will amount to only a few hundred workers (a figure of not more than 400 has been suggested by some industry representatives).

These are the direct employment impacts anticipated, but the major employment impacts will be the indirect ones reflected in the distributive industries and in government. The heavy overhead component in the Alaska petroleum industry has been referred to above as has been the impact upon government of the availability of a continuing major source of revenues from taxes, royalties, leases, etc. What this will mean to the State of Alaska, therefore, depends upon what Alaskans do with the money they receive rather than whether or not they become part of the petroleum industry's labor force.

NOTES

[1]George Gryc, "Geologic Framework of the North Slope Petroleum Province," *Twentieth Alaska Science Conference*, College, Alaska, August 26, 1969.

[2]Division of Oil and Gas, *Report for the Year 1969*, State of Alaska, Department of Natural Resources, Anchorage, Alaska, p. 6.

[3]United States Bureau of Mines, *Minerals Yearbook, 1968*, Vol. III, Area Reports: Domestic, United States Government Printing Office, Washington, D.C., pp. 71, 79.

[4]David Henderson, "Trans-Alaska Pipeline System, " *Twentieth Alaska Science Conference*, College, Alaska, August 26, 1969.

[5]Stanley B. Haas, "Marine Transport—The Northwest Passage Project," *Twentieth Alaska Science Conference*, College, Alaska, August 26, 1969.

[6]Division of Oil and Gas, *Report for the Year 1969.*

[7]J.P. Gallagher, "Economics of Petroleum Development," *Twentieth Alaska Science Conference*, College, Alaska, August 25, 1969.

[8]Alaska Department of Labor, *Alaska Economic Trends*, Juneau, Alaska, July 1970, p. 1.

[9]Alaska Department of Labor, *Workforce Estimates, Alaska, by Industry and Area*, Juneau, Alaska, 1961, 1966-1968.

[10]Alaska Department of Labor, *Alaska Economic Trends*, Juneau, Alaska, July 1970.

[11]Fairbanks Daily News Miner, *Oil and Resource Review*, Fairbanks, Alaska, September 1, 1970.

[12]*Ibid.*, September 8, 1970.

[13]Alaska Department of Labor, *Alaska Economic Trends*, Juneau, Alaska, April 1970, p. 3.

[14]*Anchorage Daily News*, "Plan for North Slope Headquarters," Anchorage, Alaska, September 14, 1970.

[15]George W. Rogers, ed., "The Economics of Petroleum in Alaska," *Change in Alaska: People, Petroleum, Politics*, Chapter 2, University of Washington Press, Seattle, 1970.

[16]David M. Hickok, "Development Trends in Arctic Alaska," *Conference on Arctic Communities*, University of Alaska, College, Alaska, July 1, 1970, pp. 10-11.

[17]F.G. Larminie, "Comments on North Slope Development," *Conference on Arctic Communities*, University of Alaska, College, Alaska, July 2, 1970.

[18]Western Oil and Gas Association, *Alaska Petroleum Industry Facts*, Alaska Division, 1965-1969.

[19]Larminie, "Comments on North Slope Development"; *Anchorage Daily News*, "Plan for North Slope Headquarters."

This article appeared as an issue of the *Alaska Review of Business and Economic Conditions*, Vol. VII no. 3. (College, Alaska: Institute of Social, Economic and Government Research) July, 1970.

ALASKA'S PETROLEUM LEASING POLICY

Gregg K. Erickson

The value of an oil lease depends upon the profits that can be made from producing any petroleum that may be discovered thereon. The fundamental problem of managing the private development of public lands is to determine how these profits, if any, are to be shared between public landowner and private developer. In making this determination, Alaska has an interest in obtaining the highest possible returns from publicly owned oil lands.

It is not always easy to know what means can best assure this. In petroleum development, the profits expected from production can only be estimated. Since these estimates are subject to adjustment as production proceeds, the ideal petroleum policy would provide for continuing incorporation of new information and a self-correcting system of profit assessment.

Alaska's present petroleum development policy, enacted in 1959, though certainly not ideal, does rely on just such a system, the market, to determine the price of competitive petroleum leases.

Competitive and Non-Competitive Leasing

Of all objections advanced to Alaska's present leasing policy, the most fundamental comes from those who object to the use of the market system, i.e., competitive bidding, as a means of transferring petroleum leases into the hands of private developers. This issue came to a head in 1969 when the Commissioner of Natural Resources reclassified as "competitive" most of the state-selected land south of the Prudhoe Bay oil discovery on Alaska's North Slope. Technically, these lands were frozen in federal ownership because of the Native land claims, but they had been selected by the state prior to (and soon after) the Prudhoe Bay discovery. Despite the fact that these lands were likely to pass immediately into either state or Native ownership on resolution of the land claims, private individuals, sensing speculative gain possibilities, submitted lease applications at the Fairbanks office of the Bureau of Land Management under the federal non-competitive leasing laws. Such offers, however, were not acted on by the Bureau, but simply were kept on file pending resolution of the land claims. What Commissioner Kelly's action essentially did was to wipe out any hope of speculative gain from such offers. Contrary to popular belief, the only loss of private investment to the government was the $10.00 filing fees paid on each 2,560 acre parcel.   (See Note No. 1.)

In arguing against the commissioner's action, speculators posed the issue of competitive versus non-competitive leasing as one of large versus small enterprise. They argued that the independent oil producer—the little guy—would be effectively denied the opportunity to participate in the development of Alaska's petroleum resources if competitive leasing was allowed. Presumably, the acquisition of such leases would require larger sums of money than such independents could possibly raise. The smaller firms, it was contended, have a right to continued existence, which right would be extinguished by the commissioner's actions. It was also argued that dominance of Alaska's petroleum industry by the major oil companies would result in their eventually "owning" Alaska, an eventuality that could be precluded by the nurturing of a healthy group of smaller companies through non-competitive leasing.

While there may be an element of truth in these arguments, they would never have been seriously proposed in regard to the public interest had it not been for the substantial private interest at stake. Despite the efforts of these private interests in the political sphere, it seems clear that the State of Alaska is firmly committed to a petroleum development policy that has as its objective the maximization of public revenue. The transfer of any substantial interests to the hands of private developers on either a first-come, first-served basis or by lottery, the two means by which non-competitive leasing could be implemented, runs counter to such a policy.

Legislation and Administration

The legislation embodying Alaska's present oil land policy was closely modeled after federal leasing laws on the assumption that industry's familiarity with these would render it acceptable. In framing Alaska's petroleum law in 1959, the lawmakers were conscious of the fact that Alaska had but one producing oil field, and that not even located on state land. The state was faced with the specter of of a serious financial crisis in the immediate future. Many felt then that the only way to avoid such a crisis, and indeed the key to the state's financial security, would be the rapid exploration of the state's several petroleum provinces, and the development of the resources that it was hoped existed there. They argued, correctly it would seem, that the state had little to lose by offering private developers a fairly large share of the fruits of the development of these publicly owned resources. (See Note No. 2.)

Most criticism has not been levied against the general laws under which Alaska's petroleum lands are leased and developed, but rather the methods by which the commissioners of natural resources have chosen to implement those laws. In addition to determining how Alaska's petroleum lands will be leased, i.e., whether competitively or non-competitively, the commissioner, acting for the administration, has almost complete authority to determine which lands shall be made available for competitive leasing, and the rate at which they will be leased. Both the Egan administration and the

Hickel-Miller administration have been criticized, the former, for moving ahead too slowly with their leasing arrangements, the latter for moving too quickly.

Petroleum Lease Market

In determining policy with regard to the rate at which prospective petroleum lands are leased, Alaska's natural resource administrators have had to take account of the market in which they were attempting to operate. This market is one in which Alaska enters as a seller, competing to various degrees with our own federal government, the Canadian federal and provincial governments, other states of the United States, and other foreign governments, in roughly that order of importance. The buyers in this market are all those who wish to purchase the right to explore and develop the petroleum resources that may be discovered on lands that, although presently non-productive, hold promise of such production. By far the greatest part of this demand is generated by the world's thirty or so fully integrated petroleum companies.

Alaska's petroleum policy makers are likely to be influenced in the future, as in the past, by conditions in this market. Of particular concern to Alaska over the past decade has been the federal government's policy of leasing offshore petroleum lands. A conscious attempt has been made to program Alaska's lease sales so as to compete as little as possible with the comparatively far more valuable offshore lease offerings. Fortunately for Alaska, the federal government during this period has been conscious of its dominance of the market for prospective petroleum lands in the United States. In an apparent attempt to maximize revenue, the federal Bureau of Land Management has leased its offshore lands at a relatively slow rate so as not to spoil its own market. This has had the effect of keeping prices for prospective petroleum lands at a high level and consequently increasing the bids oil firms were willing to submit on Alaskan land. Prior to Alaska's $900 million dollar sale in late 1969, Alaska was a very small operator. This can be seen by comparing the total of $97.6 million Alaska received in all 22 competitive sales through 1969 (see Table 1) with the more than $600 million realized by the federal government in its single lease sale in the Santa Barbara Channel in 1967.

TABLE 1
Competitive Oil and Gas Leasing of State Lands

Sale No. and Date		Acres Leased	$/Acre	Bonus Received
1.	Dec. 10, 1959	77,191	$ 52	$ 4,020,342
2.	July 13, 1960	16,506	25	407,655
3.	Dec. 7, 1960	22,867	2	35,325
4.	Jan. 25, 1961	400	679	271,614
5.	May 23, 1961	95,980	75	7,170,465
6.	Aug. 4, 1961	13,257	8	110,672
7.	Dec. 19, 1961	187,025	79	14,863,049
8.	April 24, 1962	1,062	5	5,097
9.	July 7, 1962	264,437	59	15,714,113
10.	May 8, 1963	141,491	29	4,136,225
11.	Cancelled			
12.	Dec. 11, 1963	247,089	12	3,042,681
13.	Dec. 8, 1964	722,659	8	5,537,101
14.	July 15, 1965	403,000	15	6,145,473
15.	Sept. 28, 1965	301,751	15	4,674,344
16.	July 19, 1966	133,987	53	7,040,880
17.	Nov. 22, 1966	18,590	7	136,280
18.	Jan. 24, 1967	42,398	35	1,478,777
19.	Mar. 28, 1967	2,560	1	517
20.	July 25, 1967	256,557	73	18,757,341
21.	Mar. 26, 1968	164,961	18	3,009,224
22.	Oct. 29, 1968*	60,272	17	1,042,220
23.	Sept. 10, 1969	412,548	2,182	900,218,590
	TOTALS & AVERAGE	3,586,588	$ 278 (Av.)	$997,817,985

*Competitive sale bonus received included 1/5 bonus from forfeited leases.
Source: Alaska State Department of Natural Resources, Division of Lands.

Timing Lease Sales

Alaska's resource administrators have had to weigh carefully the effects produced by leasing practices on potential revenue. Alaska's need for immediate revenue and economic development argued for placing large amounts of land on the market as quickly as possible. Another consideration was the effect of leasing in stimulating economic development. Some argued the state would develop more quickly if much land was leased. Immediate sales would encourage exploration and increase the likelihood of successful oil discoveries. Yet, such success, if it came, would undoubtedly increase the value of adjacent leased lands by many fold. Thus, the leaseholders rather than the state would gain.

Others insisted that most of the land be held until a higher lease revenue could be anticipated. Proponents of the latter view cite the experience of the Tyonek Indians, who originally had offered their land at a competitive auction that brought high bids of less than $1 million. These bids were rejected, and sometime later the lands were again put up for sale and brought several times that amount as a consequence of nearby petroleum discoveries. If the state leased only a very limited amount of land of high potential, therefore, it would be in the hope that an oil discovery would spark a land rush. If this occurred, the profits from the increased value of the adjacent leased land would accrue to the state rather than to some private leaseholder.

The state has generally followed a middle course. Beyond a certain point, offering additional acreage does not significantly increase the probability of discovery as there are obvious limitations on oil companies' exploration budgets. The most likely and first leased prospects will be drilled regardless of the total available acreage.

Spoiling the Market

Since the discovery of the tremendous reserves on Alaska's North Slope, Alaska's relationship to world markets has become far more complicated. Alaska is no longer considered a small operator. For instance, the more than $900 million spent by the oil industry on acquiring North Slope leases in 1969 is more than 50 per cent of the total expenditures of the U.S. oil industry on acquiring such rights in the United States during 1968. It must be an even higher percentage of the 1969 expenditures. Indeed, the $900 million spent in Alaska in 1969 is better than 10 per cent of all capital expenditures of the United States oil industry in 1968.

Thus, Alaska can no longer afford to ignore the effects that its own leasing policies have on the market. In disposing of petroleum lands, Alaska faces competition from only two other significant sellers—the Canadian and U.S. federal governments. In 1969, at least, Alaska dominated this market.

This dominance is significant for Alaska's leasing policy in several ways. First of all, now Alaska can clearly spoil its own market by disposing of too much land too rapidly. On the other hand, leasing at too slow a rate may provide an opportunity for Alaska's competitors—particularly the Canadians—to recapture some of the initiative that they lost subsequent to the Prudhoe Bay discovery. Recent discoveries in northwestern Canada and the subsequent increase in oil industry geophysical activity there indicate that this is happening now. These events tend to support the position of Alaska's Commissioner of Natural Resources, Thomas Kelly, who argued against postponement of the 1969 lease sale. Kelly thought that postponement might permit Alaska's competitors an opportunity to draw bid money away.

Corridor Leasing

Some critics of Alaska's petroleum administration, while not specifically objecting to the rate at which lands were leased, suggest that the state's interests would be better served by some form of "checkerboarding" or corridor leasing. In effect, such plans would require the state to reserve unto itself every other acre or tract of land in an area leased. For every tract that would be made available for private development, another equal and usually contiguous tract would be reserved to the state. This practice originated in Texas and has been followed in Alberta and elsewhere. The Canadian experience with corridor leasing has generally been a favorable one (see Table 2), and Canadian visitors have often urged Alaska to adopt a similar policy. (See Note No. 3.)

TABLE 2
Petroleum Revenues in Alberta
(in millions of Canadian dollars)

Revenue Source	1963-64	1964-65	1965-66	1966-67	1967-68
Rentals & Fees	38.5	48.0	57.0	52.0	54.0
Royalties	56.5	62.0	68.5	80.0	94.0
Bonus Bids	53.0	92.0	121.0	106.0	69.5
TOTALS*	148.0	202.0	246.5	238.0	217.5

Source: 19th Annual report of the Alberta Department of Mines and Minerals.

Almost all industry representatives, on the other hand, particularly those from larger companies, are vehemently opposed to such schemes. They contend that this pattern would seriously reduce their companies' interest in exploration in Alaska, where one of the prime attractions has been the ability to combine a large group of tracts to assure that any oil discovered will be within the confines of the discovering company's leaseholds. Their contention has some weight. Yet, losses resulting from this reduced interest might be compensated for by the increased revenue derived from the subsequent leasing of the reserved parcels. Naturally, the value of the reserved parcels would be affected by their proximity to either productive acreage or dry wells.

Although oil companies have been allowed to acquire fairly large contiguous tracts, the state has, in many cases, reserved itself large areas of land adjacent to these tracts Figure 1, showing the North Slope lands leased in the 14th, 18th, and 23rd competitive sales (including lands in the area of Prudhoe Bay), demonstrates how this policy has worked. This same figure and Table 3 show the many thousandfold increase in land values that can result from a discovery. Of course, it is possible that under a checkerboarding system the Prudhoe Bay discovery would not have been made, for lack of oil company interest.

TABLE 3
Results of North Slope Lease Sales

Date of Sale	Acres Leased	$/Acre*	Bonus Received
Dec. 9, 1964	466,180	$ 9	$ 4,376,523
July 15, 1965	403,000	15	6,145,473
Jan. 24, 1967	37,662	39	1,469,645
Sept. 10, 1969	412,548	2,182	900,218,590
TOTALS & AVERAGE	1,319,390	$ 691 (Av.)	$912,210,231

*Rounded to nearest dollar.
Source: Alaska State Department of Natural Resources, Division of Lands.

Even though strip leasing may reduce incentives, many economists believe it is the optimum means by which the state can assess and take its share of the oil profits. The system does tend to compensate for the defects inherent both in systems of early payment for exploration rights and those of deferred payment.

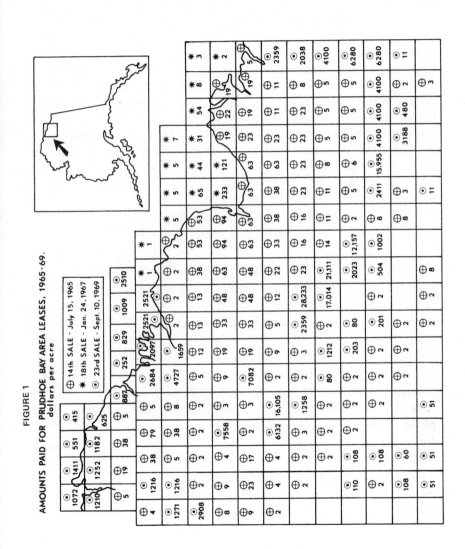

FIGURE 1

AMOUNTS PAID FOR PRUDHOE BAY AREA LEASES, 1965-69.
dollars per acre

⊕ 14th SALE - July 15, 1965
✳ 18th SALE - Jan. 24, 1967
⊙ 23rd SALE - Sept. 10, 1969

Taxation and Import Quotas

Another matter of concern to Alaska's petroleum policy makers and to the entire world petroleum industry is the future direction of the United States policy with regard to taxation and import quotas. Changes unfavorable to the domestic oil industry, like a further reduction in the depletion allowance or a reduction in the restrictions to the free flow of foreign oil into North America, would depress prices for subsequent production from Alaska's oil fields. This would, in turn, lower the prices that oil firms would be willing to pay for Alaskan land. If an oil policy maker in Alaska sensed that these changes were coming, he would rapidly lease as much land as possible prior to the recognition of such changes by the oil industry.

Severance Taxes and Royalties:
Resource Allocation

Great debate rages over Alaska's legislative policy regarding severance taxes and royalties. Both these provisions are devices for delaying the determination of the state's share of the profits until it is produced. Such delay can be advantageous to both parties, but the severance tax and the royalty provision are imperfect devices for determining the amount of "economic rent" due to the state. This rent is the residual that is left over after all the costs of production have been deducted from the market value of the crude oil. If the state wished to maximize the long-run returns from the exploitation of its publicly owned resources, it would be advantageous to collect from the oil companies no more and no less than this residual. Setting the charges too low is obviously undesirable. But if oil companies find that they are not able to meet their expenses of exploitation and production as a consequence of excessive rental charges, then they will search for oil elsewhere.

If every barrel of oil cost every operator exactly the same amount to find and produce, then the severance tax and royalty provisions would be appropriate methods for determining the economic rent due and available to the state. Unfortunately, this is far from the case. Costs of production in the state's known Cook Inlet oil fields vary from somewhere in the neighborhood of 25 cents per barrel up to about $3.00 per barrel. Consequently, severance taxes and royalties are inefficient in that they overcharge some producers and undercharge others.

The Premature Shutdown Effect

When the landowner's royalty take, as a percentage of the gross income of the producer, is much less than the producer's profits, due to very low per barrel cost of exploration, development, and production, the losses to the landowner are obvious. What is less generally realized, however, is that the landowner will also lose when his total percentage recoveries from royalties are greater than the net profits available to the producer. At the date when the total costs of production, plus royalty payment, exceed the value of the crude oil, the private operator will shut down his operations and stop paying royalties altogether. Under such circumstances the landowner will be losing potential revenue. Had the royalty been reduced, production would continue and the landowner would have continued to receive some return that would have otherwise been lost. Rigidity in royalty or severance tax rates calculated as a fixed percentage of the gross value of production results in losses not only to the landowner but also to society. This is true because the real cost in labor and materials of continuing production will still be less than the real value of the oil produced. (See Figure 2.)

It can be argued that the premature shutdown effect is not much of a problem in Alaska because of the very high productivities and low per barrel cost of Alaskan oil. Even the most expensive fields in the Cook Inlet Basin are worth keeping in operation for another few years at the present rate of tax and royalty. In the more highly productive fields in northern Alaska, it would be at least a generation before the present levies could force one of the field's operators to shut off production. Nevertheless, the time will come when any system relating Alaska's revenue to gross production will be detrimental to the state.

FIGURE 2

REVENUE FROM TYPICAL
OIL WELL

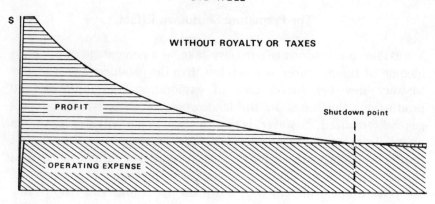

WITHOUT ROYALTY OR TAXES

PROFIT

Shutdown point

OPERATING EXPENSE

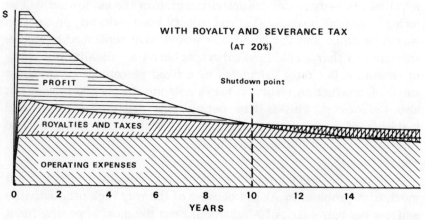

WITH ROYALTY AND SEVERANCE TAX
(AT 20%)

PROFIT

Shutdown point

ROYALTIES AND TAXES

OPERATING EXPENSES

0   2   4   6   8   10   12   14

YEARS

Royalties: Profit Allocation

Most of the controversy over severance taxes and royalties focuses on profit allocation. Clearly, the higher the severance tax rate or royalty, the greater the share of the profits that is likely to be taken by the state. Yet, royalties and severance tax differ in a very important respect. Royalties are a matter of contract between the state, acting as a landowner, and the private developer. This contract is enforceable in the courts, and the state has no special rights or privileges under the contract that a private landowner would not have under the same circumstances. As specified in the lease document, the royalty rate is fixed for the life of the lease and can be changed only by mutual consent. In a sense, then, the oil companies know what they are getting into with regard to royalties. No matter how high or low the royalty, the oil companies will at least theoretically take it into account when calculating their bonus bids. Any leases which specify a very high royalty rate would elicit relatively low bids; leases on equally favorable land with low royalty rates would bring forth much higher bids, assuming a competitive market.

Economists differ in evaluating the efficiency of royalties. While it is widely acknowledged that higher royalties will mean lower bonus bids, there is no way of predicting confidently how much lower those bonuses will be, or whether the amount lost in bonuses will be more than made up for in future royalties.

Part of this confusion arises because the bidder and the offerer may be using different discount rates in measuring the time value of money. The discount rate is essentially an expression of the fact that a dollar today is worth more than a dollar tomorrow, the rate being an indicator of *how much more* that dollar is worth today.

If the bidder uses a lower discount rate than the lessor, then both parties may find it advantageous to eliminate the royalty completely, with the landowner's share of the profits thus determined entirely by the bonus bid. The landowner may feel that he can "invest" the value of the lease, which he receives as a bonus bid, and earn a higher rate on that investment than the bidder himself believes that he could earn.

The converse is also true. If the oil company has a time value of money higher than that of the landowner, in theory at least, it will be to the advantage of both parties to eliminate the bonus bid entirely, with the landowner collecting his share of the profits only after production is under way.

Economists are not in clear agreement about the discount rates that a government such as the State of Alaska should use in evaluating the economic development of its natural resources. While this point may seem somewhat obscure, it is undoubtedly a matter of great relevance to the proper evaluation of Alaska's petroleum policies, and is one that depends as much upon political and social outlooks as upon technical sophistication in economics. Individuals who believe in a high social discount rate (and, by implication, in a relatively low royalty) are those who believe that the state should divert a greater proportion of its total wealth towards spending in the public sector. In a sense, such individuals thereby indicate that they believe "investments" in the public sector can generally be expected to earn more than those in the private sector.

Unfortunately, a problem arises in doing away with the royalty completely. Oil developers may systematically underestimate the value of the lands that they are trying to obtain, or they may have to reduce its value because of the risk of total failure. Royalty provisions in Alaska's leases clearly provide a way to remedy possible underestimation and the consequent loss of revenue.

The Speculator Problem

Complete reliance on royalties or any other system of deferred profit evaluation creates the problem of speculative bidding. Since payments to the landowners depend upon actual production, the state is left with no satisfactory means of determining who should obtain the lease. Schemes such as royalty bidding or bidding on net profit percentages have been proposed as a way around this difficulty, but they do not provide a completely satisfactory solution.

Of course, royalty bidding raises the specter of premature shutdown, but both net profits bidding, which avoids this difficulty, and royalty bidding effectively make it possible for anyone, no matter how qualified or how serious, to bid upon the lease. Because no actual expenditure of resources is required to gain control of the leasehold, such situations will attract speculators who do not have the ability to undertake actual exploration investment and may result in a very low rate of development. The percentage rates, whether they be of profits or gross production, will be bid up to very high levels. At such high levels, few if any developers will find it profitable to explore. The speculators themselves, of course, will have lost nothing.

All in all, it is probable that neither the elimination of bonuses in favor of deferred forms of payment nor the complete reliance on bonus bids to the exclusion of deferred forms constitutes an appropriate policy for disposing of the public's petroleum resources. Whatever criticisms may be directed against Alaska's present leasing policy, it is clear that any modification of it will still combine both methods of payment.

Severance Tax

Most Alaskans are less concerned with methods of profit calculation and the time of payment than with the amount of the state's share in the development of oil resources. Much attention has been given to whether the severance tax rates imposed will be fair and appropriate. Unlike the royalty, this rate is subject to unilateral change by the state legislature. Few people recognize that the uniform imposition of a severance tax is an attempt to collect payments for the right to produce publicly owned resources on a basis that does not depend on the profits derived from the exploitation of these resources. The severance tax creates ticklish problems in petroleum leasing policy simply because no one can know what it might be fixed at in the future. Even if a legislature were so inclined, it could not legally bind itself to refrain from increasing the tax rate at some later date. Quite understandably, the oil industry mistrusts a game in which the rules can be changed at any time by the state.

Alaskans cannot assume that this severance tax flexibility is altogether to the state's benefit. Oil executives do not ignore the possibility of such tax increases. This factor increases the uncertainties of the complex calculation of production costs, and there is ample evidence that most industry evaluators are very conservative in calculating how much of their profits or gross production they will be allowed to keep for themselves. While predictions of future severance taxes vary from company to company, and are not made public, it is probable that few companies figure on a tax rate of less than 12½ per cent of the gross value. Thus, they expect the state to be taking in taxes and royalties, at a minimum, 25 per cent of the gross value of their production. Their bonus bids are naturally reduced accordingly.

Assuming that oil industry assessments of the amount of oil to be discovered are reasonably accurate and that the market system works to maximize the bonus paid, as it theoretically should, Alaska will receive bonus bids that are still considerably less than the true value of the land, given the present tax rate. The only means whereby Alaska can recoup this loss is to raise the severance tax rate to a level which approximates the oil industry's expectation.

Ironically, such increases fulfill those expectations. If the state attempts to make good its loss by increasing the severance tax rate, it naturally influences future oil industry expectations with regard to the political climate in Alaska. Thus, subsequent bonuses are reduced by an even greater amount, requiring even greater increases in the severance tax to avoid new losses. What could very easily develop would be a severance tax rate at such a high level as to make premature shutdown a very real problem, with a drastic reduction in the attractiveness of Alaskan ventures. Of course, it may be that Alaska has had as much oil industry investment as it wants, and that this latter eventuality would not be too discomforting. However, *existing* fields will be producing very little revenue for the state under this situation, an eventuality which even those unfavorably disposed to the oil industry are not likely to countenance. Alaska is, in effect, put in the position of being the loser in either the short or the long run.

Industry's Expectations

If this is to be the scenario for future developments in Alaska's petroleum leasing policy, the oil industry's recent large scale investments in Alaska would appear to be somewhat imprudent. While very much aware of this problem, the oil industry people certainly do not think so. As one official put it,

> "You can't legislate stability, it has to be in the minds of the legislators and the people. We'll probably have this tax uncertainty in Alaska until the oil industry has been here long enough for people to become accustomed to it. It happens the same way in almost every new oil area. It's kind of a natural cycle and there is really not much people can do about it except wait it out."

Oil industry confidence is based on experience gained in working in other states. Apparently this background leads the industry to believe that at some point of the lower bonus bids/higher taxes/lower bonus bids cycle the legislature will, as has been the case in other states, lose its taste for a larger share of the oil pie.

Only time can test the validity of this argument. At least a part of the oil industry has invested a great deal of money in the expectation that such stability will develop. Nevertheless, there are some good reasons for having serious doubts in this regard, reasons which perhaps even the oil industry itself has failed to consider adequately.

"Taxation stability" in the other states of the United States is a direct derivative of political influence. It is essential to note that the immediate source of this influence has not been the oil companies themselves. Other states have tax stability because in every state there exists a small, well-organized army of private landowners with oil wells in their backyards. These landowners believe—quite correctly—that any increase in the rate of severance taxation will ultimately work to decrease their incomes.

Prior to the imposition of a severance tax, the profits from oil production are shared between the producing organization and the individual landowners. The assessment of a severance tax cuts the state in for a share of the profits. It is the landowners who must reduce their shares to accommodate the government. Under such circumstances, landowners have an interest in keeping severance taxes at a relatively low rate.

Yet, Alaska does not now have, nor is it ever likely to have in the foreseeable future, an analogous group of politically influential landowners. Alaska has virtually only two landowners, the state and federal governments, with by far the greatest part of the oil development on state lands. This tremendously significant fact makes Alaska unique among the 28 oil producing states.

Foreign Examples

Alaska's situation more closely parallels that of underdeveloped countries where oil has been discovered and exploited. Alaska has every option available that a Middle Eastern oil producing nation has except the right of expropriation without compensation. Like Alaska, these oil-rich countries have the ability to alter the terms under which their petroleum resources are exploited. To one degree or another, however, these countries are limited in the extent to which they can exercise this power for they, like Alaska, are dependent upon the producing firms for capital and technology and for access to world markets. In these countries, as in Alaska, the public's greatest concern in regard to petroleum policy is that the government's share of the profits resulting from natural resource exploitation be appropriate and fair.

In all situations, including Alaska's, the determination of profits is very difficult. The precise value of petroleum resources cannot be known until they are marketed. Since profits depend directly upon market value, there is no way of calculating them prior to the time that the oil is actually produced. As a consequence, as soon as one is certain about the respective profit shares of producer and government, it is too late to alter the sharing arrangement. The vested interest that the oil industry has in making the profits appear small (and by contrast, making the state's share seem large) complicates the problem of gathering data for making reliable estimates of profits. Alaska encountered this difficulty head-on in 1968, when oil industry executives appearing before the legislature on the severance tax issue adamantly refused to disclose profit information.

Despite difficulties of evaluation, a government's share of petroleum profits depends largely on the degree of dependence upon the producing firms' capital, technology, and markets. Although nationalism and political demagoguery play their part, most of the efforts by the petroleum exporting countries to reduce this dependence can be related to their desire for an increased share of the profits. The history of overseas petroleum developments makes it clear that producing countries have given a high priority to the attainment of self-sufficiency in these areas. It is also obvious that the rewards accruing to a country that obtains a measure of this self-sufficiency can be very great, as can be seen in the changing terms of the agreements between oil firms and Middle Eastern countries and Venezuela. (See Note No. 4.)

Parallel to the growth of the government's profit share in most oil producing countries there has arisen the phenomenon of the "National Oil Company," a government owned and operated firm for developing, either independently or in partnership with foreign firms, the country's petroleum resources. An example of the latter arrangement is the Canadian federal government's 45 per cent ownership (making it by far the largest single stockholder) of

Panarctic Oils, Ltd., a private enterprise which holds almost all exploration permits available in the Arctic Islands area of northern Canada. The arrangement is unusual, however, in that the Canadian government does not participate very actively in the firm's management. (See Note No. 5.)

The extent to which Alaska's relationships with petroleum developing firms will parallel those of other countries is not certain, but it is perhaps significant that at the 20th Alaska Science Conference in August of 1969, Dr. Robert Weeden, a respected Alaskan biologist and conservationist, suggested that Alaska establish for itself just such a company. Members of the state legislature have made similar proposals. (See Note No. 6.) It was Dr. Weeden's contention that without such an organization, Alaska would be unable to exercise the control over petroleum resource development that he felt was essential to the proper management and protection of the state's environment and other natural resources. If the petroleum exporting countries have attempted to gain independence of the large firms for reasons of economics and national pride, it may be that Alaska will attempt to achieve the same independence for reasons of economics and environmental control.

It should be noted that the economic returns to such independence are not unlimited. The achievement of freedom from the need for oil company help in the areas of providing capital, technology, and access to markets is only profitable if those factors of production can be supplied independently at less expense. Particularly in the area of providing markets, it may be that the international petroleum companies have inherent advantages.

NOTE NO. 1

THE PRESENT POLICY

Alaska's oil and gas leasing program for state lands includes competitive and non-competitive leases. The oil lease—regardless of the type—gives the leaseholder surface rights only to the area necessary for oil and gas exploration and development work.

State Competitive Leases

All tide and submerged lands, mental health lands, school lands, and university lands must be leased competitively. In addition, whenever oil or gas is discovered, whether or not on state lands, the state Commissioner of Natural Resources determines the extent of the area surrounding the discovery well which he believes to be productive and classifies such lands as competitive. Lands also may be withheld from non-competitive leasing and offered only on a competitive basis when it is determined by the Commissioner of Natural Resources to be in the best interest of the state.

Competitive lease awards are made to the bidders submitting the highest cash bonus by means of sealed bids at public sales. Competitive leases have a term of ten years (except five years in the Cook Inlet Basin) and the annual rental is $1 per acre. The sale dates and tract delineations are announced well in advance of the actual sale. Competitive upland leases may not exceed 2,560 acres, while tide and submerged land leases are limited to a maximum of 5,660 acres.

State Non-Competitive Leases

State lands not classified as competitive are non-competitive. Non-competitive leases have a five-year primary term and are eligible for an extension of two or five years depending on classification and on the expiration date of the primary term. The annual rental is 50 cents per acre. The fee for filing a non-competitive lease application is $20 in cash, certified check or money order, and is not refundable.

The initial opening of newly acquired general grant lands for petroleum leasing is done by means of a non-competitive opening. Such openings are scheduled as required depending upon the amount of general grant acreage received by the state. Leases on these lands can be applied for within a 30-day simultaneous filing period.

Non-competitve leases are also offered through the terminated lease list, which is posted monthly. The list describes the lands on which oil and gas leases have recently terminated because of relinquishment, expiration, default, or cancellation. Lease applications can be made within a 30-day simultaneous filing period.

After the close of the simultaneous filing period, a drawing is held to determine the priority of applicants for those tracts receiving more than one application.

Any lands not leased as a result of applications filed during a simultaneous filing period become available for leasing over-the-counter on a first-come, first-served basis.

(Abstracted from the leaflet, "Information About Alaska State Oil and Gas Leases," published by the Alaska Department of Natural Resources, Division of Lands.)

NOTE NO. 2

DISCOVERY INCENTIVES

In order to stimulate exploration interest in areas that had no prior oil discoveries, the legislature reduced the royalty rate on oil produced from the actual leasehold where a new "structure" containing "paying quantities" of oil had been discovered. For ten years from the date of discovery, the producer paid only 5 per cent rather than the normal 12½ per cent royalty rate. It is impossible to determine the extent to which this stimulated the search for oil in

Alaska, but it is generally credited with eliciting some additional effort.

By the middle 1960's, this discovery incentive appeared unnecessary for Cook Inlet development. State officials were finding the provision difficult to administer because the specific meaning of "discovery," "structure," and "paying quantities" had not been defined in the law. Whether this vagueness resulted from legislative oversight, or was a deliberate attempt to give the Commissioner of Natural Resources as much freedom as possible, is not clear. At any rate, discovery rights were requested for wells that might have been located in the same field or structure or might have penetrated the same oil-bearing sands. Consequently, discovery incentives were abolished for Cook Inlet leases in 1968 and for the rest of the state in 1969. However, because the incentive provision was still in effect during the early North Slope sales, similar disputes can be expected regarding the recent discoveries there.

NOTE NO. 3
THE ALBERTA "CHECKERBOARD" SYSTEM

The so-called checkerboarding system of petroleum leasing employed in the province of Alberta works in the following manner. For the payment of an annual fee, which starts at 20 cents an acre and escalates over the years to $1 per acre, oil companies are allowed to acquire exploration rights on a first-come, first-served basis over just about any part of the public domain. Such permits may include up to 99,840 acres and run from five to seven years. At any time during that period the permit holder may lease, at $1 per acre, up to one-half of the land in each township (36 sections) within any particular permit. The land so selected, however, may not be in one contiguous block but must be made up of separate lease parcels, none of which may be larger than a square three miles on a side, or a rectangle two miles wide and four miles long. Each such parcel must be separated from any adjacent selection by at least one mile.

Thus, it is the oil company that within the statutory time limits must decide when and what to lease, and which parcels to return to the government. As lease selection proceeds, the 50 per cent which is not selected reverts to the government as reserves, and, when the permit lapses, all unselected lands become reserves as well. These reserves are, by law, subject only to competitive bidding. If, at the time the reserves are established, oil company interest is very high, as indicated by requests to offer the reserves for sale, the government will ordinarily auction them immediately. In other cases, it may await the results of drilling which the original permit holder may be expected to undertake in the near future.

Offering large parcels without bids, at low rentals, provides substantial incentive for exploration, yet the corridor requirement assures that parts of the acreage which are proven or semi-proven by the exploratory work will revert to the state for competitive leasing. The system provides a mechanism which leaves judgment and initiative with the individual oil operator and calls mainly for automatic responses from state administrators.

(The above summary has been abstracted from "Policy Choices in Petroleum Legislation—Canada/Alaska Comparisons" by A.R. Thompson, a paper presented at the 20th Alaska Science Conference.)

NOTE NO. 4

PROFITS PARTICIPATION—A PRACTICAL ALTERNATIVE

Because royalties and severance taxes do not distinguish between profitable and unprofitable producers, many Middle Eastern countries have abandoned them as the primary means of collecting oil revenues. Instead, they have generally instituted "profits participation," or net profits taxation. Rather than taking a small percentage of gross revenues, the government participates in up to 75 per cent or 90 per cent in the new profits.

Although it occurs mainly overseas, profits participation is practiced in this country, particularly in agreements between private landowners and private developers. Indeed, the agreement between the Cliff Burglin interests in Fairbanks and the General American Corporation calls for General American to pay the former landowners a sizable percentage of all net profits realized from production on those lands.

Generally, however, profit participation is not favored by domestic oil explorers. Their reluctance probably results from ignorance of the operation of such schemes, an ideological abhorrence of government participation in business, and a preference for keeping their profits secret.

While avoiding the host of problems raised by royalties and severance taxes, net-profits taxation does have one possibly unfavorable attribute. In order to assess the amount of tax due from a producer, it is necessary that the government have a clear idea of how much money the oil producers are making and, more importantly, what their legitimate expenses have been. It has often been argued that this knowledge will be very difficult to obtain without a disproportionate investment in a small army of accountants, auditors, and field inspectors to keep the oil companies from padding their expenses, overstating overheads, and other subterfuges.

Yet, well-written agreements could provide for the reporting of necessary information without resort to such extensive investigations. After all, the net profits of every firm in the United States are evaluated once a year by the Internal Revenue Service, and in Alaska by the State Department of Revenue.

A simple method of assessing allowable deductions must be formulated before net-profits taxation will be acceptable. For example, Alaska might find it desirable to restrict the allowable expenses to the lease bonus and actual on-site expenses. The on-site expenses would be relatively easy to determine since almost all drilling is done under contract. Depreciation deductions under such a system would be allowed only on equipment actually installed on the leasehold.

Higher bonus bids might result from this arrangement since much of the uncertainty regarding future taxation could be eliminated by a contract provision stipulating that subsequent increase in the severance tax would be offset by a corresponding decrease in the state's profit share.

The net profits taxation arrangement could be easily made on future leases. Changing existing leases, however, would be more difficult. One possible method might be to renegotiate the leases, offering the owners approximately equal terms under the new system. Leaseholders fearing drastically increased severance taxes would be induced to sign new leases relatively favorable to the state.

NOTE NO. 5

NATIONAL IRANIAN OIL COMPANY (NIOC)

For purposes of comparison, the terms of a typical "Middle Eastern" type agreement (Iran, 1965) are summarized:

EXPLORATION RIGHTS

The country is divided into concessions. Exploration rights over individual concessions are sold to oil companies on a negotiated basis. Payment for these rights has been in the neighborhood of $3 per acre. After five years, 25 per cent of the land must be turned back to the government, 50 per cent after 10 years. After 12 years, only those areas that are producing oil can be retained. A minimum exploration expenditure is required, usually about $1.75 per acre.

DEVELOPMENT

All development must be conducted in partnership with the government owned National Iranian Oil Co. (NIOC), usually on a 50-50 basis. In other words, once oil is found, NIOC pays half the costs of development and gets half the production.

ROYALTY

None.

TAXES

Fifty per cent of the private operator's net profits based on actual lifting costs and realized prices. Exploration and land acquisition costs not deductible.

MARKETING

Concession holder agrees to market a portion of NIOC'S production on request.

NOTE NO. 6

COMPETITION VS. ENVIRONMENT

A biologist speaks his mind:

"Much of the abuse of the landscape at Prudhoe Bay can be traced directly to the competition among companies to find and lease the best ground in the shortest possible time. The State of Alaska's haste to get in on the bonanza — as evidenced by the eleventh hour selection of nearly three million acres south of the discovery area just before the federal land freeze went into effect and by the lease sale to be held in a few days — has contributed to the problem.

"The implication is that there has to be adequate control of the pace of development, and that this control evidently has to come from government. When rock strata under public lands are favorable for oil accumulation, and after government determines that new fields should be developed, shares should be advertised in a government-controlled exploration venture. Shares would be unlimited, and companies could bid what they think can be invested into that particular venture. Then exploration would proceed in an orderly way, with complete sharing of geophysical and test-well data. When exploration is completed, the companies would operate under a unit plan to develop the field, with shares in proportion to the original exploration bids. This process (and I admit that I will have to leave details for others to work out), would reduce competition from the exploration and drilling phases of petroleum development; those who dislike this un-American idea can take comfort from the fact that manufacture and market processes could be just as competitive as now."

(From "Arctic Oil and Environmental Degradation," a paper presented at the 20th Alaska Science Conference, August 24-27, 1969, by Dr. Robert Weeden.)

ADDITIONAL READING

Adelman, M.S. "The Alaskan North Slope Discoveries and World Petroleum Supplies and Costs," in Rogers (ed.).

Alaska Industry. (Special Oil Issues) October, 1969 and October, 1970.

Bradner, Tim. "Petroleum." *Alaska Survey and Report: 1970-71.* Stephen M. Brent and Robert M. Goldberg eds. Anchorage: The Research Institute of Alaska, 1970.

Burrell, Homer. "The Role of State Agencies in Petroleum Exploration and Development." *Proceedings of the Twentieth Alaska Science Conference.* College, Alaska: Alaska Division of the American Association for the Advancement of Science, July, 1970.

Carter, Luther J. "North Slope: Oil Rush," *Science.* Vol. CLXXI (166), October, 1969.

Engler, Robert. "New Frontiers for Old." *Proceedings of the Twentieth Alaska Science Conference.* College, Alaska: Alaska Division of the American Association for the Advancement of Science, July, 1970.

Haas, Stanley G. "Marine Transport — The Northwest Passage Project." *Proceedings of the Twentieth Alaska Science Conference.* College, Alaska: Alaska Division of the American Association for the Advancement of Science, July, 1970.

Hedland, John S. "Economic Considerations in Oil and Gas Development," in Rogers (ed.).

Henderson, David. "Trans Alaska Pipeline System." *Proceedings of the Twentieth Alaska Science Conference.* College, Alaska: Alaska Division of the American Association for the Advancement of Science, July, 1970.

Reed, John C. "Oil Developments in Alaska." *Polar Record.* Vol. XV No. 94, 1970, pp. 7-17.

Rogers, George W., (ed.) *Change in Alaska: People, Petroleum and Politics.* Seattle: University of Washington Press, 1970.

Thompson, A.R. "Policy Choices in Petroleum Legislation," in Rogers (ed.).

Tussing, Arlon R. "An Alaskan View of the Economics of Petroleum Development," in Rogers (ed.).

SECTION IV: ENVIRONMENTAL QUALITY

This article is based on an address to the Sierra Club Eleventh Biennial Wilderness Conference, San Francisco, March 15, 1969. The full text is published in M.E. McCloskey, ed. *Wilderness, the Edge of Knowledge* (San Francisco: Sierra Club, 1970), pp. 143-153.

WILDERNESS AND DEVELOPMENT IN ALASKA

George Rogers

Wilderness might simply be thought of as a residual category, that which remains after human occupation and physical use of the land has been defined. Thus, wilderness is the desert land which the farmer's plow cannot break or from which the rancher's cattle turn back. To some, this is waste land awaiting the magic touch of reclamation projects. In classical times undesirable citizens, and in Elizabethan plays wrongly deposed dukes and their beautiful daughters, were exiled to it from the human community. Wilderness was the desert to which saints, sages, and shamans retired to gain spiritual renewal and insight and to which contemporary urban man looks for similar aids to survival.

Development also has many meanings, underlying all being some notion of change, sometimes referred to as progress. As used here it will be a process over which man has some significant degree of control or conscious direction, although this sense of control seems in danger of being surrendered to non-human man-made devices, and direction left to the blind forces of scientific and market research. Its objectives might ideally be defined as improvement of the human condition and measured precisely, but inadequately, in such bookkeeping concepts as increased per capita national or regional income, or less precisely but more meaningfully in terms of distribution of income or population-income balance. The process comes in a wide range and variety. It involves exploitation of nonrenewable and harvesting of renewable natural resources, which can be done wastefully and destructively for short-run gain, or rationally with maximization of long-run benefits, the two extremes commonly being identified as exploitation and conservation. It is further modified by where man lives or aspires to live, the objectives and process differing as the mover and beneficiary, man, lives in huge urban concentrations, in modest-sized rural communities, or in the socio-economic units of the family farm.

Alaska's past development can be generalized in terms of three major turning points or transitional jumps from one form of economic and social organization to another, from one set of objectives of development to another, and from one set of attitudes or conceptions of wilderness to another. We will not attempt to go back to the first human inhabitants of Alaska, but start with the Eskimo, Aleut, Athapaskan, Tlingit and Haida variations of the human animal in residence at the time of the first European-American contacts (circa 1740). Each of these groups of the estimated 75,000 aboriginal inhabitants of Alaska represented differing social, economic and cultural systems. The basic differences between each arose from the limitations imposed and the opportunities offered by the physical environment and the natural resource base which could be harvested.

Although there were important differences, all groups shared common attitudes toward or conceptions of wilderness and development, namely that these were terms that did not exist because they would be meaningless. There was no distinction between man and nature. The other living creatures were all brothers to man. They might prey upon one another in the struggle for survival, but they all shared a broad kinship of the living. The Tlingit hunter would beg forgiveness of his brother the bear for taking his life in order to provide food; or if seeking something else, might ask for permission of his brother the bear to pass unmolested through the bear's fishing territory. There were no uninhabited places on land, on or under the sea, or in the air.

Regions we would classify as uninhabited teemed with spirits and supernatural forces — good and evil — which had to be avoided, thanked, appealed to, or appeased. In this there was no meaningful distinction between man and the natural environment, between inhabited space and wilderness. All was unity, and the rituals of man's life reminded him of this.

Development or progress, as we think of these terms, had no meaning. Change had taken place and continued to take place, but measured in terms of the memory of living man it was too slow to be recognized as such. Man operated or reacted as an opportunist, adapting to changes in the physical environment and the yield of the resource base. Success was measured in survival, failure to adapt, in death. These were the givens in the life of man. Man was not the manipulator, the changer.

Starting in the mid-eighteenth century and accelerating toward the end of the nineteenth and beginning of the twentieth century, Alaska's aboriginal self-sufficient and limited stage of economic development was disrupted and in many regions overthrown by outside forces of colonial development for the benefit of distant interests. The change in "ownership" of Alaska from Russia to the United States really changed nothing else. After purchasing Alaska, the United States merely increased and expanded the Russian colonial period of extraction and exploitation of a highly specialized narrow range of natural resources. A few statistics, which I have repeatedly quoted before, sum this whole period up better than a volume of words. In the decade 1931-40, immediately before World War II, average annual value of all out-shipments from Alaska totaled $58.8 million, of which canned salmon accounted for 55.1%, gold 26.6%, other fish products 6.4%, furs 4.4%, and miscellaneous 6.5%. The colonial nature of this period was further indicated by the average value of in-shipments of $28.4 million, of which the three leading items were tin cans, petroleum products, and alcoholic beverages.

The physical environment as well as wilderness were simply things to be ignored or to be ruthlessly subjugated if they got in the way of the cheapest and easiest means of extracting the desired resource. Development was not only a highly specialized process, but it was short-term with the mining of renewable as well as nonrenewable resources. The aboriginal or indigenous people, now referred to as "Natives" in the colonial tradition, were treated in the same manner. Development was a simple linear process which either pretended there were no side effects or ignored everything but the desires of the exploiter. The colonial mentality of Alaska's post-World War II period has its contemporary counterpart in the highway engineer who believes not only that a straight line is the shortest distance between two points, but the only route between two points.

In terms of population and economic activity, this period passed its peak about the turn of the century. By the decades of the twenties and thirties, it was clear that colonial Alaska was nowhere and was going nowhere. In 1937 the National Resource Committee took a long, careful look at Alaska and its resources and in effect wrote them off as being of no real national significance in the foreseeable future. No forced development or even modest programs encouraging development were recommended. The Departments of War and Navy, still refusing to recognize the existence of the airplane, declared Alaska to be of no military value, but rather a distant and difficult-to-defend outpost. The only positive note was sounded by one of the staff, Robert Marshall, who declared in a special supplemental statement to the final report of the committee, "Alaska is unique among all recreational areas belonging to the United States because Alaska is yet largely a wilderness. In the name of a balanced use of American resources, let's keep Alaska largely a wilderness."

The outbreak of World War II and the discovery of Alaska's strategic importance in the defense of North America in the air age was another major turning point. The natural resources of the colonial period declined in importance, both absolutely and relatively. Defense construction and support of the defense establishment became the basic economy of Alaska, accounting directly for more than half of total employment and resident income, and indirectly much more. Space became a militarily valuable resource, second in importance only to location. Wilderness became grist for the defense mill as bombing and later missile firing ranges, training areas, or simply as buffer zones in which invading ground forces might become lost and bogged down. Development was a by-product. The size of the defense economy increased or decreased in response to national policy decision, technological changes, and shifts in the international situation. But within this were important developmental forces and the seeds for the next turning point. Defense activity involved directly or indirectly large numbers of people. Alaska's population rose from 75,000 in 1940 to 228,000 in 1957. These were people from politically developed parts of our nation and they were not satisfied with the limited self-determination represented in territorial political status. The statehood movement came to life and Alaska became a full member of the union of states.

It is open to argument whether statehood played a role in launching the era of resource development Alaska is now experiencing, but there is no question that the political context has changed the objectives of development. The political act of creating the State of Alaska carried with it the objective of creating and sustaining a level of economic and social development sufficient to keep the new ship of state afloat. Long-term and resident interests now had to be considered. Elements of the old colonialism might still lurk in the Japanese investment in timber, fish, and petroleum development and in domestic United States and British investment in petroleum development of the North Slope. But the new colonialism can no longer be overt or go its own way unchecked. Government development programs are not simply promotional efforts, but include overall planning attempting to realize the fullest potential, both direct and indirect, of any major development prospect which appears on the horizon. Controls aiming to minimize adverse effects are being devised and the needs of Native people are being discovered. All of this adds up to the necessity of considering the interests and desires of persons residing in Alaska and the sort of place Alaska might become as a result of development activities. It is no longer a place to be exploited and then forgotten or discarded. Or is it?

Statehood is not the happy ending to the Alaska story—only a new beginning. We today face another transition and a crisis. Whether development is to be solely for nonresident interests or should contribute to the creation of a resident society within Alaska was at least technically answered by the granting of statehood. But the new Alaskans speak in a babel of voices when it comes to guiding this development. When he was a mere millionaire, Walter J. Hickel announced in an interview shortly after statehood that we were to engage in the building of a Fifth Avenue on the tundra. People sympathetic to that view can now point with some pride to their accomplishments in at least the two major population centers of the state. A few years ago when Norman Mailer was visiting Alaska, the chamber of commerce people in Anchorage made the mistake of dragging him before the local TV cameras and asking him what he thought of their beautiful city. His hosts were thrown off balance and the show hurriedly terminated when he replied that as he landed at the airport and was being driven into the downtown center, he said to himself, "Hell, I've been here before. This is the American nightmare." And, indeed, it is all there with a special northern accent. Urban sprawl and slums in the subarctic represent human discomfort and misery surpassing that of their counterparts in more temperate zones. Pollution of water and air are accomplished more quickly than in tougher, more southern environments (in winter the air pollution over Fairbanks rivals that of any California city). Our major centers can boast the rates and varieties of crime, violence, ugliness, and filth typifying any major city elsewhere. The transplant has not yet been rejected by the Alaska body politic.

The crisis is further deepened by the last frontier syndrome. Many Alaskans, including political leaders, think of themselves as heroes in a TV western. In the northern version of the last frontier, as in the western version, wilderness is to be despoiled and destroyed as valueless, a nuisance, or a threat. This usually includes the human beings who were already there. Unfortunately, many Alaskans hold this view without realizing it or questioning it. But the story will not be repeated in its entirety. Like the buffalo, the caribou may not vote; but unlike the plains Indian, the Alaska Eskimo, Aleut, and Indian are a political force to be reckoned with.

Our present crisis does not arise solely from conflicts and uncertainties within ourselves and the political boundaries of our Brave New World. New outside forces are present in the awesome power of our technicians. Shortly after the granting of statehood, the Atomic Energy Commission made a bid to convert Alaska's arctic lands into a vast testing grounds for what they euphemistically called "nuclear devices" and for the demonstration of what was called, also euphemistically, the new science of "engineering geography." The Corps of Engineers promoted the construction of a dam at Rampart Canyon on the Yukon River which, had it been constructed, would have been capable of generating the second or third largest block of hydro-electric power in the world, but which would have had the unchallenged distinction of creating the world's largest man-made lake. Another technical marvel has been announced as a possible accompaniment to the development of petroleum resources of our North Slope, an 800 mile pipeline across Alaska.

This leads to the final element in our present crisis with which I wish to deal here, the impending oil rush and boom on our North Slope. The details are well known, but unless you live in or are interested in the North, you may not be fully aware of the emotional content of these developments and their possible consequences. I have just come from participating in two conferences sponsored by the Arctic Institute of North America and each concerned with aspects of northern development. Although their announced subjects and purposes differed, they both shared a sense of urgency and an unannounced and unintended dominance by oil in the Alaskan and Canadian North.

The largest and most publicized was a symposium on "Arctic and Middle North Transportation" held in Montreal and attended by over three hundred representatives of industry and government. The reason for the large attendance (another three hundred applicants for admission were turned away because of space limitations) was oil, not transportation as such. To me the meeting presented a model of what has been happening to people in the North or who are interested in northern development. The general air was one of intense excitement stimulated by an urge to discover how to cash in on what looked to be the biggest thing ever to hit the North. One variation of this theme was stated in a keynote address by a senior vice president of a Canadian bank who urged his colleagues to stake out their claims to a part of the action (in Canada) before it all was taken up by the Americans, British, Japanese, and, above all, the French. The conference gave over to rampant colonial development forces because consideration of human factors and values, including the physical environment, was absent. Oil was everything. This was not stated in so many words, but the meaning was clear. The oil companies are faced with the task of getting the petroleum out of the ground and to market as efficiently and economically as possible. This is their prime objective. There was no other interest represented at the meeting to exert any modifying influence. The objectives of the several Canadian and United States government transportation lobbies appeared to be simply to see that their particular form of transport got top priority in the consideration of means of getting oil to market.

In such an atmosphere, wilderness values could only be thought of in defensive terms. But they need not have been if the model of general public values and motivations presented had included a concern for the human beings affected or involved in the development and appreciation of the place of wilderness in the making of the whole man. At the least, there would have been discussion of means of regulating and controlling the transportation aspects of exploration and development activities in order to minimize damage to these values. There might have been consideration of the public interest as opposed to the limited self-interest of the industrial combinations and individuals seeking to draw personal gain from the impending developments. There might even have been a recognition of the basic madness of development that required the destruction of one physical environment, the North American Arctic, to extract petroleum from the ground to be converted into materials to be used elsewhere to despoil another physical environment through air and other forms of pollution, to say nothing of the promotion of wholesale manslaughter on the highways.

Human values as such were absent from the Montreal symposium, but they were at the center of the conference on community development in the North, this one at Dartmouth College. The Dartmouth conference involved about fifty architects, engineers and social scientists, most of whom had been involved or interested in the planning of new communities in response to industrial development and other needs in the northern regions of North America and Europe. The sense of urgency also arose from the impending petroleum boom in the North. But it was a different sort of urgency based upon the participants' firsthand knowledge of what development had meant to the human condition and the environment in the past, a concern that future efforts of the planners result in something better and an awareness that whether or not they did anything to improve these prospects, the industrial developments were going forward without them. As a minimum, the conference followup hoped to open avenues for expanded and continuing interchange and communication between engineer, architect, and social scientist to the end that the planning process take into account the whole man and his place in his environment, and launch programs to educate or influence top decision makers in directions leading toward the ideal of new northern communities or other social units fit for human living.

I drew great hope from the Dartmouth meeting, for it represented builders who knew that they were not engaged simply in providing shelter and sanitation, but consciously or unconsciously were engaged in creating new environments, good or bad, within which people had to live. Not only were they aware of what they were doing,but it was clear that they were all motivated by a desire to promote human happiness as well as to make possible the industrial developments which were the basis of their employment. The introduction of human values into the development process, of course, is not unique to this conference. In recent years it has received growing acceptance. Even the bookkeeper mentality of the professional economist has been able to accept an extended definition of natural resources that goes beyond things that enter directly into production to include physical environmental factors which indirectly condition the production process. These "amenity resources" can include wilderness values depending upon the sort of lives people want to fashion for themselves. This awareness and desire is growing, but there is need for further education to promote wider appreciation and use of wilderness to enrich our lives.

In the concluding chapter of my book on the future of Alaska, published in 1962, I made these observations,

> The land hunger which in the nineteenth century stimulated the settling of the west, cannot be reckoned with as a force in the peopling of Alaska, where land ownership, as such, is seldom productive of standards of living found elsewhere in the states today. But something akin to the same drive—in terms of a yearning for open space and remaining wilderness values—may generate a different sort of movement into the U.S. northland. City people, as their environment becomes more congested and their travel more prescribed by networks of monotonous highways, may look to Alaska for fulfillment of their recreational needs, and the present technological revolution in transportation is steadily bringing Alaska's scenic resources closer to them in terms of time and money. Properly recognized, conserved, and developed as the need emerges, Alaska can find in its wilderness an element which, with the state's forest and fisheries wealth and minerals and hydroelectric potential, could give it the type of balanced development we all hope for.

These observations were not put forward in a spirit of romantic idealism, but as hard-nosed realism. Unless wilderness is included within the meaning of the term "development" in Alaska, the future of Alaska will revert to being simply another version of the colonial periods of the past. Beyond Alaska, wilderness and development must be brought together into such a unity if the North is to survive. In this the North and Alaska are models of the universe of all mankind.

This article, prepared in August 1970, appears in *Polar Record* (published by the Scott Polar Research Institute, Cambridge, England), Vol. 15, No. 97, 1971, pp. 479-494.

WILDLIFE AND OIL:
A SURVEY OF CRITICAL
ISSUES IN ALASKA

Robert B. Weeden and David R. Klein

Throughout the Arctic, serious questions have arisen regarding environmental and cultural by-products of petroleum exploration and development. Perhaps nowhere has there been greater public concern than in Alaska, which has experienced commercial oil production since 1958 near Cook Inlet and which is now working out plans for development of the Prudhoe Bay pool.

One such question is how the Alaskan biota will fare in this new and highly volatile situation. In this paper we survey the most clearly defined points of conflict between petroleum development and wildlife populations and evaluate society's capability to meet challenging new circumstances in renewable resource management. To some extent the problems—especially those relating to institutions and statutes—are peculiar to Alaska, but many similar problems face Canada and other Arctic nations, both in social and ecological parameters.

We shall first define problem areas geographically, each of which carries its lessons and warning. Generalizing from experience to date, we then point out some constraints that affect the public's ability to protect its interests in resource management during

exploration, field development, and production-transport phases of
petroleum industry activities.

The North Slope, Exploration and Initial Development

On 18 July 1968, reserves of oil estimated to be in excess of 10
billion barrels were discovered by Atlantic-Richfield Oil Company
near Prudhoe Bay, 200 miles east of Point Barrow. This discovery
sparked extensive exploration along the entire Arctic coast of North
America, particularly in the Mackenzie River delta of Canada's
Northwest Territories and in the central and extreme western parts
of Alaska's North Slope, the name applied to 60,000 square miles of
treeless tundra north of the Brooks Range. Commercial quantities of
oil may exist in formations favorable to oil underlying the Beaufort
and Chukchi seas.

Oil-related activities on the North Slope are a multi-faceted
ecological force whose total impact has yet to be assessed.
The most important biotic effects appear to stem from: (1) the
disturbance of vegetation and soil on uplands; (2) the removal of
gravel from streams, shorelines, and ridges; (3) possible behavioral
reactions of tundra animals to oilfield facilities and activities; (4)
hunting and harrassment; and (5) oil pollution and waste disposal.

The most apparent and widespread effect of human activities
on the North Slope is scarification of the tundra, which is caused
by tracked vehicles when the surface soil is thawed, by heavy
vehicle traffic in winter and by deliberate removal of vegetation in
construction activities. The linear scars of those activities are now a
permanent and unsightly feature of the tundra scene north of the
Brooks Range. There are few areas remaining west of the Arctic
Wildlife Range where tracks are not visible from small aircraft. By
far the worst scarring was done between 10 and 30 years ago by
caterpillar tractor trains used in seismic exploration for the United
States Navy in Naval Petroleum Reserve No. 4. Concentrated
activity in 1968 and 1969, between Naval Petroleum Reserve No. 4
and the Arctic Wildlife Range has also resulted in unsightly
scarring. State and federal prohibitions, first imposed in 1969,

against the use of tracked vehicles on thawed tundra should virtually eliminate this problem in the future. The aesthetic damage of these tracks is bad enough, but biotic degradation also occurs simultaneously. For example, Burns (1964) found that the operation of tracked vehicles along the tundra and channels of the Yukon-Kuskokwim delta resulted, after thawing of exposed ground, in the formation of water-filled ditches that altered drainage patterns on streambanks. Mink dens on the banks of streams were flooded, and persistent ice in the ditches prevented the mink from digging new dens. Similar abuses have accompanied other oil-related projects, such as the winter haulage road from Fairbanks to the North Slope. Near Point Barrow, new erosion channels have drained several lakes.

On sloping ground erosion of the subsoil in vehicle tracks often occurs and accelerates with each summer thaw. Such erosion ditches can carry excessive silt loads into small tundra streams that may be important as spawning and brooding areas for grayling and Arctic char. Where degradation of the permafrost and erosion does not occur, compaction of the vegetation by vehicles may change the plant compostion from lichens to a sedge complex. Both plant types are important to caribou, but lichens are winter forage, which is often in limited supply, whereas sedges are summer food of widespread abundance.

Large quantitites of gravel are required for foundations at camp and well sites and for road construction and air strips. If used properly, gravel insulates the permafrost and prevents it from thawing. Away from the coast, gravel is found only in drainage channels and its removal can threaten fisheries by increasing stream turbidity and by removing or silting over spawning beds. As with so many other problems of tundra management, the design of criteria for mining operations in gravel lags far behind present need because detailed knowledge of fish populations—where they are, when they migrate, where they spawn, their vulnerability to added silt loadings of river waters, etc.— is lacking.

On the flat coastal plain of northern Alaska, any ground elevated a metre or so above the general surface provides favored den sites for Arctic Foxes, Red Foxes, mink and wolves. Unfortunately, the same sites are useful to humans because they provide a view and a firmer and drier substrate for travel or camping, and they are usually snow-free in winter. A clear example of such conflict exists on sand dunes of the Sagavanirktok River near Prudhoe Bay, where oil companies have bulldozed burial pits for garbage and where a pipe storage area was levelled. Destruction of vegetation that stabilized the dunes threatens their very existence and, of course, the foxes that denned in them. Pingos occasionally suffer the same abuse and should be specially protected.

Waste disposal has been a major health, aesthetic, and ecological problem in the Arctic for many years. Intensive oil activity has aggravated the problem both in volume and on a geographical basis, but it has also provided the impetus to find suitable treatment and disposal systems. In terms of wild animal populations, inadequate disposal of organic waste attracts scavengers to campsites thereby exposing the animals to humans and vice versa. Arctic Foxes, altogether pleasant to watch, tend to chew on plastic or rubber-coated cables, and knowledge that they can carry rabies may lead to their destruction in an over-reaction to the threat they may pose to human health. Leaseholders in Prudhoe Bay have financed an active fox-trapping program.

Grizzly bears, wolves, and wolverines also scavenge in garbage pits and they too are sometimes destroyed wantonly or because they pose a threat to humans. Although it is hard to assess the toll of animals thus taken, we know that the populations of large arctic predatory mammals are sufficiently endangered that unnecessary killing should not be tolerated. Technical solutions to the problem of waste disposal are not well developed, although high-temperature incineration, treatment of organic wastes such as sewage, and deep burial or collection and transportation to permafrost-free regions may be employed.

Disposal of solid waste was not a problem in the early history of mechanized exploration: useless and waste material was simply discarded. This practice is no longer acceptable to the public or to responsible members of industry. The tundra is still scarred by rusting equipment, fuel cans and barrels, detonating wire and other solid waste accumulations which cause aesthetic damage and, in the case of rusting fuel containers, pollution. Abandoned wire left occasionally entangles and kills caribou. Although such mortality is not likely to be biologically important, it is an unnecessary source of public dismay and criticism.

At one time there was widespread apprehension among Alaska biologists that the legal harvest of wild game animals on the North Slope would rise sharply with the advent of oilworkers. The passage of time has somewhat diminished this fear. Oil companies prohibit guns in work camps, which means that their employees must do their hunting elsewhere. Employees tend to work long hours while in the Arctic, then to fly home or elsewhere (at company expense) for rest and recreation rather than seeking it in the north. Legal hunting pressure has undoubtedly increased in arctic Alaska but data are lacking on the effects of this increase.

On the other hand, as the scope of environmental change wrought within a large oil field becomes more apparent, biologists are increasingly concerned by the behavioral reactions of animals to the change. The number of persons working on the North Slope at any one time may not be great—at present there probably are some 2,000 employed in exploration, development, or supporting services in the area—but relatively few persons are employing a tremendous amount of capital equipment, mostly in fixed facilities (roads, airstrips, campsites), fixed machinery (wells, generators, etc.) and in aircraft or ground vehicles, the latter including hundreds of pieces of earthmoving equipment. It is hard to image a local fauna, which until recently had lived in a land almost empty of people, able to survive indifferent both to the noise and the re-arrangement of the landscape going on today.

Unfortunately, biologists have almost no answers to the behavioral questions asked. Are tundra birds adversely affected by hovercraft, helicopters, and large low-flying aircraft? How do migrating marine and land animals react to the stench of flared natural gas or to burning waste in sumps? Will caribou maintain their usual migration paths with dozens of roads, camps, airfields, and feeder pipelines athwart their lines of movement? Will ungulates, attracted to salt licks formed by the NaCl used in drilling, ingest toxic materials at these sites? Does the harassment of bears and other large animals by aircraft increase their mortality rates?? There is some evidence of social dislocations and other adverse effects. For example, some Canadian biologists fear that continual dispersal of muskox herds by helicopters is exposing them to increased predation. Mountain sheep in Canada have abandoned parts of their range after disturbance, and re-occupation of abandoned range appears to occur very slowly. Whether heavy air and vehicle traffic in the central Brooks Range will affect the sheep there is conjectural but probable.

Sponsored by industry and by government agencies, several research and technical groups are making steady progress in working out the solutions of many vexing problems that management of an oilfield in a tundra environment must face. Waste disposal systems and housekeeping practices are improving, and new overland vehicles with light surface-loading factors are being tested. Nevertheless, there is an urgent need for more detailed information on the distribution, abundance, and habits of wildlife of the North Slope, and particularly for experimental and observational information on the reaction of various species to different sorts of human disturbance. Rigid protection also is required of areas especially important to wildlife, such as coastal lagoons and barrier islands for waterfowl and the several caribou calving grounds, where stresses on the fauna from human activity should be minimal or absent.

Transporting Oil: The Trans Alaska Pipeline

The pace of oilfield development at Prudhoe Bay has recently slackened pending agreement on a system for transporting oil to refineries and markets. Of several suggestions made by the petroleum industry, the most likely and the one that could soonest be available is the Trans-Alaska Pipeline System (TAPS), a proposal to pipe oil to Valdez for transhipment to tankers.

TAPS would traverse about 800 miles of terrain, most of it federal land. In June 1969, the TAPS[1] consortium submitted to the United States Department of the Interior a general design and route proposal with their request for a construction and right-of-way permit. Department officials accompanied the permits with detailed stipulations which, combined with close field surveillance, would protect soil, water, vegetation, and wildlife from serious or permanent damage. However, geological engineers of the Department of the Interior did not think the design proposed by TAPS adequately prevented stress to the hot-oil pipeline when frozen ground around it thawed and subsided. The department has requested more soil data and TAPS' new design will probably be submitted in the late winter of 1970-71.

Wildlife biologists watched early developments of TAPS with considerable dismay, largely because there was no firm information available about the proposed route or its design, and because implementation of the project appeared to be moving so fast that there would be no time for pre-construction inventories and ecological studies. At present—and it is important to remember that no final construction plan is yet available—there are three areas of major concern relating to the impact of the pipeline on wild animals: (1) the possibility of pipeline breakage or leakage leading to massive oil spills, (2) disruption of seasonal movements of ungulates, (3) severe silting of streams by continued erosion along the pipeline's right-of-way.

The southern half of TAPS would traverse several major fault zones and seismically active areas. With the example of the severe earthquake in 1964 fresh in mind, no one pretends there is absolutely no danger of pipeline rupture because of earthquakes, but no one appears willing to estimate just what the risks are. The biological effects of a rupture would vary from negligible to very serious depending on where, when and how much crude oil escaped.

Geologists and some engineers have felt there is also a considerable risk of breakage if a pipeline carrying hot oil is laid in frozen soil with high moisture content (Lachenbruch, 1970). If no design for burying pipe in such areas can be found, probably large portions of the line (up to 40 per cent) would be carried on pilings, a technique that would reduce the risk of rupture from oil subsidence but would increase the risk of puncture by bullets of sportsmen and others. It might also interrupt migrations of caribou, moose, and mountain sheep, particularly if the pipeline were not high enough to allow free passage of large animals beneath it.

More than 300,000 caribou use the North Slope during certain portions of the year. They are divided into a northwestern or Arctic herd of about 200,000 animals and a northeastern or Porcupine River herd of approximately 100,000 animals. Especially during the summer months, the herds use the wet coastal plain that is now the scene of intensive oil development. Portions of the Porcupine River herd traditionally calve on the coastal plain as far west as the Canning River area, and the main calving area of the Arctic herd is near the headwaters of Colville and Utukok rivers (lat. 69 degrees N, long. 159 degrees W).

The tradition of seasonal movement is maintained by the older caribou, especially the females, which return to the calving areas they have previously used. If caribou are forced to use other areas for calving or for winter feeding, younger animals begin to use new areas, thereby disrupting the cohesiveness of herd movements. One can only speculate on the possible effects on caribou movements of disturbances associated with oil development. The Richardson Highway between Fairbanks and Valdez transects a major caribou migration route, which the TAPS pipeline would also transect, and the animals have continued to cross the highway twice each year. On the other hand, the traditional movement of caribou across Steese Highway, north of Fairbanks, has ceased in recent years, although whether the highway has been a causal factor is not known. In Dovrefjell, Norway, a railroad has disrupted normal movements of wild reindeer and prevented their using an extensive wintering area. Disrupted migrations can impose heavier population pressures on the remaining portion of the range and ultimately result in a population reduction.

What has been stressed above for caribou is less of a threat for moose, because their movements are neither concentrated nor extensive. However, TAPS will be confined to valley bottoms and low lying areas along most of its route and it will therefore cross units of good moose range. On the North Slope, moose are restricted to tall willow stands in the larger river valleys, which offer food and concealing cover, and pipeline and road construction will probably frighten them from many of their small habitats. Moose would possibly be threatened by the refilled ditch of the pipeline which, in wet areas or those underlain by permafrost, may produce a mire that would trap animals attempting to cross it. Moose are occasionally known to become helplessly mired and die in artificially created water holes within experimental moose enclosures of the Kenai National Moose Range. Seismic lines, constructed on Tuktoyaktuk Peninsula, Northwest Territories, by scraping the vegetation from wet tundra, have developed into mud-filled moats through degradation of the permafrost and have effectively blocked movement of domestic reindeer.

The third major concern of biologists is that large amounts of silt may enter clear streams important to grayling or salmon populations. Techniques for minimizing silting are fairly well known, and government inspection of field operations should ensure that these practices are followed. Two questions still remain, however. One is whether permafrost degradation along a large proportion of the pipeline will result in periodic erosion problems over decades. The other is whether natural or induced re-vegetation of exposed soils will proceed fast enough to reduce erosion problems. The TAPS consortium and government sources are supporting several studies of the latter question through the University of Alaska. Preliminary results are expected about 1972-73.

Several Canadian firms are interested in running a natural gas pipeline from Prudhoe Bay east-south-east through Yukon Territory and Mackenzie District to mid-continent markets. This pipeline would be nearly the same diameter as the TAPS pipeline and would carry gas at ambient temperature or below. Construction would pose problems and hazards similar to those of an oil line. Because natural gas will be produced simultaneously with oil in the gas-rich Prudhoe

Bay field, and because by state law this gas cannot be flared off, some provision for transporting the gas must be made. If natural gas and crude oil lines can be built along one right-of-way and at essentially the same time ecologic and aesthetic damage will be minimized.

Prince William Sound:
Ecological Problems at a Tanker Terminal

Crude oil pumped through TAPS will be transferred to tankers at Prince William Sound for shipment to Puget Sound and to other refineries on the west coast of the United States. Despite automation in many aspects of the transfer, the pipeline will bring a considerable permanent rise in the population of Valdez, now a town of 1,000 supported by ship-to-truck freighting, commercial fishing, and tourism. The growth will bring new pressures on the area's wildlife, particularly on black and brown bears, mountain goats, deer, salmon and waterfowl. The most serious possible effect on wildlife, however, is from oil spilled offshore as ballast disposal from tankers, from discharge of treated ballast at shore facilities, from infrequent but massive spills caused by tanker collisions, rupture of ships, or shore facilities during earthquakes, and from accidental or negligent mishandling of oil-loading equipment.

The biggest single source of pollution in daily operations will be treated discharge water from onshore ballast-cleaning facilities. Ships coming to Valdez to load crude oil will be carrying sea water in their tanks for ballast. Ballast normally is 50 to 60 per cent of the pay load volume. As TAPS will initially be handling 600,000 barrels of crude oil per day, and 2.2 million barrels per day at peak capacity, the volume of ballast to be discharged ranges from 300,000 to 1.1 million barrels a day.

By the time the TAPS terminal is in operation, most ships entering the port will probably be equipped with gear for cleaning ballast water so that, when it is discharged into the open ocean (as it is now legal to do) or into shore ballast tanks, there are from 50 to 100 parts of oil, by weight, per million parts of effluent. TAPS has agreed to install shore facilities that will release effluent containing no more than 10 parts per million. These are rigid requirements by today's technological standards and will require both physical and chemical treatment (flocculation) of the ballast, and incineration of the remaining sludge.

even if this was reduced to 10 parts per million

Nevertheless, there will still be a great deal of oil in the cleaned ballast water. Assuming a concentration of 10 parts per million, and assuming 1.1 million barrels of ballast discharged per day, there will be about 3,700 pounds (12 barrels) of oil pumped into upper Prince William Sound every day. No one at present knows what the fate of this oil will be, nor what effects it will have on marine life before it disappears through auto-oxidation, biodegradation, or sedimentation.

Little attention has been focused on the problem of massive oil spills in the tanker lanes between Alaska and the west coast of the United States, probably because the responsibilities for prevention and for assessing liability are scattered among many federal agencies, the oil industry, and the shipping industry. A simple calculation shows the very high probability that huge volumes of crude oil will be spilled at sea. According to McCaull (1969), an average of one unit of oil is spilled at sea or in port through tanker mishaps for every 1,000 units carried. At two million barrels a day, an average of 2,000 barrels of crude oil would be spilled every day from ships loading at Valdez. (The spills, of course, would not be daily, but infrequent and massive.)

Because the public is concerned and the news media give oil spills headline treatment, governments and industries are increasing efforts to improve the rather frightening record of tanker safety to date. A major conference on oil-spill technology was held in New York City in December 1969, and the United States and Canada are exploring the possibility of an international treaty to prevent oil pollution in the Arctic. Oil pollution in the Arctic Ocean north of Canada will obviously pose a major problem. Here questions of sovereignty are combined with concern that oil spills in cold Arctic waters will last much longer and do more ecological damage than in warmer waters.

In attempting to predict the biological effects of oil pollution in Prince William Sound, one immediately thinks of the species that use the habitats most affected: the inter-tidal zone, the surface meter of water, and quiet bays with minimal water exchange. Species affected would include the marine mammals, marine and shoreline birds, some shellfish, and salmon and other fish of commercial value. The foregoing is a narrow view of the situation because (1) oil deposited on beaches, on marine plants, or on the substrate anywhere can disturb the entire littoral and benthic community, and (2) oil in surface waters can affect plankton and juvenile stages of macrofauna, with direct or chain effects on other life forms. The lack of sufficient information to support a total community approach forces a focus on only the most obvious problems.

Prince William Sound supports a valuable commercial fishery. According to a recent survey (United States Department of Interior, 1970) the estimated total potential value of the fishery resources of the area is $9.7 million per year. Recent average annual harvests have included 3.7 million pink and chum salmon, halibut worth $1 million, 20,000 tons of herring, 1 million dungeness crabs, 75,000 king crabs, 147,000 tanner crabs, 600,000 sockeye salmon, and 1 million pounds of razor clams. (The last two fisheries are in the Cordova-Copper River area at the eastern fringe of Prince William Sound).

Nearly half of the pink salmon in Prince William Sound spawn in the intertidal zone at the mouth of streams. Of all of the commercial fish species, this population and shellfish living in intertidal or shallow waters may be the most vulnerable to oil pollution.

At least 1,000 sea otters live in the shallow waters around the islands of outer Prince William Sound. Because this animal spends much time on the surface of inshore waters, and because of the characteristics of its fur and heat-exchange physiology, biologists fear that it may be exceptionally vulnerable to oil pollution. Several thousand sea lions and many harbor seals live in Prince William Sound; killer whales, blackfish, and occasional fur seals pass through it.

Sea and shore birds are numerous in the sound, although there are no quantitative data available on their abundance or distribution. The area of highest waterfowl numbers in the region is the Copper River delta near Valdez. Here many species of ducks, at least 10,000 Canada geese, and close to half of the Alaska population of trumpeter swans nest. During spring and fall, the concentrations of shorebirds and waterfowl are very large; their use of seaward areas at these times exposes them to the effects of oil pollution more than during the breeding season. The sound itself supports marine birds year round, with seasonal fluxes of species composition and of total abundance; it is also used by humans for recreation and sightseeing.

To protect the resources of Prince William Sound serious obstacles must be overcome: fragmented goverment-business responsibility for preventing pollution; limited financial resources of public agencies; insufficient knowledge of the effects of oil pollution; and unsatisfactory technology for cleaning up spilled oil.

Five federal and three state agencies have statutory responsibility in some aspect of oil pollution problems in Prince William Sound. Perhaps sharing reduces the strain on any one agency, but this benefit is more than outweighed by inevitable difficulties in coordination. In adjacent Cook Inlet, where state and federal agencies have confronted oil pollution problems for a decade, an informal conjoining of forces has increased operational efficiency several steps above total confusion. This concept, formalized through a task force with field level authority, could help solve problems looming in Prince William Sound. The role of the task force would be four-fold: it would be the interface between government and industry in the area of oil spill prevention; it could be the nerve center for surveillance activity, including provision of men to accompany tankers entering the sound; it could have the operational authority for clean-up activities which, it is to be hoped, can be charged to the polluter; and it could be the plaintiff for government in cases of judicial action against polluters.

Bristol Bay: A Germinal Problem
in Resource Conflicts

Bristol Bay is underlain by continental shelf and is just southeast of the seasonal southern limit of the Arctic pack ice. The bay and adjacent uplands comprise a rich and diverse biological area partially exploited by commercial fishermen, lodge owners, and big game guides. Most of the region's 5,000 people (largely Eskimos and Indians) live along three major salmon streams in the upper reaches of the bay, the Naknek, Kvichak, and Nushagak rivers.

In commercial terms, the red (sockeye) salmon is by far the most important member of Bristol Bay's fauna. Annual harvests averaged 8.2 million red salmon in the years 1956-67 but past catches have exceeded 24 million. A near-record catch of 20 million was landed in the summer of 1970, but the catch is shared by so many small gill-netters over such a short season that annual family incomes among resident fishermen are low.

Alaskans and visitors from all over the world enthusiastically angle in dozens of excellent clearwater streams and lakes draining into Bristol Bay for salmon, trout, grayling and char. Others also fly to Bristol Bay to hunt big game in spring and autumn on Alaska Peninsula. Moose and brown bears are plentiful and rather easily hunted in the shrublands of this region, especially in the treeless southern two-thirds of the peninsula. The number of bears taken is so great that many guides are concerned and game managers are alert to the need for increased investment in research and surveys and in better management practices. A herd of approximately 11,000 caribou lives in the central section of Alaska Peninsula, providing a moderate harvest both for subsistence and for sport.

The waters and shores of Bristol Bay receive four migrations of birds annually. In spring a major part of the world population of emperor geese, black brant, cackling (Canada) geese, and Steller's and spectacled eiders, as well as huge numbers of pintails, scaup, old squaw, surf and common scoters, king and Pacific eider ducks follow the Bering Sea side of Alaska Peninsula northward to their coastal arctic nesting grounds. The bay is more than a simple way-station;

most species spend several weeks there awaiting the breakup farther north, preparing themselves physiologically, nutritionally, and behaviorally for the critical first few days after arriving at their nesting areas.

Summer is the season for a more pelagic avifauna. Sooty and slender-billed shearwaters—literally by the millions—arrive after concluding their breeding season in the Southern Hemisphere. Murres, guillemots, puffins, and kittiwakes in huge numbers nest on cliffs on the north side of the bay. Moulting male and immature ducks summering in Bristol Bay are joined in autumn by waterfowl from the nesting grounds coming to feed before flying to southern wintering areas. The very large eelgrass beds studding the lagoons around the entire rim of Bristol Bay are especially important during this September-October feeding period. Izembek Bay, at the extreme south end of the bay, supports almost the entire continental population of black brant for several weeks in the fall. In winter, vast flocks of hardy sea ducks, alcids, cormorants, and other birds ride out the storms there at the southern edge of the Arctic pack ice.

Geological maps show a large sedimentary basin underlying—so far as is known—all of Bristol Bay and all but the mountainous backbone of the Alaska Peninsula. The geology is favorable for the presence of oil and gas; both offshore and onshore seismic explorations have been carried on for a number of years. The federal government has sold onshore leases along most of the coastal area of the Alaska Peninsula. In 1968, the State of Alaska leased 165,000 acres offshore from the lower peninsula.

If substantial oil and gas reserves were to be discovered in Bristol Bay, it is very likely that development would proceed rapidly, because marine transport of petroleum products to the United States west coast would pose few special problems. Such development would raise all the familiar questions — the fate of salmon fisheries, waterfowl, and other natural assets — that have plagued oil-producing regions for a century. Bristol Bay may well prove to be the region where Alaskans put to crucial test their concepts and practice of multiple-use resource management.

Beginning with a few individuals in agencies that manage the renewable resources of the area, interest in the potential conflicts of resource use has grown over the past two years. Evidence is mounting that this concern is strong enough to find managerial and political expression:

(1) The Commissioner of the Alaska Department of Natural Resources has refused applications for offshore leases in Izembek Bay on the grounds that eelgrass beds and waterfowl would be endangered.

(2) In 1968, the United States Secretary of Interior wrote to the Western Oil and Gas Association that, "I cannot overemphasize my grave concern for the safety of the fish and wildlife resource in the Bristol Bay area ... no oil exploratory or development work should start in that area until the industry can assure that its operations will be carried out without polluting the environment ..."

(3) Secretary of the Interior Walter Hickel said in *US News and World Report* (10 November 1969) that the Bristol Bay region was high on the list of national priority wilderness and wildlife areas.

(4) In May 1970, the Alaska State Legislature passed a law prohibiting mineral, oil or gas leases or permits for the inner part of Bristol Bay, the heart of the salmon harvesting area. However, this bill was vetoed later by Governor Miller.

(5) The Department of the Interior in 1970 included Bristol Bay in a list of eight of the nation's estuaries that stand most urgently in need of comprehensive management planning and requested an appropriation from Congress to start such a program.

A combination of the complete exclusion of oil exploration from areas of exceptional value to fish and other wildlife and of generally firm controls on oil exploration and oilfield operational techniques could reduce ecological risks and environmental losses to tolerable levels. Some initial work in identifying such high value areas has been done and a few areas have been given some measure of protection. Others—such as the lagoons along Alaska Peninsula where waterfowl congregate—need but do not have special management designation. Neither is the situation satisfactory with respect to geophysical exploration and test-drilling techniques; uplands are still being scarred unnecessarily by heavy vehicles and streams are still endangered by silting. Brown bears and caribou, both valuable animals, will be confronted by hazards similar to those of the North Slope.

Other Areas of Petroleum Exploration

There are many areas of petroleum exploration in Alaska besides Prudhoe Bay, Cook Inlet, and Bristol Bay. Sharp interest is being shown in the Icy Cape area, both onshore and offshore. Seismic exploration has been followed by test-well drilling in the Nelchina Basin and seismic work has been done elsewhere. The present slow pace of Alaskan exploration is expected to accelerate when Prudhoe Bay fields go into production and when the moratorium on public land leasing and disposal is lifted, following settlement of aboriginal land claims. It would take too much space to describe here the varied ecological situations of each of the potential oil areas. Alaskan resource managers must, in the short time left before petroleum exploration accelerates, obtain effective protection (including exclusion of exploration, if necessary) for areas of critical, ecological, scientific and scenic importance, and they must apply the lessons learned in the Alaskan Arctic to similar operations on other public lands.

Overall Status of Wildlife

With such notable exceptions as the sea otter, fur seal and Pacific salmon, Alaska's wildlife and fish populations have been largely free from the over-exploitation and destruction of the habitat that has characterized wild animal populations in other parts of the world. Even today less than two per cent of the land in Alaska is devoted to agriculture, mining, industry and residential use. The sea otter has now recovered from near extinction and is reestablished throughout most of its original range; the fur seal now numbers over two million and is managed under the terms of an international treaty. Salmon that spawn in Alaskan streams support an intensive fishery under a close management that strives to prevent repetition of past over exploitation, although this effort is becoming more difficult under the increasing pressure of foreign and American fisheries in the North Pacific and Bering Sea.

In spite of the present bright picture, certain elements of Alaska's fauna appear particularly vulnerable to intensive oil development. Grizzly, brown, and polar bears are eagerly sought as trophies by sport hunters and they provide the base for commercial guiding. Increasingly restrictive regulations governing their take will be required in the future. The wolverine and wolf will also require closer protection. The anadromous fish in Alaskan fresh waters will be greatly reduced if road and pipeline construction and other activities associated with oil development result in extensive pollution and destruction of spawning beds. The marine environment, because it is the site of mass transport of oil, is perhaps the area for greatest future concern. Intertidal vertebrate and invertebrate fauna and birds appear to be most directly and severely affected by oil spills. Although several oil spills have recently occurred in Cook Inlet and the Gulf of Alaska, with large losses of birds and other forms of marine life, very little is known of this potential threat to Alaska's ecology, either from the standpoint of the vulnerability of the species involved or of the mechanisms that would break down petroleum products in Alaska's cold seas.

Critical Issues

Commercial oil extraction raises two critical issues with respect to renewable resource management: (1) direct effects of exploration, development, and shipping on wildlife populations and habitats, and (2) problems that stem from human population growth and industrialization made possible by petroleum extraction.

We cannot shrug off the effects of direct attrition on wildlife populations as oil exploration and development proceed in one area after another in Alaska. Seismic operations, gravel extraction from streambeds, road and drill site construction, minor spills of fuel oil, harbor development, and other aspects of oilfield work all take their toll. The industry is becoming more familiar with northern operations, however, and this knowledge, together with public pressure to minimize damage to vegetation, terrain, and wildlife, have resulted in tangible improvements in procedures and technology. The days of summer travel on thawed tundra with cleat-tracked vehicles, for example, are all but finished.

There remains one major uncertainty regarding direct effects on wildlife: the question of the behavioral reactions of wild animals to oilfield activity. There may be twenty roads athwart the path of migrating caribou in the central Alaskan Arctic today, and there may be fifty in a few years. The amount of ground covered by these roads is perhaps trivial—but will the roads and their traffic so confuse and disturb the caribou that they will stop using the area altogether? Other questions of this sort were posed earlier in this paper.

Oil spills are the greatest potential threat to wildlife and fisheries of all of the direct effects of oil exploration and development. Very few major oil spills have occurred to date: the death in mid-winter 1969-70 of tens of thousands of sea birds east of Kodiak Island, owing to the discharge of oil ballast from tankers is the prominent exception. The threat is real, however, and the perception of it by the public, industry, and the government is the *sine qua non* of effective prevention. Some progress is being made, but breakthroughs in detection capabilities, spill-prevention technology, and clean-up technology are sorely needed.

The advent of "big oil" in Alaska has changed the entire economic picture in the state and could trigger a sharp rise in population and industrialization. These changes would not come as a direct accompaniment of the petroleum industry—the oil industry itself is capital-intensive and highly automated—but as an outgrowth of state investment decisions. The state receives a very high rent from its oil resources directly through leasing and taxation—revenue from the sale of leases on the North Slope in September 1969 was nearly equal to the total annual income of all Alaskans in 1968. If the state chooses to invert these revenues in programs designed to stimulate population growth, to settle uninhabited areas, to build transportation systems, and to subsidize new industries, there will be enormous consequences to all phases of Alaskan resource management.

The degree to which wildlife managers will be able to cope with the new problems generated by petroleum industry and derivative activities is too large an issue to discuss here. However, certain institutional constraints affecting the outcome warrant mention. The first is an organizational problem. In Alaska two levels of government (state and federal) have wildlife management responsibilities and, within each level, the agency and animal management responsibility is not the agency with primary control of the land. The State Department of Fish and Game and the Federal Bureau of Sport Fisheries and Wildlife manage the fauna, while the federal Bureau of Land Management, federal Forest Service and Alaska Department of Natural Resources control the land. (The Bureau of Sport Fisheries and Wildlife is, however, proprietor of approximately 20 million of Alaska's 365 million acres of land.)

This splitting of authority is not necessarily impractical or undesirable in the broad sense, but it does create serious problems of coordination and cooperation. There have been notable instances of cooperation in Alaska, but there have been many other cases of conflicting purposes, attitudes, and procedures. There is no formal binding structure, and thus cooperation is sporadic and dependent largely on personalities. Several formal "master agreements" have been signed by agencies, providing some continuity of cooperation as administrations change. The two fauna management agencies and, especially, the Alaska Department of Fish and Game either take what circumstances give them or assume a defensive stance, rather weakly bolstered by statutory authority over land use activities.

The second constraint relates to the question of public versus private initiative in petroleum development. There is in the United States (as elsewhere) an historic assumption that oil production is an overriding land use. This assumption, plus the passiveness of land managers towards petroleum exploration, has put the initiative firmly in the hands of private industry.

Without suggesting nationalization of the oil industry, we think there is a clear need for governments to accept a more active role in determining where, when, and how petroleum will be sought and produced. Some fundamental questions need to be asked. In view of the long term environmental effects of converting fossil fuels to heat, carbon dioxide, and various atmospheric and water-borne pollutants, should society try to reduce per capita petroleum consumption? Are there areas where we should forego oil and gas extraction? If so, what criteria (such as geological instability or exceptional surface values) should be used to decide? Should new oilfields be put into production before the probabilities of disastrous and chronic spillage en route are greatly reduced?

A third constraint is the state of environmental science and its application to technological problems in the Arctic. A large body of environmental and ecological knowledge was accumulated before demand for arctic science rose two years ago. Unfortunately much of the information was out of focus with respect to current needs, and much more was not readily available to people who needed it -- or, worse still, it was ignored altogether. By and large, the petroleum industry, spurred by competition, has moved faster than knowledge of local conditions safely allowed. For example, one oil pipeline in Cook Inlet ruptured five times in a two-year period, primarily because the scouring action of underwater currents was underestimated. TAPS purchased pipe for its proposed 800 mile line from Prudhoe Bay to Valdez before confirming its route plans and before permafrost engineering knowledge could support safe construction. Large areas of tundra and taiga have been denuded during oil-related construction, but there is not enough knowledge of basic plant physiology or plant ecology to support a revegetation technology.

The International Biological Program has drawn together much of the past research in northern Alaska and has stimulated efforts to discover the basic features of tundra ecosystems. A new focus on marine environments will be achieved through the recently initiated Sea Grant program. Industry itself is supporting a considerable amount of investigation. Some of these investigations are attempts in good faith to strengthen problem-oriented research, but a small portion of them appears to be little more than window dressing in response to public pressure. Nevertheless, the total effort directed towards science in the Arctic is rising annually. The greatest need now is to establish systems whereby this science can be applied effectively in decision-making and in technological contexts.

NOTES

[1]Since this article was written TAPS has been replaced by the Alyeska Pipeline Services Corporation (ALPS). Although detailed plans of this new organization are not yet known, the effects on the ecology of whatever area the pipelines pass through will be the same.

This article was prepared for the Conference on Productivity and Conservation in Northern Circumpolar Lands, Edmonton, Alberta, Canada, October 15-17, 1969.

MAN IN NATURE:
A STRATEGY FOR ALASKAN LIVING

Robert B. Weeden

People move to Alaska for many reasons, and because of the distance and cost of moving, the reasons rarely are trivial. Major population increases have come in boom times; one might infer that the lure of economic benefits has been paramount. But recessions have followed the booms and those with purely economic motives often have gone back "Outside" where, if they were going to starve, they could do it in a comfortable climate. Even in our exciting times in Alaska a man spends $1.32 for what he could buy in Seattle for $1.00; he earns only $1.21 for a dollar's worth of labor by national standards. Clearly the Alaskan is not as well off as the average American.

Or is he? Is there something in the air, the romance of Alaska that creates the captivating incentive that money fails to provide? Do people stay because they expect to take part in a legend? I think they do. In Alaska people perceive and respond to a uniqueness comprising the freshness of history, the indefinable lure of "frontier," and, above all, the wilderness. Despite the comings and goings of boomers, I think the heart of Alaskans is in Alaska.

If ever it was important for a people to gauge accurately their own feelings about themselves and their environment, it is true in Alaska today. History and Nature have proffered an array of choices that our civilization has never seen before. The only decision we cannot make is to stay aloof from change. If we Alaskans do not make our own choices, others will happily do it for us.

The most obvious element in the situation is the economic upheaval since the September 10, 1969 oil lease sale in Anchorage. On that day Alaskans, who had earned a total personal income of a little over a billion dollars in 1969, received slightly over $900,000,000 in lease payments and bonuses on state lands near Prudhoe Bay. The expectation of significant continued income from future lease sales and from oil and gas production suggests that the rather desperate search for revenue characterizing the decade after statehood is over.

An equally important ingredient is that the inherent character and productivity of the land are largely undiminished. Over vast areas of the state there is hardly any evidence of human use. Air and water are as pure as anywhere in this polluted world. Renewable resources are (with a few exceptions) harvested below or barely at annual production levels. Surface transportation nets cover only one-fourth of the state, sparsely. In short, the present array of choices is not greatly diminished by past mistakes or heavy capital investments.

Third, a major group of Alaskans, the approximately 60,000 Indians, Eskimos, and Aleuts of the state, may suddenly gain economic and landowner stature such as they have never had before. These people face individual and group choices that are in many ways more difficult and unsettling than those confronting other Alaskans.

Fourth, the richness of the present opportunity is largely due to the recognition by Alaskans that their new wealth brings new responsibilities of decision. To some the responsibility is mainly fiscal: to invest for greatest dollar return in time. Others see the social good that could come from expenditures for education, sanitation, public works, or various welfare programs.

In this context it seems both appropriate and urgent that there be full and vigorous public debate of various strategies for Alaskan living. Among the several alternatives, I am urging one that involves exceptional recognition of Nature as an integral part of the human environment. If this style of life touches the hearts and minds of Alaskans we will necessarily have to adopt bold policies relative to population growth and industrialization. These, in turn, will require that specific tactics of resource and environmental use immediately be brought to bear on current political and economic decisions.

The general idea is simple. I see Alaska as a place where people elect to withhold the full force of their technical and procreative powers so as to reap the rich harvest of tangible and intellectual resources the wild north can promise. I do not propose turning Alaska into a permanent nature preserve, administered by some monstrous conservationistic bureaucracy. Neither do I propose that Alaska welcome industrialization unreservedly, mimicking the unenviable environments technology has spawned all over the world. The middle road is not, in this case, a politically viable compromise, because walking it will be much harder than taking either of the other paths. Rather, I chose it because I believe in diversity of opportunity—economic, materialistic, creative, recreative—as a prime element in the good life. Not everyone wants to be a bird-watcher. Not everyone should be ensnared in the television syndrome.

Policies for Leaders

If this idea is to work, Alaskans and their governments must adopt three basic policies: limited population, selective industrialization, and environmental consciousness. All are indispensable. All are fraught with emotional polarities, and their acceptance and institutionalization will be extremely difficult.

There is no need to belabor the now-obvious perils of excessive population. In policy terms, whereas much of the world cannot long survive without a reduction in population, and whereas America itself must take steps to limit further population growth, Alaska is one of the few self-supporting units of government that can justify conceiving of and working toward an optimal population (which may be at a level somewhat higher than our present quarter-million people). The concept of optimal population, admittedly, is poorly defined. To me it means the general population level at which people enjoy the widest freedom of cultural and economic pursuits. There is an obvious interaction of dollars, culture, and population; a few rich people could finance a performance of an opera, but it takes more middle-income people to do the same thing. "Optimal population levels" may be dynamic rather than static, rising and lowering as cultural and environmental shifts take place.

The life style I advocate will be impossible unless we develop and practice a policy of population regulation. We will need to limit the number of births among Alaskans through legalized abortion, birth control measures, incentives for small families, or other methods and combinations that are acceptable and effective. We will have to restrict immigration, possibly approaching this tricky problem from a strategy of reducing the incentive for people to immigrate, rather than by barring entry to those who knock on the door.

The spacing or geographic distribution of people is an equally important subject. In Alaska, big settlements have been growing bigger and small places have been getting smaller for several decades, with a net annual increase in total state population. Roughly one-third of all Alaskans now live in Anchorage and its satellite communities. Another one-third live in the towns of Fairbanks, Palmer, Kenai-Soldotna, Ketchikan, Juneau and Sitka. The trend toward urbanization is essentially conservative of landscape, and it should be encouraged in Alaska. Towns and cities should be made more attractive in both opportunity and appearance. Conversely, out-dated programs such as the Homestead Act (by which the federal government gives large acreages to private persons, ostensibly for agriculture but now for other uses including land speculation) should be abandoned. These programs result in the scattering of people along road systems, leading to high costs for services, and degradation of the countryside.

(The entire mix of federal, state, and local government programs for hinterland development are in dire need of overhaul, reappraisal, coordination, and redirection. Again, Alaskan conditions favor concerted, long-term land planning because large blocks of land are under jurisdiction of a few public agencies responsible for management in the public interest. There is an unbreakable two-way relation between public lands management, access and transportation, settlement patterns, and population policy.)

The second policy, that of selective industrialization, is closely tied to the first. If we reject outright the conventional myth that population growth is a necessary handmaiden to progress, we do not have to look for industries that "provide jobs"—and end up attraction 102 job-seekers for every 100 jobs they offer. We can foster industries that are capital-intensive rather than labor-intensive, and select those least likely to degrade the natural environment through noxious effluents or outputs. We can also reject extravagant power generation projects justified with self-fulfilling projections of demand from processing industries and population growth; neither the manufacturing plants nor the increased population are desirable. Traditional tax enticements to new industries could be scrapped unless they carry out the environmental or social policies of the state.

Out of a total civilian work force of about 100,000 people in 1968, approximately 91,000 had jobs. Over one-third of all working people were employed in trades and services, about 6 to 8 per cent each in transportation, manufacturing (including logging), contract construction, and smaller proportions in mining, financial, and other occupations. The main sources of "new money" in the Alaskan economy have been federal government expenditures, commercial fish, oil and gas, forest products, minerals, and tourism, in order of decreasing dollar value. In 1969 the great increases in oil and gas revenues (mostly lease payments and bonuses, not production) have changed the relative ranking of these sources of money, and the new picture may hold for a number of years.

The important point for this discussion is that revenue from the Cook Inlet and arctic oilfields has given Alaska a tremendous bank balance after many years when federal expenditures were the critical factor in survival of the economy. Assuming that gas and oil revenues from those fields will be high for several decades, and assuming a continued net inflow of federal dollars, there is no need for economic policy that strains the productive capacities of renewable resources, and no need for aggressive expansionism in mining, tourism, manufacturing, and other industries. There is a greater need to turn our attention to the serious social inequities in our local economy, a prime example being poverty and joblessness among Alaskan Natives – a condition that is worsening rather than improving as our total dollar flow rises.

The third policy, which I coined "environmental consciousness," depends on Alaskans adopting Aldo Leopold's "land ethic." Incorporated into government it would become "ecomanagement," a term Jaro Mayda coined[1] to express the broad new tasks of conservation, encompassing all individual aspects of environment, the whole concept "environment" (since this is more than the sum of its parts), and the interplay of man and environment. Operationally this policy would seek always to maximize the full spectrum of human benefits from the use of space and other natural resources, not merely to maximize revenue. It would defend man against himself in the common environmental problems of air, water, and noise pollution. It would be the basis for defense of those delightfully "useless" animals, plants, and empty miles that may be the ultimate salvation of man, and which unquestionably are an important foundation for scientific knowledge, artistic creativity, and personal recreation and pleasure.

Petroleum in the New Alaska

As I said earlier, adopting these policies would mean completely different approaches to environmental management. Alaskan oil developments provide an excellent and timely example; I will describe the current situation briefly and suggest two steps to take immediately to cope with the oil giant.

If the first guesses of petroleum geologists are correct, close to one-half of Alaska and its offshore waters may be underlain by oil or gas-bearing strata. This includes most of the state outside of the Alaska Range, Brooks Range, and mountainous interior areas. Some private seismic work or drilling has occurred in practically all of the oil regions of the state, but two, Cook Inlet and the central Arctic have had the lion's share of attention. The first production wells were spudded on the Kenai Peninsula in 1958; the Swanson River field was developed there and, together with about 16 wells offshore in adjacent Cook Inlet, this field produces all of Alaska's present output of about 200,000 barrels per day. A small refinery exists near Kenai, but most Alaskan oil is shipped as "crude" out of shore facilities on the east and west sides of Cook Inlet.

Exploration and production activity in the inlet and on the Kenai Peninsula gave Alaskans a fairly clear idea of the sorts of problems oilfield development brings. The network of thousands of miles of intertwining tractor trails across marshes, forests and alpine areas jolted people into sharp awareness that even looking for oil causes problems. Strictly enforced regulations helped: anyone who compared the seeded roadsides and healing "cat" trails on the Kenai National Moose Range with the debris and scarring on state lands just outside the Range could see this readily. Air and water pollution came, as inevitably they will. A cloud of smoke is sometimes visible for miles when wasted natural gas is flared from the inlet's wells. Hundreds of oil spills from tankers, wells, and pipes have been recorded by government agencies. A few big ones have killed ducks or befouled the nets of fishermen (Cook Inlet has an important commercial and recreational salmon fishery). Life in Anchorage has changed, too, with the advent of oilmen and boomers. No longer a small town serving nearby military bases and tourists, Anchorage has swept into an era of burgeoning population, acute land allocation problems, and school and public service expansion suggesting that, like Alice, someone ate from the wrong side of the mushroom.

But Anchorage had its growing pains and Kenai its land scarring before oil. Petroleum development simply intensified and added new facets to the problem. It is in the Arctic, with its virginal and vulnerable landscape, that the impact of oil is most obvious. The gnawing scars from seemingly harmless trails of construction vehicles, the puzzles of permafrost engineering, the unsuitability of ordinary sanitation techniques, the fantastic longevity and visibility of debris, the oil spills, the huge demand for gravel for camps and airstrips, the question of whether caribou will be frightened and displaced by surface feeder pipes and the general bustle of oilfield operations—these are now commonplace topics of conversation in the north. Technological man has burst upon the Arctic, a stranger. He can ride roughshod for a time over the tundra to his shining golden visions, but always nagged by the feeling he could do much better. Science cannot yet be of much help. Government is an uncertain watchdog, alternately barking and licking its chops.

Bigger questions for Alaska lie beyond Prudhoe Bay and Cook Inlet. Can petroleum be shipped out of Alaska by pipeline, tanker, or any other means without chronic and catastrophic oil spills? Will the arctic oilfield, now confined to the central Arctic north of the Brooks Range, expand west into the huge Naval Petroleum Reserve No. 4 and east to the lovely Arctic National Wildlife Range? Will the semi-secret explorations in Bristol Bay and on the Alaska Peninsula turn that fabulous big game, waterfowl, and salmon paradise into another Prudhoe? Can offshore drilling in the savage Gulf of Alaska or the Beaufort Sea be done without a series of Santa Barbaras? Will the next big strike be on the delta of the Yukon River, where Secretary of the Interior Walter Hickel is said to have more than a passing financial interest at stake?

In view of these and other managerial complexities that neither industry, state, nor federal governments have been able to solve, I propose a complete shutdown for at least three years of all further oil and gas exploration in Alaska and adjacent waters, outside of present lease areas in Cook Inlet and the central Arctic. In my judgment the immediate and permanent benefits from this action would far outweigh any temporary reduction in revenues to geophysical contractors or to the State of Alaska. First, this action would let the oil and gas industry turn its full attention to getting known petroleum reserves into production and to market safely and with minimum losses to the environment. Second, the moratorium would give governments time to establish a full range of regulations for oilfield conservation and for the protection of the landscape and wildlife. Even more critical is the need for resource agencies to obtain the staff and funds to explain and enforce these regulations, and to establish training programs jointly with industry. Third, universities and others could begin basic, full-scale studies of tundra and taiga disturbances, so that better evaluations of the regulations would be possible. Fourth, and very importantly, oil companies and the government could steadily improve techniques of slant drilling, seismic systems, helicopter, hovercraft, and overland vehicle usage, and sanitation, so that future exploration could be done in safety and with minor and tolerable damage to the land. Fifth, the State of Alaska could study its new role as rich man, learning how to make the most social mileage out of its financial windfall. Finally, the moratorium would allow resource agencies and private groups to develop sound proposals for lands to be reserved permanently from oil and gas exploration, based on their importance to science or exceptional wildlife, scenic, or recreational values.

Eventually more of the potential oil lands would be explored. This should come on the initiative of the government, not industry. It should be done when the national and global situation clearly calls for development of new reserves, and it should be done on lands selected by the government. And, as oil and gas are public resources under public land, the public, through government, should dictate the conditions and techniques of exploration. I suggest that a separate industry-government corporation be established to explore each parcel as it is opened up, with companies and individual entrepreneurs bidding for a share in the venture. The corporation would then conduct all exploration work with the best technology available, sharing geophysical data within the corporation. This would eliminate the haste and secrecy that have caused such wasteful and destructive duplication of seismic lines, shot holes, camps, roads, airstrips, test wells, and gravel pits in the Arctic. Petroleum discoveries would be developed by the private members of the exploration group, under a unitization plan, dividing proceeds in the ratio of original bids for exploration. I am convinced that if we act sensibly, using the knowledge we have or can soon develop, the Arctic, Cook Inlet, and perhaps other oilfields can be developed into showpieces of public and private cooperation. Alaska would necessarily have to sacrifice some of her wildness, some of her cleanness of landscape, and some of her outdoor playgrounds and classrooms, doing this not blindly but in full knowledge that a good bargain has been struck by men for men.

Alaska and the World

The future Alaska I rather wistfully envision would have more people than now—perhaps 500,000 or so—but they would be in the same population centers as now. There would be awesome stretches of semi-wilderness where people lived who prized solitude, or who enjoyed making their way from the seasonal fruits of the countryside. There would be relatively smaller stretches of true wilderness, balanced by local areas where facilities were developed for the enjoyment of nature by large numbers of visitors. There would be a comfortable network of roads where needed, planned, mile by mile, to display and preserve the countryside and to host appropriate commercial, residential, and recreational uses. Public revenues would come from the usual range of personal and corporate taxes and from the state's share of Alaska resources extracted for private profit: oil, gas, fish, minerals, timber, water. Alaskans would be teachers, scientists, civil servants, tradesmen, miners, fishermen, loggers, financiers, artists—a reasonable sample of the whole range of occupations open to modern societies.

Anyone who knows Alaska will remark that what I have in mind is simply to perpetuate the present. Today's Alaska, however, is a result of a complex and dynamic history. The economic, psychological, and global events that made Alaska what it is are already pushing it towards something else. That "something else," I fear, is a repetition of the dollar-rich, culture-poor, trash-and-poison-ridden landscape so characteristic of industrial America. Changing this destiny requires a revolution in the attitudes of every man (and especially of those who lead), towards his own sources of happiness, his own life style, and his own environment.

In a very real sense, what I am proposing is not only a milieu for Alaskans but an opportunity for the world. The world needs an embodiment of the frontier mythology, the sense of horizons unexplored, the mystery of uninhabited miles. It needs a place where wolves stalk the strand lines in the dark, because a land that can produce a wolf is a healthy, robust, and perfect land. The world desperately needs a place to stand under a bright auroral curtain on a winter's evening, in awe of the cosmic cold and silence. But more than these things the world needs to know that there is a place where men live amidst a balanced interplay of the goods of technology and the fruits of nature. Unless we can prove that a modern society can thrive in harmony with the land, the bits of wildness we salvage in Alaska will be nothing more than curious artifacts in the sad museum of mankind.

NOTES

[1] Jaro Mayda, 1967, "Environment and Resources: From Conservation to Ecomanagement," School of Law, University of Puerto Rico.

ADDITIONAL READING

Cooley, Richard A. *Alaska: A Challenge in Conservation.* Madison, Wisconsin: University of Wisconsin Press, 1962.

Brown, Tom. *Oil on Ice: Alaskan Wilderness at the Crossroads.* San Francisco: Sierra Club, 1971.

Evans, Charles D. "Environmental Effects of Petroleum Development in the Cook Inlet Area." *Proceedings of the Twentieth Alaska Science Conference.* College, Alaska: Alaska Division of the American Association for the Advancement of Science, July, 1970.

Glasgow, Leslie L. "Federal Responsibilities in the North—The North Slope Task Force," *Proceedings of the Twentieth Alaska Science Conference.* College, Alaska: Alaska Division of American Association for the Advancement of Science, July, 1970.

"Interview with David Brower." *Alaska Daily News.* September 3, 1970.

"Interview with Robert B. Weeden." *Alaska Construction and Oil.* July 1970.

Rogers, George W. (ed.). *Change in Alaska: People, Petroleum and Politics.* Seattle: University of Washington, 1970. Part IV and V.

Tussing, Arlon R., and Erickson, Gregg K. *Mining and Public Policy in Alaska.* College: Institute of Social, Economic and Government Research. 1969.

SECTION V: RURAL DEVELOPMENT

This article appeared in *Polar Record* (published by the Scott Polar Research Institute, Cambridge, England) Vol. XI no. 96 (1970) pp. 291-299.

RURAL ALASKA'S DEVELOPMENT PROBLEM

Gordon S. Harrison and Thomas A. Morehouse

Introduction

Economic development programs in rural Alaska face barriers created by ethnic and cultural variations from the standards of urban, industrialized western society and by the virtual absence among the Native population of the local capital and technical capabilities that are needed to achieve economic self-sufficiency. In addition, public and private agencies inevitably assume a dominant role, with respect to the local population, when they invest in or assist Native villages or rural regions, a fact that compounds the problems of change. The objective of modernization may get in the way of the objective of self-determination, to the detriment of both. These problems confront programs for vocational training, housing, transportation, community facilities, community organization, cooperative enterprises and small business development—virtually the entire range of programs intended to support or to trigger further development and ultimately to increase self-sufficiency in Alaska's Native villages and rural regions.

This article explores the general character of the development problem in Native Alaska and the prospect for change. The focus is on social and political obstacles to significant improvement in the economic condition of the rural Alaska Native population. It is assumed that such change will continue to depend heavily on a flow of financial and technical assistance from outside the region; there is generally no base for economic growth in the region itself.[1]

Characteristics of Rural Alaska

About 70 per cent of Alaska's 60,000 Native people live in some 180 villages of 25 to 2,500 population, scattered over a half-million square miles. The median population of Native villages is about 160. Only a dozen of these villages are located on the state's road system: access to all others is primarily by air, but also by boat, snowmobile, or dog team.

The Native population constitutes about one-fifth of the state's total population. Eskimos make up about one-half the total; Indians, three-eighths; and Aleuts, one-eighth. These groups live in separate and fairly well-defined regions of the state: Tlingit, Haida and Tsimshian Indians live in the panhandle of southeast Alaska; Athapaskan Indians in the interior, most of them along the Yukon, Tanana, and Kuskokwim rivers and their tributaries; Eskimos live along the northern and western coasts; and Aleuts occupy the southern part of the Alaska Peninsula and the Aleutian Islands.

Almost all Native housing is grossly substandard, health conditions are extremely poor (in 1966, the average mortality age for Natives was 34 years), and education levels are very low. Lacking adequate resources, technical skills, and opportunities, the Native peoples cannot themselves generate the wealth and technology needed to improve their condition materially.

The large majority of Alaska Natives lack training and opportunities for permanent wage employment. They are classified as unskilled labor and have incomes well below the poverty level as defined by the federal government. Wage employment and ᐧbsistence activities are highly seasonal. Unemployment approaches

80-90 per cent during the winter and falls to 25 per cent during the summer, when commercial fishing, canning, construction, and fire-fighting jobs become available. More than half the Natives are jobless most of the year, and their cash incomes generally fall considerably short of what is needed to live in villages where prices for essential goods are often twice as high as in the other states. Subsistence hunting, fishing, and gathering, together with welfare payments, must, therefore, meet a significant portion of a family's minimum needs.

As summed up by the Federal Field Committee for Development Planning in Alaska,

> For some Alaska Natives who live in cities, social and economic problems are enormous, and for some who live in rural areas, such problems may be but few. But broadly told, while joblessness is high and income levels low among Natives generally, these conditions are worse for those in villages. While educational achievement is low among Natives generally, it is lower for those in villages. While the health status of Natives is poor across the state, it is poorer for those in villages. While opportunity for progress is limited for most Natives, *it is virtually absent for those in villages.*[2]

Rural Development Windfalls?

The view is becoming widespread that Alaska is turning an economic corner and that its social and economic problems will soon be solved in both urban and rural areas. This view, unfortunately, is not a realistic one, at least not for the immediate future. The three developments most prominently mentioned in this connection are: (1) new jobs and general economic growth created by the oil industry, (2) settlement of Native land claims, and (3) the state's prospective oil wealth.

First, the new jobs created directly by petroleum development may ease the problem of Native employment somewhat, but this increase clearly will be no panacea. Just as with military construction in the early 1950's, a spurt of high-wage employment may be sustained for a few years, but it will then fall off sharply. Moreover, with job training programs for Natives lagging, and with workers being imported from outside the state, the number of short-term jobs filled by Natives is likely to be small. For those who will benefit directly from the new employment opportunities, as well as for those who do not, long-term social and economic assistance programs will continue to be necessary.

Second, whatever the time and the specific terms of the Native land claims settlement, it will not lead automatically to solution of rural Alaska's many ills. The settlement will consist of land and money: putting these resources to work will require organization, leadership, many kinds of knowledge and skills, and technology—all of which are now, and are likely to remain, in very short supply in rural Alaska.

Third, these same constraints on the productive use of money apply to the state government. Alaska has not shown great creativity nor expended much energy in attempting to face—let alone to solve—the problems of rural Alaska, even on a small scale.

If these developments promise no easy answers or short-cut solutions to Alaska's rural problems, it is apparent that the concentration of population and investment in selected regional growth centers is equally inadequate. It has been widely held that the populations of small villages were naturally gravitating to centers such as Barrow, Kotzebue, Nome, and Bethel, with the result that many villages were growing smaller and would eventually disappear. It has also been assumed that this changing pattern would, at least, lead to greater efficiency in the administration of economic and social development programs, if they were directed to a more concentrated and accessible Native population. Although some villages will, no doubt, wither away, and the regional centers will continue to grow—some at rapid rates—the limited evidence now available suggests that many small villages, probably most of them, are likely to remain in existence for some time to come.[3]

In other parts of the United States, local unemployment often provides the push, and the lure of jobs often provides the pull for economically rational movements of population. In rural Alaska, too,

... there is a willingness to move to take jobs. But — owing to a preference for village life, a sense of being ill equipped for city life and jobs, an inability to command adequate salaries given their lack of education and training, or to a combination of reasons — the willingness of village adults to move to obtain temporary work is far stronger than it is to make a permanent move in order to obtain employment.[4]

Social and economic problems are, therefore, likely to persist: oil development, land claims settlement, and prospective state wealth will not make them go away. Voluntary movements of population probably will not do much to increase efficiency of programs or to ease administrative burdens. Current federal and state programs must continue to fill the wide gap between the basic needs of the Native peoples and the resources and capabilities available to meet them. New programs will be needed, not only for the additional funds they can provide, but also for the concepts and techniques they can develop and apply in Alaska's rural regions. All such programs, whatever their individual strengths and weaknesses, need to be viewed as part of a comprehensive and long-term rural development strategy.

Problems of Development Strategy

A comprehensive development strategy should combine economic and socio-political elements. In essence, the aim of economic development is to increase per capita productivity and income, and the aim of socio-political development is to enable the people to manage their own affairs. Although easily stated, these aims are large and complex objectives, and, in practice, they are not easily reconciled, particularly in environments that are outside the economic and cultural mainstream of urbanized and industrialized western society.

Not only is economic development extremely costly in rural areas, but attempts to organize people to help themselves may run directly counter to deeply entrenched attitudinal and behavioral patterns.

To be frank, a sense of progress — a recognition that change is
possible and that alternatives offering a better life are, or can be
made available — is not too often encountered as a feature of peasant
society in the underdeveloped world. In many cases, leadership
functions have for so long been monopolized by out-group individuals
and institutions that even the concept of autonomy of action is
alien.[5]

Conditions in some parts of rural Alaska come very close to this
state of affairs, especially where, underlying the structural
constraints, value is attached to non-competitive and non-striving
behavior. This situation poses a major challenge to development
because the means of achieving a better life must include a local
willingness to strive for it. Such willingness is difficult, if not
impossible, to achieve where non-economic benefits in the form of
higher educational levels, better housing, and improved health are
either inconceivable or seem beyond reach. On the other hand, if the
benefits are within realistic range, and are so perceived, they can
supply the motivation needed and can act as catalysts to increase
productivity at the same time that they contribute directly to
economic growth themselves. Thus, a large investment in "human
capital" has to accompany investment in economic enterprise.

More still, however, is involved than high cost and a local
willingness to change. Local leadership and administrative capabilities
are needed if development is not to be imposed from outside.
Demands on local leaders and administrators must be carefully
matched to their capabilities, neither over-estimating nor
under-estimating them. The more unbalanced the demands and the
capabilities become, the greater the tension between the economic
objective of increased productivity and income and the
socio-political objective of self-determination. If the link between
these objectives breaks, distortions are likely to occur: economic
development may become mere short-run exploitation or simply a
bad investment and socio-political development may result only in
increased dependence or despair. While the objectives must be clearly
articulated, there is, unfortunately, no formula for ensuring this
accomplishment. It is only certain that a sense of timing, the
integrity of the program, and an intimate knowledge of and respect
for the people involved are of immeasurable help.

There is still another set of constraints and hazards in programs of economic and social change, and it has to do with the politics of development. Regardless of the people's willingness and ability to change, the innovations required in development strategies may be resisted by established economic interests, particularly when assistance policies involve re-allocations, not just increases, of resources. For example, at the local level in rural Alaska, the private merchant-trader, who has built up a highly diversified business and who has established strong credit ties with villagers, will tend to oppose the creation of cooperative stores that may break his monopoly; at the regional and statewide levels, the major fishing and canning interests will tend to resist the establishment of new fish marketing cooperatives, especially when such cooperatives might bring in other large buyers that have the power to challenge their domination of the Alaska market. In general, therefore, such interests must be identified and their strengths assessed before decisions can be made to avoid, compensate, outmaneuver, or simply to ignore them.

In sum, an effective strategy for economic and social development must combine, (1) investment in both social services and economic enterprise, (2) development of indigenous leadership and administrative capacities, (3) resolution of conflicts with dominant economic interests and structures, and (4) maintenance of relationships between assistance agencies and client groups that keep central direction and assistance in balance with local responsibility and autonomy.

Execution of such a strategy requires multi-faceted, comprehensive, and long-term commitments. It is clear that no single assistance program, or even several small-scale ones, can carry the full burden of economic and social change in rural Alaska. Federal and state government programs in rural Alaska have typically been of a single-purpose, one-shot, or short-term nature. Although often laudable in purpose and for the immediate benefits they have provided, programs for the development of education, housing, health care, employment and training, transportation, and community facilities, for example, have been under-financed and widely scattered. None of the approximately 60 federal, state, and quasi-governmental agencies[6] involved has designed its programs as components of any over-all planning and development process, and none of these agencies appears to have the scope, status, or authority necessary to initiate such a process. An organizational solution is, however, not enough. Whatever the character of development plans and of implementing vehicles, there must be Native receptivity to self-help and helping-hand programs.

Native Attitudes Toward Economic Development

Apart from a small circle of young, acculturated, articulate, and enterprising Native leaders, who are almost constant participants in rural development board meetings, conferences and planning sessions, the notion of economic development is dimly perceived, and then in a confused way, among Alaska Natives. Rural Alaska Natives tend to be highly adaptive to innovations that ease and enhance individual and community life. They have readily adopted products of modern technology into their homes, and they have eagerly received into their communities tangible state and federal rural development projects. Even so, their relationship to these projects, to the idea of economic development, and to white society in general, is mainly one of adaptation and response.

Outside of the panhandle of southeast Alaska, the role of Alaska Native communities in the development process has been essentially passive, although in some notable cases it has been creatively active and is, in general, becoming less passive.[7] Most of the following observations apply to Eskimo, Indian and Aleut communities in northwest, interior and southwest Alaska.

Eskimos, in particular, have been responding defensively to western society since their initial contact with Russians late in the 18th century. More than 150 years of exposure to whalers, fur traders, gold prospectors, missionaries, school teachers, and government administrators have resulted in the general abandonment of traditional modes of economic existence, the radical alteration of traditional community organization, the transformation of social structures, and substantial destruction of cultural identities.[8]

The condition of poverty, which most Native communities now experience, is largely a product of the white man's world. Commercial exploitation of whale and seal stocks and the introduction of firearms into Native hunting patterns contributed to a catastrophic depletion of the biological resources that were the economic base of traditional society. A money economy has displaced traditional patterns of subsistence and created an expanding need for trade goods and social services, but not the means of obtaining them. The living standard of white society is the criterion for unfavorable comparison with the living standard of Native society, although, from some points of view, the living standard of the Native peoples is higher than ever before. There is, therefore, an understandable confusion, ambivalence, and passivity among Natives today with respect to the dominant white society and its numerous, eager, and often contradictory schemes for economic development.

Indeed, years of contact with federal, territorial, and state agencies have created an undercurrent of skepticism, suspicion, and outright hostility among villagers to "briefcase bureaucrats," who sweep through the villages to announce new programs, plans, schemes, surveys, and research projects, very few of which ever profit the village in a direct or discernible way. A common Eskimo word for a white man, *gussuk*, has pejorative overtones and is a reflection of the unhappy state of Eskimo relations with whites from beyond the village.

Development organizations and agencies establishing relationships with Native villages encounter subsurface resistance to their efforts merely because of the *modus operandi* they are forced to adopt. For the most part, they are Anchorage-based, white-dominated institutions, the employees of which earn exorbitant salaries by Native standards and fly in and out of villages—sometimes in a single day—to check books, give advice, or call a council meeting to transact business. Some development agencies, to their credit, have anticipated latent Native hostility and have attempted to counter it with a courteous, respectful, business-like approach to village problems. Despite the sensitivity of such agencies to Native attitudes and despite direct pay-offs to the villages, no agency has been totally successful in dispelling the usual village skepticism toward *gussuk* organizations operating from remote, cosmopolitan Anchorage.

The failure of agencies to dispel Native doubt and hostility is largely due to tension stemming from still another source, the rivalries and jealousies over control that inevitably arise between central funding agencies and their sponsored projects. Money is wanted, but the strings that go with it are resented. This tension becomes especially acute when one of the avowed purposes of a program is to promote local autonomy: the desire for self-determination outpaces either the local capacity to assume responsibility or the agency's willingness to transfer real authority. Even today, the appearance of a new development agency in a village generally represents the sacrifice of local control over some further sector of village life.

Whites control virtually every organization touching village life, and villagers know this. They have little or no control over the organizations and institutions that affect village life. Inspiration for specific rural development projects generally comes from a small number of Native leaders and urban whites, who are searching for practical ways to alleviate rural poverty in Alaska and who know that some federal and state funds may be available for such projects. The futility of serious attempts by villagers to bring a new health clinic or school to their village has proved to many that the celebrated virtues of local initiative are largely mythical. While cooperatives, educational programs, and other community development projects are touted by their sponsoring agencies as the product of local initiative, the local people know that the critical decision whether or not to finance them was made somewhere "outside," in the mysterious bureaucratic world of white men. Community support for programs is sought after they have been initiated.

Native management is a key concept in the development of rural enterprises. Cooperatives based on Eskimo fishing and on arts and crafts, for example, are ultimately to be fully Native-owned and operated. However, neither Eskimo cultural tradition nor Eskimo social history has fostered the development of business management skills. Traditional experience has not put a premium on competition and personal aggrandizement and has not involved extensive trade or commercial exchanges. Eskimo culture stresses adaptation to and accommodation with the forces of nature rather than their manipulation and change. Leadership roles involving firm exercise of authority are alien to a culture that customarily employs extremely subtle and informal techniques of behavior control. In fact, both cultural and historical influences in Eskimo life have led to the formation of values, attitudes, and behavior patterns that are antithetical to those of the modern business manager. Practical experience in business management is limited among Eskimos because, among other reasons, white traders have dominated the commercial life of most villages. General skills in mathematics and English are also in short supply in the villages, where, until recently, education has been poor in quality and limited in quantity. Acculturated and educated Eskimos are usually attracted to well-paid, permanent, and secure employment in urban and regional centers.

Finally, local Native leadership, with only rudimentary experience of business management, has little understanding of formal organizational procedures. On many occasions, the failure to grasp the intricacies of bureaucratic methods has caused tension between development agencies and Native villages. Representatives have arrived at meetings in Anchorage ill-informed or ill-prepared and unable to express adequately the interests of their communities. Applications for financial support have not been approved because forms were late or incomplete. The disappointment and confusion caused by such misunderstandings have complicated the activities of all rural Alaska development agencies.

Conclusion

By almost any measure, the record of development programming in rural Alaska has been dismal. Historically, the development of village Alaska has meant false panaceas, which initially generated hope, cooperation, and a willingness to innovate and experiment, but which usually resulted in despair, apathy, cynicism, and increased distrust of assistance agencies. It has meant projects designed, controlled, and imposed by agencies outside the community. It has meant isolation of a project from other community or rural development efforts. It has meant that few, if any, attempts have been made to judge the immediate effects of projects to form better policies and to produce tested strategies. It has meant capricious extensions and withdrawals of support, with little regard for the preparation needed to make effective use of programs or the time required to achieve significant and lasting results.

The question remains whether the new opportunities for change that are now emerging in rural Alaska can be more effectively exploited than the record of the past would suggest.

NOTES

[1] See Federal Field Committee for Development Planning in Alaska, *A Subregional Economic Analysis of Alaska.* (Anchorage, 1968) and *Alaska Natives and the Land.* (Washington, D.C.: Government Printing Office, 1968).

[2]Federal Field Committee for Development Planning in Alaska, *Alaska Natives and the Land.* p. 35.

[3]A.E. Hippler, "Some Observations on the Persistence of Alaska Native Village Populations," Research Note A1, Institute of Social, Economic and Government Research, University of Alaska, 1969; Dorothy C. Jones, "Changes in Population Structure in the Aleutian Islands," *ISEGR Research Note A-2,* Institute of Social, Economic and Government Research, December, 1970; and Joseph D. Bloom, "Recent Population Trends of Alaska Natives," *Alaska Medicine,* January, 1971.

[4]Federal Field Committee for Development Planning in Alaska, *Alaska Natives and the Land*, p. 56.

[5]T.R. De Gregori and O. Pi-Sunyer, *Economic Development: The Cultural Context.* New York, John Wiley and Sons, 1969, p. 39.

[6]Prominent federal agencies include the Bureau of Indian Affairs, Public Health Service, Economic Development Administration, Farmers Home Administration, Office of Economic Opportunity, Bureau of Commercial Fisheries, Forest Service, and Federal Aviation Administration. At the state level are the Department of Education, Rural Development Agency, Department of Health and Welfare, Department of Labor, Department of Economic Development, Local Affairs Agency, Department of Public Works, Department of Fish and Game, Alaska State Housing Authority, and others. Quasi-governmental agencies include the Rural Alaska Community Action Program, Alaska Legal Services, Community Enterprise Development Corporation, Alaska Village Electric Cooperative, and others. In addition, there are "agencies within agencies" whose lack of coordination often matches that of the inter-departmental and federal-state levels.

[7]G.W. Rogers, "Party Politics or Protest Politics: Current Political Trends in Alaska," *Polar Record*, Vol. 14, No. 91, 1969.

[8]D. Jenness, *Eskimo Administration; 1. Alaska.* Arctic Institute of North America, Technical Paper No. 10, 1962.

This article was prepared for the First Far East Conference on Regional Science, Tokyo, Japan, September 11-13, 1963.

ECONOMIC DEVELOPMENT IN SOUTHEAST ALASKA AND ITS IMPACT ON THE NATIVE POPULATION

George W. Rogers

Southeast Alaska is a large archipelago and a narrow strip of the mainland lying along the northwest coast of the North American continent. Politically, it is an all but separate appendage of the State of Alaska, while geographically it is a continuation of the continental Pacific Mountain system and is closely related to the coastal region of British Columbia. It comprises all that land and intervening waters lying east of the meridian of 141 degrees west longitude, north of latitude 55 degrees north, and west and south of the Alaska-Canada boundary line from Portland Canal to the 141st meridian.

Within this region lies a land area of 35,527 square miles, 60 per cent of which is a mainland strip and the balance consisting of the hundreds of islands comprising the Alexander Archipelago. The mainland strip consists of a mountain range or ranges rising from a few thousand to 18,008 feet above sea level. The crest of the mainland lies within approximately 25 miles or so of tidewater and is covered with snow and ice caps which feed numerous glaciers. It is cut by six of the larger rivers of the region which originate in the interior plateaus of British Columbia and Yukon Territory.

The islands of the Alexander Archipelago account for the remainder of the region's land area. Six of these islands exceed 1,000 square miles in area, ranging from 2,770 to 1,084 square miles. Nine islands range from 773 square miles to 127 square miles in area.

Land, however, accounts for only a part of the region's total area. The total region is roughly 400 miles long by about 120 miles in width from the Canadian boundary to a line connecting the seaward shores of the western isles. Its approximate composition, therefore, is about forty four per cent mainland, thirty per cent islands, and twenty six per cent water area. The first two elements in the composition—the mainland and the islands—are laced together by the third element which forms an intricate system of inland seaways nearly all of which is navigable by small craft, and the mainline of the system, the Inside Passage, by ocean-going steamers. There are 9,000 miles of shoreline around the contours of the islands and mainland.

Long before the European discovery of southeast Alaska, it supported one of the heaviest concentrations of aboriginal population found in the western hemisphere north of the areas of highest civilization in Mexico and Central America. In aboriginal times, it was known as the "territory of the Tlingit," one of the several "nation groups" among the coastal Indians of the northwest Pacific. With the exception of a beachhead of colonization established on the southern end of Prince of Wales Island by the neighboring Haida, the territory of the Tlingit was identical with that of the State of Alaska's present Southeastern Senate District. Not only did this region provide the means of support for a relatively heavy concentration of population, it also provided the economic means for the elaboration of a primitive culture rich in art, oral literature and social and legal organization.

This high aboriginal culture arose from an ample natural resource base. The land and the sea were divided among clans within the broad bounds of the Tlingit people and managed by local geographical units through tribal groupings of the clans. The land provided the timber for housing, canoes, and other artifacts as well as game, fruit and vegetable foods, but it was the marine resources which provided the principal source or wealth and well-being. The sea afforded rich harvests of salmon, halibut, cod, herring, "olachen" and other fish. The sea also provided tremendous quantities of edible mollusks, abundant marine game—hair seal, sea lion, porpoise, whale, sea otter—and important plant matter. The sea and the inland waters were the very source of life to the Tlingit and their culture and held the same place of veneration as does the abstraction "land" in Western cultural heritage.

A second principal cause of the rise of this high aboriginal culture was the degree to which a division of labor had been established among the people. Not only was there a division of labor among the members of each community group according to individual talents and skills, this specialization went beyond the individual and was organized upon a community basis. The inland waters which provided the basis of the aboriginal wealth, also provided the natural highways for the lively aboriginal commerce which made possible this specialization of labor and a further elevation of general living standards. If these protected waterways had not existed, communication, trade and social intercourse would have been difficult due to the mountainous nature of the terrain and there would have been no unified territory of the Tlingit nor any culture of the level they were able to achieve.

The waters of the region, therefore, served the double purpose of being the source of aboriginal life and the means of its unity and rich elaboration.

Following the ill-fated attempts to establish outposts near Yakutat (1796) and Sitka (1799), the Russians through force of arms were able to re-establish what was to become the capital of their Alaskan empire at Sitka in 1804. From that date until the transfer of Alaska to the United States, the economy of Russian America was based upon the fur trade and this, in turn, primarily upon the harvesting of the sea otter. In addition to trade with the Tlingits, furs were secured by company hunters plying the inland and coastal waterways of southeast Alaska in flotillas of skin kayaks. This colonial economy, although more narrowly based than the aboriginal, was likewise primarily oriented to the harvest of marine resources. Among the several factors which influenced the Russian decision to sell its Alaskan holdings to the United States in 1867 was the decline of the sea otter trade which had provided the main element in the basic economy of that period.

The year 1878 stands as an important starting point in the economic development of southeast Alaska. In that year the first salmon canneries in Alaska were erected at Klawock and Sitka and within eight years canneries were operating in all areas of the region. The size of the canned salmon pack continued to expand rapidly, the peak being reached with the 1941 season. The year 1878 was also the year in which the first full-fledged gold mining camp in Alaska came into existence at Windham Bay. Discoveries extended throughout the region and production continued until World War II brought the closing of the last of the large operations in 1944. Gold values reported since then have been primarily from old mill cleanups. Significant values were realized from other natural resources, but canned salmon and gold were the economic lifeblood of southeast Alaska from the 1880's until the early 1950's.

During the period 1906 through 1957, a total of 6,489,480 fine ounces of gold were produced by the region's lode mines, and 107,543,175 standard cases (48 one pound cans) of canned salmon came from the region's canneries. Converting these quantities to 1957 prices (average 1957 wholesale price for canned salmon), the value of the products of the lode gold mines was $227,131,738 and the salmon canneries was $2,446,600,000 (more than ten times the value of gold at 1957 prices). As in the case of the aboriginal and Russian periods, therefore, the region's economy under American rule until the mid-twentieth century has been heavily oriented to marine resources.

The indigenous peoples accommodated themselves readily to the new commercial fishing industry. Existing labor skills were readily adapted to the new industry: men continued to fish, but with larger boats and somewhat different equipment; women continued to clean salmon and shellfish, but for a cannery rather than the family unit. The industrialization of fisheries also required little change in traditional ways of life. Tied to regular fish runs, the seasonal rhythms of life were little changed. Settlements were already oriented to a marine-centered life, so dislocations or relocations of population did not occur. During the period 1929 to 1950, the participation of the indigenous people in the commercial fisheries was almost constant in absolute and relative terms. More than ninety per cent of those of normal working age participated in some phase of fishing or processing each season.

Basic Change—The Economic Impact

Since the mid-century, the region's economy has been undergoing basic changes. Following the closing of the last lode gold mining operation in 1944, except for a brief export of significant values of uranium in the late nineteen fifties, the minerals industry of the region has been virtually nonexistent. Fisheries products have experienced almost continuous decline, falling from the 1941 high total output of 255,590,000 pounds prepared for market to the 1955 low of 86,580,177 pounds. The cause of this decline has been simply over-exploitation and depletion of the salmon resources and although heartening rehabilitation progress has been made since 1955, production can never recover its past high levels.[1]

But the region is not limited exclusively to marine resources. The major land cover is that of the dense coastal rain forests of the Pacific Northwest, predominantly western hemlock and Sitka spruce. Approximately 73% of the region's land area is within the Tongass National Forest which contains an estimated 146 billion board feet of commercial timber, 92 billion board feet of which is economically accessible under present conditions. Because of the marine character of the region, its forests fringe the many miles of shoreline of islands and indented mainland, about three-quarters of the timber being within two and a half miles of tidewater and the rest rarely extending inland more than four or five miles and reaching altitudes of no greater than 1,500 feet. The waterways of the region provide a ready-made system of trunk or main "roads" and the feasibility of logging much of the timber directly into tidewater reduces the need for feeder roads.

Despite the extent and generally good commercial quality of these forest resources and the natural means provided for their economic harvesting and movement to mills, until 1954 they had been subjected only to a modest harvest to provide special cuttings of high-grade spruce logs for export during World War I and World War II and small annual harvests primarily for local timber requirements. In 1954 a mill initially producing 300 tons daily (later increased to 525 tons) of high alpha pulp for use in rayon and cellulose acetate production went into operation at Ketchikan and late in 1959 a similar mill at Sitka started with an initial capacity of 390 tons per day for export to Japan. The average annual timber cut in the Tongass National Forest jumped dramatically from an average of 55 billion board feet for the five year period 1949-1953 to 189 billion board feet for 1954-58 and 317 billion board feet for 1959-1961.[2]

The generalized impact of these developments and shifts in the basic economy were registered in the composition of total natural resource products and employment patterns. A comparison of the value of products from natural resources in the five years immediately preceding the launching of the pulp industry revealed that 86.7% was accounted for by commercial fisheries. This is representative of the composition of earlier periods with a modest shift toward "land resources" before 1955 when gold was being mined. With the addition of one pulp mill, the relative importance of marine resources dropped to 53.3% for the period 1954-1958 and to 43.3% for 1959-1961, while the importance of "land resources" rose from 13.3% to 46.7% and 56.7% of the value of all natural resource products for the same periods.

Although generated within the region, much of this value went outside in the form of profits and other payments to absentee business interests and wages to non-resident seasonal workers. However, the changes did have important and beneficial impacts on the personal income received by residents. Comparing the data for the calendar years 1950, 1955 and 1960, not only was the relative distribution between various forms of income payment changed, but both the total and per capita amounts were increased. The region was more prosperous and its residents, *on the average*, more affluent.

Another profound change in the region's economy has been the introduction of the first major year around industry (other than government and "distributive" industries). In the past, general development and settlement has been handicapped by the extreme seasonality and uncertainty of fishing and fish processing and the lack of off-season job opportunities. This has meant that after the brief and intense activity of the fishing season, the indigenous population has had to round out its annual support from subsistence food gathering and welfare payments. The additional labor required has been met by a regular migrant labor force much as is done in many agricultural regions. In the new timber industries, the seasonal pattern is comparatively minor, resulting from the effects of winter weather conditions upon logging activities and the regular year-end shut down of the pulp mills for major repair and rehabilitation, etc. Unlike fisheries, the forest products industries require a resident labor force on a year around basis.

These are the impacts upon the economy and general employment. Now we must turn to the people involved, and this will be done in very broad terms of the impact upon the indigenous and the non-indigenous populations.

Basic Change—The Social Impact

The popular and official view on the expected impact upon the indigenous population of the expansion of forest products industries was stated by the Governor of Alaska before a congressional committee in 1947. "I know of no one thing that will be more beneficial to the economy of the Indian population than the development of this pulp and paper industry . . . It means a new day in the Indian economy. It means that instead of being obliged to subsist for twelve months on the rather uncertain earnings of three or four months' fishing, they will have something that will keep them employed all year around, and I can think of nothing that will equal that in benefit."[3] This conclusion appeared too obvious for further comment. Thousands of new jobs would be created just at a time when fisheries income and employment were falling at an alarming rate. All non-Indian persons concerned appeared to have no doubt that the readjustment would be automatic, immediate and complete.

Seven years after the opening of the first pulp mill, however, the actual experience has been that there was virtually no impact upon the Indian population as a result of the introduction of the new industry and its new jobs and income. For his basic livelihood, the Indian continued to cling to fishing and fish processing despite their depressed condition. This has called for expanded federal and state relief programs within the region. In 1953 and in 1954 the president of the United States declared that a major economic disaster existed in those areas dependent upon fishing and a program of agricultural surplus commodities distribution was instituted in addition to the more customary cash relief programs. Annually the Alaska legislature has appropriated money for a continuing program of work relief in the villages. The only significant geographic movement of Indian population within the region away from the ancestral villages has been into the town of Juneau and the Mount Edgecumbe center, the principal sources of public assistance. An occasional Indian found employment in the mills or logging operations, of course, but these are only minor exceptions to the generalization that these people have not received the expected benefits of employment and income from the new industry.

Although these conditions can be observed by the resident or visitor to the region, their verification by statistical means is difficult because employment records are not collected on the basis of race and the U.S. Census data are for the month of April, an offseason month in Alaska. A few indicators of the impact of these developments on the Native and non-Native (a less cumbersome terminology of the technically more correct indigenous and non-indigenous) people can be gleaned from a comparison of selected data from the 1950 and 1960 census reports. Despite the creation of a whole range of new employment opportunities, the participation rate of the normal working-age Native population actually declined between 1950 and 1960, while that of the non-Native population enjoyed a significant increase (refer to Table 1).

TABLE 1.

EMPLOYMENT STATUS, APRIL 1950-APRIL 1960*

	Persons 14 Years old and Over	Gainfully Employed	Participate Rate
April 1960			
Native, total	5,408	2,015	0.373
Male	2,591	1,168	0.451
Female	2,817	847	0.301
Non-native, total	18,271	11,663	0.638
Male	10,224	7,935	0.776
Female	8,047	3,728	0.463
April 1950			
Native, total	4,858	1,849	0.381
Male	2,562	1,309	0.511
Female	2,296	540	0.235
Non-native, total	15,703	9,402	0.599
Male	9,309	6,851	0.736
Female	6,394	2,551	0.399

*Computed from data in U.S. Bureau of Census, *1950 U.S. Census of Population*, P-B51, Alaska, Tables 25 and 26; *U.S. Census of Population, 1960*, PC(1)-3B, Alaska, Table 28, and PC(1)-3C, Alaska, Tables 83 and 87.

The economic shifts within the decade of the 1950's was accompanied by a 25% increase in total population (refer to Table 2). Breaking this data into geographic areas and major racial classifications, there appeared to have actually been a movement of Native population away from the two centers of new economic development at Ketchikan and Sitka. (The location of the major Bureau of Indian Affairs health and education center at Mt. Edgecumbe near Sitka introduces some abnormalities into the picture, but the generalization would appear to apply.)

Both of these comparisons indicate that the new jobs were filled by more intensive utilization of the non-Native population and a significant immigration of additional workers from outside Alaska. The developments appear to have had virtually no impact upon the employment situation of the Native people.

The failure of the increasingly underemployed Indian to move into the new job markets has perplexed many other Alaskans. The Indian already appeared to have made a transition from an aboriginal local-consumption-oriented economy to a modern commercial economy geared to fisheries production for overseas markets. He no longer ran naked or dressed in skin garments but bought his clothes, food and household goods from the same sources as other Alaskans. Most of his income had long been received in the form of negotiable commercial instruments or "legal tender" for fish sales, wages and welfare payments. He has enjoyed full citizenship rights under United States rule, is an apt politician and an active voter.

The experience of the past few years, however, has demonstrated that the difficulty and extent of the remaining transition was underestimated. The marine-based economy which developed from the late nineteenth until the mid-twentieth century required relatively minor adjustments in traditional means of securing a livelihood and no change in the seasonal rhythm of life. The new emerging economy is primarily land-based, urbanized, requires new and more specialized labor skills, for all practical purposes is almost nonseasonal, and requires a labor force accustomed to working at a set employment within specified time limits of the day throughout the year.

TABLE 2.

GEOGRAPHIC DISTRIBUTION OF POPULATION INCREASES, 1950-1960*

	Total Region	Ketchikan Area[1]	Sitka Area[2] Mount Edgecumbe[3]	Sitka Area[2] Balance	All Other Areas
April 1960					
Native	9,242	2,778	1,435	1,402	3,627
Non-native	26,161	9,064	449	3,404	13,244
Total	35,403	11,842	1,884	4,806	16,871
April 1950					
Native	7,928	2,581	718	1,447	3,182
Non-native	20,275	6,904	429	1,956	10,986
Total	28,203	9,485	1,147	3,403	14,168
Percentage Increase 1950 to 1960					
Native	16.6	7.6	99.9	(3.1)[4]	14.0
Non-native	29.0	31.3	4.7	74.0	20.6
Total	25.5	24.8	64.3	41.2	19.1

[1]Ketchikan and Prince of Wales election districts.

[2]Sitka election district.

[3]Bureau of Indian Affairs major health, boarding school and vocational training center. 1950 to 1960 increase due to expansion of programs drawing native Alaskans from entire state.

[4]The decrease between 1950 and 1960 may be due in part to the movement of native population from the city of Sitka to Mount Edgecumbe as facilities were made available between 1950 and 1960, and in part due to different methods employed in collection of census data.

*U.S. Bureau of the Census, *U.S. Census of Population, 1960*, PC(1)-3B, Alaska, Tables 23 and 28; census data for 1950 from unpublished census worksheets as tabulated in G.W. Rogers, *Alaska in Transition*, Baltimore, 1960, pp. 358-59.

Not only is there a shift in the natural resource base of the economy, but the organization of economic activity has changed. This requires a whole new set of skills from the Indian wishing to make the transition from fisherman to mill operative or lumberman, plus an entirely different attitude toward work and life. The fisherman is a man of many skills and talents, and within the rigid limits imposed by nature and economic necessity makes his own decisions as to when, where and how much he will work. As an industrial operative, the former fisherman will be required to learn one narrow set of skills intensively and be willing to submit to the discipline of working under the direction of others who will make his work decisions for him. The acceptance of public welfare assistance might appear to involve no greater loss of human dignity than the acceptance of such terms.

The importation of technically qualified workers from outside the region has also had its unanticipated results. Economic feasibility studies took into consideration the higher cost of living in estimating labor costs, but did not take into account the cultural characteristics of the imported workers and the physical conditions imposed by the region. The new labor recruit has not "taken" to the sort of life offered by the region. Although there has been an increase in the number of new Alaskans, they have tended to be a very restless lot.

Only one example will be cited. The automobile is the most prized possession of the highly mobile industrial workers of the United States and together with the superhighways represents a whole way of life. The new worker brought his family car along just as naturally as he did the family. But the topographic features of the region—the many islands, mountainous terrain, breaking of the mainland portion by deep fiords, etc.—make any significant milage of local roads costly and a fully interconnected system an impossibility. The difficulty in realizing maximum pleasure from an automobile in such country has contributed to worker discontent and to the unexpectedly high rate of labor turnover. During a strike in 1961, the Ketchikan local of the pulp and sulfite union included in its negotiating contract a proposal that the company pay for the barging of workers' family cars to Seattle and return as a part of their regularly paid vacation benefits. The agreed upon compromise provided that the company subsidize the rental of cars at Seattle and pay milage rates beyond for workers who spend their vacations outside. This is only one of the costs of retaining outside labor recruits.[5]

Another set of human adaptations, therefore, are called for in considering the recruiting of labor from non-Native sources. This involves the adaptation of man to a new physical environment. Although the economy has shifted to the land, life within the region is still dominated by its marine nature and must be amphibious in turn. As in the case of the need of the Indian to adapt to a new social and economic environment, this will not be simple and will be costly in the long run if not recognized as a real problem.

Goals and Problems of Further
Economic Development

The Southeast Alaska region can be summarized in terms of a few strategic elements and their interactions. Physically the natural resource base is both marine and land oriented and its essentially marine nature imposes an amphibious way of life upon its inhabitants. The economy can be divided into three major levels, the relative importance of each varying over time. The first is the aboriginal subsistence hunting and fishing economy which still operates in a limited way. The second would be commercial fishing and processing for export to outside markets. This is a highly seasonal activity, and also highly nonresident in orientation. Not only are its markets outside the region, but much of the labor force must be imported for the brief working season and much of the means of production are owned by nonresidents. It is a typical colonial economy with the greater share of the income produced within the region and from its natural resources being distributed elsewhere in the form of wages to nonresident workers and profits to nonresident proprietors. Finally, the third economic level embraces the development and exploitation of land resources—at present primarily forest products, but also in the past and possibly in the future, mineral resources. It is more resident-oriented in the distribution of income produced than is the second level. Although much of the capital for this development must come from outside sources, the industries included require a year around resident labor force.

The aboriginal subsistence level stands at the lowest end of the scale of economic development in terms of effective use of natural resources and material well-being produced. The basic cause is technological, but also is due to the combination of the serious decline in the once abundant salmon runs and the recently accelerated increase in the indigenous peoples due to operation of public welfare and health programs. The second level has been on the decline since the mid-1930's and at best afforded only seasonal employment and limited resident income. The third level has increased importantly and shows promise of further increases. Existing forest-products plants, if operated at their full rated capacities for three shifts a day, would utilize less than half the U.S. Forest Service's annual allowable sustained-yield cut of timber, thus leaving considerable room for additional expansion. The State of Alaska's most immediately promising iron and copper development potentials are located within the region.

Because the first two levels were based upon the same general natural resources, there has been interaction between them in the past. The people identified with the aboriginal economy found seasonal employment and cash income in the colonial economy of commercial fisheries, but they also were forced to surrender their salmon base to heavy industrial exploitation and eventual destruction. There has been no interaction between the first two and the third level. Their natural resource bases are entirely different and there has been a very high degree of labor immobility.

The goals of economic development in this region are quite obvious. The third level should be expanded. It would result in fuller utilization of the natural resource base, diversify the economy and introduce into it very desirable elements of stability and balance, and provide a means for improving the welfare of the inhabitants of the region. Studies and investigations have been launched by public and private agencies to foster this development. As a result the natural resources of the region have had more intensive investigation and evaluation than those of the balance of the State of Alaska. From the background of this basic data, there have been studies of transportation and costs of development. The probable requirements in capital and labor and the competitiveness of resulting product outputs in domestic and overseas markets are well known. The U.S. Forest Service has organized the forest resources into four "working circles" with hubs at the principal population centers of the region and utilizing the patterns of waterways provided.

The actual realization of development appears to wait only for further publicity of the potentials known to exist and the appearance of the markets and other conditions assumed in the models of projections. All of these factors are external to the region itself, as the nature of development will still be colonial, or modified colonial, with export of raw or semi-processed products to markets in the continental United States and Japan.

Drawing upon the experience gained from the introduction of two new pulp mills, it could be concluded that the truly strategic factors remaining for study and consideration relate to the region itself—the degree to which the people at present living here (the people who are a product of conditioning by the physical character of the region) can provide the required new labor force and the living requirements of the additional labor which must be imported and their compatibility with the physical conditions imposed by the region.

For practical economic, quite aside from humanitarian, reasons, there is an urgent need for more widespread intelligent and sympathetic understanding of the Indian's problem of transition. The region's further economic expansion will be hobbled should it be saddled with the economic burdens of an increasingly unproductive sector of its population. There is also a need for determination of what the physical region imposes and offers in the development of a satisfying life for new immigrants. Unless it is possible to develop a citizenry adapted to the region, the newly established enterprises will continue to be plagued with the added cost burden of continuing high labor turnover.

For purposes of analysis it should be possible to devise simple statistical measures to assist in gauging progress and determining needs in these adjustments. At present measures of participation in the employed labor force by racial groups are available only at ten-year intervals in the regular U.S. Bureau of the Census reports. These are also a source of measures of the general population mobility, an indirect index of labor turnover. Current measures are needed and could be devised from labor data collected in connection with the administration of unemployment insurance programs and other sources.

Beyond devising measures of participation and turnover, the strategic factors bearing on the economic development of the region clearly call for the combined skills of the geographer, sociologist, anthropologist and others as well as the economist. It is in providing the interdisciplinary focus needed in devising the analytical and policy means for increasing the interaction between the levels and elements of the southeast Alaska region that regional science could be of the greatest value in promoting the region's economic development.

NOTES

[1]U.S. Fish and Wildlife Service, *Alaska Fishery and Fur Seal Industries: 1941*, Statistical Digest No. 5, Washington, 1943, pp. 19-21; and *Alaska Fishery and Fur Seal Industries: 1955*, Statistical Digest No. 40, Washington, 1957, pp. 32-39.

[2]From U.S. Forest Service records, as published in G.W. Rogers and R.A. Cooley, *Alaska's Population and Economy*, *Vol. II*, *Statistical Handbook*, State of Alaska, March 1962, p. 208.

[3]"Hearings Before Committee on Agriculture, House of Representatives, 80th Congress, First Session, on House Joint Resolution 205," May 26, June 14, July 1-3-9, 1947, p. 45.

[4]The strike and contract negotiations were fully covered in the local press. The *Daily Alaska Empire*, September 20, 1961 summed up the settlement.

Data from which this paper was developed have been published as "Some Observations on the Persistence of Alaska Native Village Populations," *ISEGR Research Note A-1* (College, Alaska: Institute of Social, Economic and Government Research) September, 1969.

PATTERNS OF MIGRATION, URBANIZATION
AND ACCULTURATION

Arthur E. Hippler

This article delineates the broad patterns of migration, urbanization and acculturation of Alaska Natives. These three conceptual categories involve different levels of abstraction: migration is the physical and observable movement of peoples; urbanization is the outward but less directly observable process of adaptation to an urban environment; acculturation is a general, abstract notion referring to the process of social and psychological accommodation with a new culture. There is a complex interpenetration of these phenomena, and an elucidation of it can provide a framework within which to view the dymanics of Alaska Native life.

Prior to contact with Euro-American civilization and for a significant period thereafter, northern and western Alaska Natives tended to live in small, dispersed, impermanent settlements, often composed of individual families or extended families. Periodically, depending upon the subsistence and ceremonial calendar, people would come together into groups—often of several hundred. With the exception of a few permanent villages, such as Point Hope (Tigara), Barrow and a few others, there were almost no large permanent settlements in the northern and western parts of Alaska[1] during this period. Gradually and for a variety of reasons this dispersed population came to be concentrated in permanent villages.

There appear to be several stages in this process of agglomeration, some of which are completed and others of which are still underway. With the advent of traders, missionaries and in more recent times medical and educational practitioners in the outlying areas of Alaska, Native Alaskans began to settle in groups where they could take advantage of new services. Such settlements were the beginnings of the present villages. As greater economic complexity was introduced into the rural areas through trapping and mining, and as Natives came to need more money to buy the newly discovered Euro-American material goods, the population began to gravitate toward those communities that could offer some cash employment. Alternatively men, and sometimes women, would leave villages for extended periods of time to travel to cash work in canneries, construction jobs, etc.

Thus, villages came into being with populations of up to several hundred persons. At the same time, migration was occurring both from these villages and from the remaining small family settlements into the larger regional villages of Barrow, Kotzebue, Bethel and Nome. As this process accelerated, still a new dimension of migration emerged. Many Natives began leaving the small settlements, villages and the regional centers for the urban areas of Fairbanks and Anchorage.[2] Thus, there have been overlapping waves of migration starting before the turn of the twentieth century and resulting in settlement in larger and larger communities.

Noteworthy is the fact that this agglomerative movement is not uniform in terms of age grouping. Although incomplete data makes all conclusions tentative, population curves suggest that older individuals are staying in the villages and young adults are moving to the regional centers and cities.

An expected consequence of a predominant out-migration of young adults is a declining number of births due to the smaller number of couples of childbearing age in the villages. These developments should lead to a static or declining population. But while some small villages are declining in population, the majority of villages are not.[3] Instead it appears that the population is still increasing in most villages. This probably reflects the drastic decline in infant mortality within the last two decades and the consequent greater number of living children for each of the remaining young adult families.

Several implications can be derived from this data. Though some very small villages may be absolutely disappearing, villages as such do not appear to be disappearing with anything like the rapidity that one may assume at first glance.[4] Though in some cases small villages have a rate of increase lower than that of the Native population in the area as a whole, the large absolute number of young children in the villages suggests that unless these children out-migrate en masse upon reaching adulthood (for which there is no present evidence) the villages will remain, and grow. At the same time, large numbers of villagers are migrating to the regional centers and cities, bringing with them special problems.

This pattern of migration from smaller to larger population centers has not been accompanied by a commensurate pattern of Native urbanization.[5] Although only sketchy information exists concerning Alaska Native urbanization, the broad dimensions of the process appear to be the following.

Alaska Natives come into urban centers where the white population exhibits overt and covert racial prejudice. (I have noted elsewhere some of the reasons for and characteristics of this behavior).[6] These Natives find well paid employment to be almost unavailable, in part because of racial prejudice and discrimination, and in part because of their inadequate formal educational preparation. They are blocked from both economic and social access to the fuller richness of the urban environment.

The principal reasons for movement to urban areas appear to be a desire for cash work and a desire for the excitement of city life. Few find work, but many who remain do find a form of urban excitement in the bars, which are important socializing centers. The new urban immigrant appears to rely heavily on friends and acquaintances (usually from his own village) who have preceded him, and it is typically through the filter of their perceptions and experiences that he comes to perceive and experience the urban environment.

One of the results of this urbanization process is an immediate and continuous negative contact with the police of Fairbanks and Anchorage. Many Natives feel that the police are prejudiced against them and harass them continually. Many police, in fact, do object to Natives as "dirty drunks" who congregate on street corners and defile the city. In general, the police exhibit a general lack of tolerance for cultural differences with regard to Alaska Natives.

In the absence of employment opportunities, many city newcomers learn how to acquire unemployment insurance and other forms of assistance and learn how to manipulate "help" agencies as part of their routine of life. Most of their urban white contacts are either with authorities who disapprove of them, such as the police, and agency personnel with ambivalent attitudes, who must be manipulated for survival. Also, there are servicemen on pass, construction workers from the North Slope oil explorations, and the variety of drifters, predators and prey who inhabit the undersides of cities, and who through their interaction with Natives pass on selected aspects of the dominant culture's values.

Many Natives faced with what is essentially an unpleasant, or at least confusing, urban experience, return to the village of their origin. In relating their experiences, they produce expectations of the urban environment which condition the perceptions of future migrants. Thus cities come to be seen by many Alaska Natives prior to their visits to them, during such visits, and after, in a way which would seem deeply distorted to many whites.

Both the migratory and urbanization phenomena exist within an overall framework of the general acculturative experience of Alaska Natives. This experience appears to involve for individual Natives severe personal pathologies.

Personal prestige for men has been eroded by a decline in the importance of the role of the hunter and minimal possibilities for entering fully into the cash economy. The decline in subsistence activities has resulted in similar depreciation of self perceptions among women, who are seldom required to sew, tan, fish and prepare materials for the camp and the hunt as in the past.

Thus, many Alaska Natives have internalized a generally self deprecatory attitude. Generations of school teachers and missionaries, often for what they felt were the very best of reasons, have overtly and covertly attacked Native life ways, attitudes, values, religion and family life. Moreover, expectations by teachers that Natives would do poorly have become in many cases self-fulfilling prophesies.[7]

One might almost say that Native-white interaction has been so structured as to prevent Native achievement in the white world. Native failures are then pointed to by many whites as justification for the policies of segregation and prejudice which have been instrumental in creating those failures.

Within this interlocking web of complex migratory patterns, selective urbanization and general acculturation stress are some further complexities.

Some Alaska Natives do well in school and bring more sophisticated (by western standards) perceptions of the village, Alaska and the world back to their homes. Some stay in their villages and become leaders and local powers. Some stay and become simply private persons. Others leave and bring a more critical and sometimes angry voice to the urban environment in which they reside.

A few Natives come to the cities with an educational level, value structure, and adaptational ability that permits them to acquire a job and income, and to enter at least into the broadest definition of the mainstream of American life. There is no hard data presently available on the number of people in this category.

This differential impact of urban life and the differential ability to understand and manipulate the social order may well be producing a strong class system among Alaska Natives. The caste system of the past, in which all Natives ranked inferior to whites, appears to be undergoing modification into a more complex caste-class system, in which differential acculturation and urbanization are the key factors.

NOTES

[1]This pattern is, of course, substantially different for the Natives of southeast Alaska, where large villages existed as permanent settlements.

[2]Adequate information especially through time on the number of Natives in urban regions in Alaska is poor. Our best present estimates suggest 2,000-2,500 Natives in Fairbanks (perhaps 500 Eskimos) and 6,000-9,000 Natives in Anchorage (perhaps one half Eskimo).

[3]It may not even be true for the small villages where it appears to be so. The high variability in individual village size through time and the small numbers involved make any statistical statement risky.

[4]Independent confirmation for this comes from Arlon R. Tussing and Robert D. Arnold, 1969: While migration to urban places in Alaska and to other states is occurring, villages are not vanishing from the scene today, as is often assumed. There are 12 fewer separate Native places (of 25 or more persons) than were indicated in the 1950 census, but more than 80% of the places continuing to exist are larger than they were seventeen years ago.

[5]Urbanization in this context means the ability to adapt to and manipulate the urban environment and to develop behavioral and value patterns commensurate with the urban American norm. Urbanization is one aspect of the larger process of acculturation.

[6]Arthur E. Hippler, "Some Unplanned Consequences of Planned Culture Change," in *Higher Latitudes of North America: Socio-Economic Studies in Regional Development.* Boreal Institute, University of Alberta, Occasional Publication No. 6:11-21, 1968.

[7]There is now some evidence that such perceptions on the part of teachers strongly color pupil response and achievement.

This article was prepared in 1968 for the Federal Field Committee for Development Planning in Alaska and is excertped from Chapter VI of *Alaska Natives and the Land* (Washington, D.C.: U.S. Government Printing Office, 1968).

THE ECONOMIC CONSEQUENCES OF A
LAND CLAIMS SETTLEMENT

Arlon R. Tussing and Douglas N. Jones

It is a fair generalization that Alaska Natives as a class are not owners of commercial property assets. Nor are they possessors of the acculturation, education, training or experience to take advantage of the new job opportunities in the kind of economic growth now occurring in the United States and in Alaska. This generalization is confirmed by a variety of statistical series, which show that the economic position of Alaska Natives, and of the communities in which they live, is steadily falling further behind statewide averages.[1] It is a common notion that any obstacles to economic development resulting from the impasse over Native claims hurt the interests of Alaska Natives above all, but this is a serious exaggeration. On balance, it appears that Alaska Natives as a group now have little if any stake in a continuation of the present pattern of regional economic development. It follows also that they have little stake in a resolution of their protests and claims for the sake of removing obstacles to economic development, unless that resolution involves either the creation of new kinds of economic opportunity for individual Natives or Native groups or a substantial transfer of commercial assets to them.

The Native interest in economic development as it touches on a resolution of the protests can be subdivided into four concerns:

1. *Protection of the Indigenous Way of Life.* Commercial development of Alaska's natural resources or the population growth it supports may endanger, or compete for, resources required in the subsistence economy. Native groups seek land title to increase their control of, and ability to protect, these subsistence resources.

2. *Employment Opportunities.* Exceptionally high rates of unemployment result from a shortage of job opportunities for Alaska Natives at their present levels of education, training, and acculturation. Federal and state agencies in Alaska, particularly in the forestry and fishery fields, use primary processing requirements and other policies as means toward creating otherwise uneconomic employment within the state. Native groups aspire to control land and water resources in the hope that their own management of them can be used to create jobs specifically for Natives.

3. *Property Income.* The prospective value of mineral and timber rights and of urban land now in public ownership in Alaska is on the order of hundreds of millions and probably billions of dollars.[2] It is not surprising that Native groups look toward the potential income from public lands as a means of directly alleviating the poverty of their constituents and of providing the capital for Native enterprises. The example of the Tyonek Indians, who have used their oil revenues to build houses and village facilities and to invest in urban real estate and construction, as well as to raise their individual incomes, has been a powerful one.

4. *State and Local Revenues for Education, Health, Welfare and Community Development.* Regional economic growth can normally be expected to expand the revenue base for state and local government. In addition, the state receives income from mineral leases and timber sales both on state and on federal lands. The extent to which the growth of

state and local revenues benefit Alaska Natives depends, however, on precisely how they are spent. In the absence of a comprehensive strategy on the part of the state for dealing with the problems of the Native people, Native groups can be expected to continue to rank this interest in economic development considerably lower than the previous three.

Any forecast of the pace and pattern of economic development in Alaska is limited by the accuracy of its assumptions and must be accepted with great caution. The same caution is required with respect to forecasts of the economic consequences of any legislative package designed to settle the Native claims. The following remarks are intended to set out in what general direction will be the probable effect on the economic status of the Natives and on Alaska's general economic development of the individual elements of various settlement proposals, including those before the Congress.

Protection of Subsistence Resources

None of the legislation introduced so far deals in a definitive way with protection of fish and wildlife stocks used in the indigenous economy, or with protection of Native access to these stocks. With the partial exception of migratory wildfowl, fish and game are a matter of state title and state responsibility. Article VIII, Section 3, of the state constitution appears to preclude establishing proprietary rights in fish or wildlife harvests.[3] Under these circumstances, the only provisions of any of the existing bills which might effect exclusive Native access to fish or wildlife resources would be large grants of land in fee simple, or unrestricted grants of the surface estate. Such measures, while not conveying a property right in fish or wildlife, would enable Native proprietors to post the land against entry by others for hunting, fishing, or trapping.

Congress might, however, protect public access, Native and non-Native, to fish and wildlife by providing that state-selected land and other land withdrawn from the public domain in Alaska for other purposes remain open in perpetuity to (all) the public for hunting, fishing and trapping. Under either of these provisions, the harvest in fact available to Natives would still depend upon state management and regulations.

The general economic impact of legislation in this area would depend upon the amount and location of lands and waters involved. There might conceivably be local effects on recreation and tourist-oriented enterprise, but these effects in the aggregate are not likely to be large.

Grants of Homesites, Townsites, and Special-Purpose Locations

The absence of title to land occupied by Natives in Alaska villages is clearly an obstacle to financing homes, businesses, and community facilities. The grant of title to these lands would just as clearly have a beneficial effect on the village economy. The same is true of grants of land for expansion in the vicinity of each village. One necessary reservation here is that, unless some provision is made for future exchanges of land or otherwise for the occupation of new sites, families and communities may be tied to places which turn out to be poorly located from an economic or physical standpoint.

Grants of land title for homesites, businesses, community facilities, and special-purpose locations such as fish camps and burial grounds should not be expected to have any negative effects on general economic development. Some question might be raised about sites in existing withdrawals such as national forests. The total area of land involved is so small, however, that we can find no instance in which such transfers would subvert the purposes of the original withdrawal.

Individual Land Grants

The aggregate impact of granting individuals fee simple ownership, or title to either the surface estate or the mineral estate, on large tracts of land is extremely difficult to predict. It is obvious, however, that the benefits would be very unevenly distributed, both because of the wide differences in value of land resource, and because of wide differences in individuals' ability to manage and exploit these resources. Some individuals would undoubtedly become very wealthy, while a great number would probably not benefit at all.

It is not clear whether such a provision would on balance speed up or retard commercial development of Alaska resources. What probably can be said is that the time horizons of individual proprietors would be shorter, and their focus narrower, than would be the case with government management.

Land Grants to Native Corporations or Native Associations

There is no reason to expect the quality of management employed by Native associations to differ from that available to the state. Generalizations about management policy, however, are extremely speculative. On balance, ownership by Native corporations, like private ownership in general, would probably result in a more rapid rate of development and a greater concern for maximizing the economic returns from the land resources than would management by government agencies. For instance, Native corporations would probably not require primary processing of extractive products or "sustained-yield" timber management except where they were clearly justified in dollar terms. Native corporations in attempting to maximize their net incomes from the land would pursue a multiple-use policy, and in doing so would probably be able to resolve conflicts among competing commercial land uses more economically and more satisfactorily than would government. On the other hand, to the extent their policies reflected a single-minded concern with the commercial revenues of the land, they might be less concerned than would government with such nonmonetary and collective values as those of wilderness and scenery.

The previous treatment assumes that Native corporations would manage their land grants for their income rather than distributing them to individuals or selling out in order to distribute the proceeds. The impact of either of these policies on Native welfare would approximate that of individual land grants and individual cash settlements, respectively. Grants of commercially valuable land managed for its income by Native corporations could be expected to provide an income flow to individual families and to provide a source of capital which Native enterprise could invest in other lines of business and capital for community improvements. It would also provide openings for the development of Native managerial talent.

Individual Lump-Sum Settlements

It is again difficult to generalize about the impact of lump-sum individual payments on Native welfare except to say that the effects would vary immensely among individuals. Some Natives undoubtedly would invest their money very effectively; but because of poverty, lack of education and of commercial attitudes, a great number of recipients would undoubtedly soon be no better off than they were before receiving the grant.

For the same reason (i.e., the Natives' high propensity to consume), the lump-sum settlement to individuals would probably provide stimulus to the general Alaska economy, but this stimulus would be of a "one-and-for-all" nature and would leave little lasting impact on Alaska income or employment.

Individual Cash Annuities

Substantial cash grants to individuals, distributed regularly over a long period of time, might be expected to make a contribution to Native living standards proportionate to the size of the grant, and to be a corresponding stimulus to the regional economy. It is not clear, however, that such payments would be any different in principle or in effect from increased, universal, public-assistance distributions.

This study is not the proper place for a full discussion of the philosophy and economics of welfare. Existing public-assistance programs are under critical examination throughout the United States, and several alternatives are being widely considered. It is appropriate to point out here, however, that some kind of family income maintenance program will be required in rural Alaska for many years. We would hesitate to generalize about the relationship of public-assistance payments to the feelings of self-respect and to the economic motivations of Alaska Natives, but it is clear there is a close connection among them in the thinking of the cultural majority in America. "Unearned" income is regarded as degrading and disgraceful if the recipient gets it because he is poor and unemployed. But such income is highly respectable if it comes from the ownership of land or securities. This consideration suggests that, dollar for dollar, public funds distributed to Alaska Natives may be more effective in raising their social and economic status if done wisely as part of a land-claims settlement than if done as public assistance.

Cash Settlements to Native Associations or Corporations

A large cash settlement distributed to a Native corporation or corporations, if treated as investment capital rather than distributed to individuals, could be expected to provide a continuing stream of income to individuals as well as a source of funds for enterprise and for community development. It would also provide openings for the development of Native management talent. Beyond this it is difficult to generalize, because the impact both on welfare of individual Natives and on overall economic development would depend on the investment policies pursued, and on the managerial skills provided by, or hired by, the Native groups.

Share of Revenues from Public Lands
(And/or Outer Continental Shelf)

ᵃⁱ ⁺ⁱ Distribution to Natives of a specified share of revenues from all or from certain kinds of public lands in Alaska would have effects on Native welfare similar to that of cash disbursements and would vary similarly depending on whether the payments were to individuals or to Native corporations. In the latter case, they would vary depending on the managerial skills available to, and the policies of, those corporations. Unlike grants of commercially valuable lands to individuals or to Native corporations, land and resource management would remain à government responsibility and would probably be pursued with a broader range of policy objectives than would be the case under private ownership. The flow of funds to Native individuals or groups would begin sooner than they would in the case of grants of land title, unless the latter included lands presently under mineral lease.

Any increased investment or expenditure in the state resulting from these payments would clearly be an impetus to overall economic development, except to the extent they preempted a share of royalties, lease payments, or timber sales revenues which would otherwise accrue to state or local government. The net effect on economic development in the latter case is not clear.

Tax Exemption

Tax exemptions could have significant fiscal implications for the state and local government. The real estate exemption of S.B. 3586, for instance, keeps all the lands granted off the property tax rolls whether they are "in fee or in trust." This provision applies as well to any minerals associated with the land grant which could otherwise be made subject to *ad valorem* levies where tax bodies existed. Conceivably, these sums might amount to considerable amounts of public receipts foregone. Some caution is appropriate here, however, in that too early and too much land taxation can result in confiscation of the land, which results would clearly be counter-productive to the policy resolution intended.

The probelm here seems to be to distinguish among the different purposes for which land might be granted. In the case of homesites, fishing camps, and the like, or of lands granted to protect subsistence activities, maximum insurance is required against confiscation because of the owner's inability to pay taxes. In the case of grants of commercially valuable land for income purposes, however, the point is to get them into a productive, income-earning position and, indeed, to get them on the tax rolls. To the extent that these lands are in fact capable of producing income, there is no obvious justification for keeping them off the tax rolls simply because they happen to be owned by Natives or Native groups.

Any provision, however, that initial cash payments under the act are not taxable means simply that any monetary settlement is effectively larger in disposable income than its nominal dollar amount.

The provision in S.B. 3586 relating to Section 501 of the Internal Revenue Code indicates that another "nonprofit" enterprise would be created, a corporate status which is currently under serious review by government and public-finance scholars alike. In a state the vast bulk of whose land a great proportion of whose capital assets are already exempt from taxation, there seems to be no economic justification for this further departure from tax uniformity.

Corporate Organization, Trusteeship, and Property Alienation

To the extent that lump sums, tracts of commercially valuable land, or a share of the revenue from public lands in Alaska are transferred to Native corporations, a major purpose is to assist tne Natives as a group to get a firm footing within the money economy and the capitalistic organization of the United States. Other aspects of the claims settlement may be designed to protect those Natives and Native communities which wish to maintain intact their nonmarket economy and their distinctive ways of life. But legislation providing a special role for Native development corporations is directed toward economic equality for Natives with other Americans, and toward their economic integration into the life of the nation. For this reason, provisions establishing any trusteeship over the capital assets of the Natives, including land, or establishing a special status for Native development corporations, should be carefully examined and the time span of these provisions carefully considered.

The desire to protect a vulnerable people from exploitation or expropriation must be balanced against the desirability of giving them early control over their own livelihood and their own assets, and against the community's interest in avoiding franchise to private monopolies and special privilege. While restrictions on land transfer or stock sales to non-Natives provide some protection to the improvident and the gullible, these restrictions will sharply reduce the value of the assets involved. Land which cannot be alienated cannot be mortgaged. If the land is the owner's only capital asset, he is tied to it economically as securely as if he were a serf. Stock in a Native corporation which can be sold only to eligible Natives is *ceteris paribus* worth less than stock which can be sold to anyone; stock which cannot be sold at all is, of course, worth even less. To the extent that the property of individual Natives or of Native corporations is encumbered either by law or by covenant, the value of that property will be reduced, the economic freedom of the Natives impaired, and the most productive use of land and capital discouraged.

The bills so far presented to Congress for settlement of the land claims include two distinct approaches to protecting both Native assets and the public interest during a prolonged transition to full equality. One approach would hold much of the Natives' assets in trust and would rely heavily on the discretion of the Secretary of the Interior. The second approach, together with or separate from the first, provides a multitude of special provisions for Native development corporations, including tax exemptions and restrictions on the disposal of their assets and on stock ownership. Congress may wish to consider whether either apparatus is really necessary, if the Native development corporations commence with sufficient economic scale in terms of cash, land title, revenue shares, or some combination thereof, to reduce uncertainty about future income to acceptable levels, to distribute its benefits widely among the Native communities of Alaska, and to engage first-rate professional management. In this case, the public interest, Native and non-Native alike, might best be served by the early transformation of the Native development corporation into one with all the rights and responsibilities of other businesses in our economy.

NOTES

[1] James W. Sullivan, "Personal Income Patterns in Alaska," *Alaska Review of Business and Economic Conditions*, Vol. VI, No. 1, Institute of Social, Economic and Government Research, College, Alaska.

[2] The value of these properties is measured either by the amount for which they could presently be sold, or by the present capitalized value of the revenues which could be expected from leasing them or selling their products. Hence, for instance, since the Prudhoe Bay oil strikes, the leasing of additional land for oil and gas exploration on the Arctic Slope could be expected to yield several hundreds of millions of dollars in bonuses alone. The amount of timber sale revenue flowing to the government from timber sales on federal and state forest lands in Alaska has not been a central concern of management policy; but if managed by private owners on commercial principles, these forests might have an asset value in the billions of dollars.

ADDITIONAL READING

Arnold, Robert D. "Characteristics of the Economy of Village Alaska and Prospects for Change." *Proceedings of the Twentieth Alaska Science Conference.* College, Alaska: Alaska Division of the American Association for the Advancement of Science, July 1970.

Bloom, Joseph D. "Recent Population Trends of Alaska Natives." *Alaska Medicine*, January, 1971.

Federal Field Committee for Development Planning in Alaska. *Alaska Natives and the Land.* Washington, D.C.: U.S. Government Printing Office, 1968.

Federal Field Committee for Development Planning in Alaska. *A Subregional Economic Analysis of Alaska.* Anchorage, 1968.

Jenness, Diamond. *Eskimo Administration: Alaska.* Arctic Institute of North America. Technical Paper No. 10. July, 1962.

Jones, Dorothy C. "Changes in Population Structure in the Aleutian Islands." *ISEGR Research Note* A-2, College, Alaska: Institute of Social, Economic and Government Research, December 1970.

Wolf, Grace. "Native Politics: An Overview." *Proceedings of the Twentieth Alaska Science Conference.* College, Alaska: Alaska Division of the American Association for the Advancement of Science, July, 1970.

ABOUT THE CONTRIBUTORS

Gregg K. Erickson, formerly a Research Assistant at the Institute of Social, Economic and Government Research, is now Administrative Assistant to the House Resource Committee, Alaska State Legislature.

Gordon S. Harrison is Assistant Professor of Political Science at the Institute of Social, Economic and Government Research.

Arthur E. Hippler is Associate Professor of Anthropology at the Institute of Social, Economic and Government Research.

Douglas N. Jones is Legislative Assistant to U.S. Senator Mike Gravel.

David R. Klein is Leader, Alaska Cooperative Wildlife Research Unit and Professor of Wildlife Management at the University of Alaska.

Thomas A. Morehouse is Associate Professor of Political Science at the Institute of Social, Economic and Government Research.

Scott R. Pearson is Assistant Professor of Economics at the Food Research Institute, Stanford University.

George W. Rogers is Professor of Economics at the Institute of Social, Economic and Government Research.

Arlon R. Tussing is Associate Professor of Economics at the Institute of Social, Economic and Government Research.

Robert B. Weeden is Professor of Wildlife Management at the University of Alaska.